Universal Design

Universal Design

The HUMBLES Method for User-Centred Business

FRANCESC ARAGALL
Design for All Foundation, Spain

and

JORDI MONTANA
ESADE Faculty of Business Administration, Spain

GOWER

Published by
Gower Publishing Limited
Wey Court East
Union Road
Farnham
Surrey
GU9 7PT
England

Gower Publishing Company
Suite 420
101 Cherry Street
Burlington
VT 05401-4405
USA

www.gowerpublishing.com

Francesc Aragall and Jordi Montana have asserted their moral right under the Copyright, Designs and Patents Act, 1988, to be identified as the authors of this work.

British Library Cataloguing in Publication Data
Aragall, Francesc.
   Universal design : the HUMBLES method for user-centred business.
   1. Universal design. 2. Management by objectives. 3. Product design – Social aspects.
   4. Product design – Environmental aspects. 5. Design – Human factors
   I. Title II. Montana, Jordi.
   658.4'012–dc23

Library of Congress Cataloging-in-Publication Data
Aragall, Francesc.
   Universal design : the HUMBLES method for user-centred business / by Francesc Aragall and Jordi Montana.
      p. cm.
   Includes bibliographical references and index.
   ISBN 978-0-566-08865-0 (hbk. : alk. paper)
  1. Product design. 2. New products. 3. Product management. I. Montaqa, Jordi. II. Title.

   TS171.A69 2011
   658.5'752–dc23

                                   2011025334
ISBN 9780566088650 (hbk)
ISBN 9781409440024 (ebk)

Printed and bound in Great Britain by the MPG Books Group, UK

Contents

List of Figures

Acknowledgements

We would like to thank all the representatives from companies mentioned in this publication that have enriched it with their texts, materials and experiences.

We would also like to acknowledge the dedicated work of the Design for All Foundation team led by the Foundation's Director, Imma Bonet, of ESADE's Professor Isa Moll, and of the Gower editorial team.

Their assistance in designing and their support in co-ordinating the publication have been crucial to the success in transforming our ideas and texts into the book that you have in your hands.

Executive Summary

Were you satisfied with the treatment you received at airports during your last trip? Have you ever had difficulties using some of the functions of your new mobile phone or your TV remote control? Do you suffer from any physical problem, any allergy, or have any belief or habit that you would prefer not to have to explain, in order to avoid standing out in a crowd? Have you ever had problems opening the packaging of a product or understanding the instructions for using an appliance? Have you ever had the feeling that you have not been treated as a "normal" customer? Have you stopped using a product or a service you were interested in because it turned out to be inconvenient?

If none of these questions remind you of unpleasant moments – CONGRATULATIONS! Either you live in the best of all possible worlds or you are very tolerant.

However, have you ever considered that your company may be generating dissatisfaction among your customers and users? Do you know how many potential customers have not even heard of your products or services because your methods of communication or their presentation are alien to them? Do you know why there are customers who are loyal to your competitors?

Please note:

- Customers are changing their attitudes, and are growing more demanding from very different perspectives.
- Customers are becoming better informed and are more discerning when it comes to purchasing products or services.
- Given an infinite supply of goods and services, people buy by desire, by necessity, or by a mixture of both.
- No one wants a product or service that is difficult or even impossible to use, and if someone does purchase it, then they will feel frustrated and speak ill of it.
- In a competitive environment, the companies that succeed are the ones that:
  - best meet customers' and users' desires and needs, and even anticipate them, forecasting demographic trends, innovative lifestyles, new technologies and emerging markets;
  - create a solid reputation for commitment to their customers, their users and society.
- Currently, companies study the wishes and needs of customers on a superficial level, knowing very little about their users.

- The less a company knows about its customers, the greater the risk of losing them. Many companies could significantly increase their sales if they knew more about their users and adapted their products and services to their needs.
- Many customers reject products or services because they are not sufficiently respectful of diversity, they are not safe enough, or what they offer is neither healthy nor functional nor understandable, or is not aesthetically acceptable in terms of potential customers' age, gender, culture, creed, sexual orientation, size and build, capacities or state of health.

Thus, any company that wants to lead its market sector must be able to understand its products and services from customers', consumers' and society's perspectives. In order to do this, it is necessary to understand human diversity and to be able to satisfy each potential customer's diverse needs and desires.

The strategy to meet this challenge is called Design for All.

Design for All seeks to build environments, products and services that are adapted to the needs and wishes of all people, regardless of their age, gender, ability, culture, beliefs, values, sexual orientation, and so on.

The Design for All strategy makes it is possible to achieve market growth, increase customer loyalty and improve the company's reputation.

Design for All's implementation needs to include all areas of the company, including marketing, production, design, administration and human resources. Although it is true that we have seen positive results when Design for All has been implemented in just a single department of a company, the best results are obtained when the strategy is integrated into the overall culture of the organization and is strongly supported by top management.

Even though the expected outcomes justify the effort, implementing this strategy is not an easy task. This is why Francesc Aragall developed the HUMBLES method in 2007 to guide companies through Design for All's innovation process, allowing them to adapt more effectively to the needs and wishes of potential users.

The HUMBLES Method to Implement Design for All

Design for All can be applied in each and every area within a company, from the purchasing department to human resources or customer support to the finance department or production. However, to apply it consistently, we believe that Design for All is best deployed on a product-by-product or service-by-service basis within the business. In this way, you can rest assured that its implementation will not involve conflict with existing working practices, and that the experience gained in applying the method to an individual product or service can be applied in future implementations, fully permeating the culture of the organization.

The HUMBLES method is based on experiences of companies of various sizes from different sectors in a number of countries. We have distilled from these the most successful procedures and results, from the perspectives of profitability, innovation and reputation, presenting them in a systematic way.

HUMBLES is an acronym whose seven letters represent the seven stages in a progressive approach – the name is a remarkable coincidence, because dealing with challenges with courage and humility leads to success and recognition. The seven phases of the HUMBLES method are as follows.

HIGHLIGHT DESIGN FOR ALL OPPORTUNITIES

Decide whether the application of the Design for All principles to your company's products or services can provide new values, increase sales, improve customers' confidence, discover new lines of innovation, and so on. In short, using your own thoughts or relying on external advice, try to imagine the new opportunities for your company that can result from this development and product improvement strategy.

USER IDENTIFICATION

Who are your customers, and who are your users or consumers? Do you know the extent of diversity among your customers? Are you unwittingly excluding a sector of the public you could appeal to?

Remember that your potential market is made up of those people who are interested in your offer and have enough purchasing power to afford it and have access to it. Are you losing a target market because people are not interested in your products or services or don't know about them? Or is it because your products don't suit their budgets, or because many people cannot gain access to or use your products or services to the full? Do you know who they are?

MONITOR INTERACTION

The clients and users of your products expect positive and enjoyable experiences from each of the relationships established with your company and what it offers them. From observation of the client/user–service/product relationship, we can obtain valuable information about their needs, expectations, consumer habits, and of course, conflicts and shortfalls.

Is the way the product or service is introduced acceptable and friendly to all potential customers? How do users interact with your product or service? Is this the way you expected? Have they benefited from it more or less as you expected?

Indeed, through observation, but also from complaints and suggestions, from the comments of employees or the media, we can identify a number of black spots (perhaps some are just grey) that can be improved.

Is what your company is offering safe and healthy for all potential customers? Does it offend any of their beliefs or values? Is it easy to use and understand? Is it attractive enough?

BREAKTHROUGH OPTIONS

Once aware of the aspects of the client's or user's or consumer's relationship to your product or service that can be improved, we must then determine which of these issues to address in terms of the company's strategy, the resources available, the chances of success, the contribution towards meeting your objectives, and so forth.

There is no single way forward. Aspects of product, reputation, materials, costs, human resources, processes – to name just a few – will determine how to improve the relationship between your product and the user. There are many elements to take into account, and these must be organized and managed so that they contribute to developing a common strategy.

LAY OUT SOLUTIONS

Is it possible to improve products or services without increasing production costs, or even reducing them? Should you improve the product, or develop a strategy of diversification? How could you reduce the time to market without compromising the quality of the design process? Will you tackle the design challenges using your own resources, or hire outside experts? How will you seek feedback from users before launching or improving the product?

EFFICIENT COMMUNICATION

Once you have decided to launch a new product, you must communicate effectively to potential clients and users the solutions and improvements that you have decided to implement. Otherwise, your efforts so far will be completely useless. Communicating in this way will enable you to improve your company's reputation among your customers.

Have you developed a good communication strategy – both internal and external? Are the chosen messages acceptable and tailored to the diversity of the potential audience, or are you driving away consumers without being aware of it?

SUCCESS EVALUATION

To finish the process and make sense of it, it is important to evaluate the achievements, both those linked to economic results that are immediately tangible (increased sales or customers, a successful launch of a product compared to previous ones, and so on), and the intangible ones (greater co-operation between the areas of the company, a better attitude towards customer orientation in key departments, improved corporate reputation, and so on). Through the collection of such data, your company can gather momentum to implement Design for All for other products or services from a new perspective. As you will see, every time you apply the HUMBLES method, your efforts will improve, since you will have a more experienced and motivated team that will end up developing an excellent company for your customers and for society as a whole.

Throughout the explanation of the HUMBLES method, we will describe experiences of outstanding businesses such as Santa & Cole, Simon, BIC, Volvo, Axel Hotels, IKEA, Sears Roebuck, Fiat, IDEO, Bank of America, Transports Ciutat Comtal, Fujitsu, Sol Meliá Hotels, Ferrocarrils de la Generalitat de Catalunya, Oxo, the Design for All Foundation, i2Cat, Muñecas Llorens, Nespresso, Nestlé, Altro Supergrif, Tata, Radio Taxi 033, Philips, Panasonic, TOTO, IED, Eismann, La Selva, Pastas Gallo, Rafael Marquina Design, Normann Copenhagen, Hal Cash, Bebé Due, Yves Saint Laurent, Evax, Braun, Logitech, Razer, TENA and Hitachi. This will reveal how implementation of Design for All in each company has proved to be an engine for success.

Don't worry – our objective in writing this book was not to create another "snake oil remedy" that promises to solve with one method all your company's problems. Quite the contrary – what we aimed to do was to find and structure the common denominators of the good practices of many companies that have improved their results thanks to understanding that respecting the diversity of their clients and users is a key factor for business success.

The HUMBLES method is flexible, allowing you to implement it to whatever extent you choose, and even to use it to focus only on issues that are critical for your company at a given time.

Definition of Concepts

In this book, we will refer to certain concepts that can have different meanings in other contexts, so we will first clarify our own usage.

Buyer: A person or entity that acquires the products and services of a company and pays a price for them.

Client: A regular buyer.

Consumer: A person who uses a perishable product or specific service, whether or not he or she has paid for it. Thus, someone who buys a plane ticket and uses it personally is at the same time a client and a user, while a child who drinks a soda bought by his or her grandfather is only a consumer. Similarly, someone can be the user of a fork that a restaurant has provided.

The difference between a buyer/client and an user/consumer is very important, since companies may know a fair amount about the former, but not much about the latter.

Costumer: A person who purchase and or use the products or services.

Design for All: An intervention strategy focused on company environments, products and services in an effort to ensure that everyone (regardless of their gender, build, physical, sensory or intellectual abilities, age, sexual orientation, creed, lifestyle or any other aspect of human diversity, including future generations) is able to enjoy all the opportunities and activities offered by our society.

Although it is true that in the past there were some differences, nowadays the concept of Design for All is identical to strategies known by different names in certain geographical areas, such as Universal Design, Inclusive Design, Utenta Ampliata or Conception Universelle.

Given the historical origin of the concept, many authors have focused exclusively on functional differences in terms of age or disability. This is not at all the focus of the Design for All concept we will present in this book.

Potential client: Someone who is not yet a client, but could become one.

Prescriptor: A person close to the client who advises him or her about the purchase of a particular product or service. This person could be an interior designer, but also a company clerk who chooses a specific car rental agency for his or her superior; it could also include family members who suggest where to go on holidays. A prescriptor may also be a friend who has had a good experience with a service and advises us to use it.

Product: A material object that a company offers to its clients.

Service: An immaterial object that a company offers to its clients.

User: A person who uses a non-consumable product or specific service, whether or not he or she has paid for it.

The HUMBLES Method

CHAPTER 1

Highlight Design for All Opportunities

In this chapter, we will deal with the letter H of HUMBLES ("Highlight Design for All Opportunities") by analysing whether it is likely to be worthwhile for your company to apply Design for All as an aid to achieving its goals and discovering new market opportunities.

In order to do this, we must first remember that Design for All aims to satisfy the needs and wishes of any type of user in the best possible way. Unlike other strategies, Design for All focuses above all on conveying pleasant experiences to users and consumers, not forgetting the clients and prescriptors.

The potential market for a given company is the group of people that is interested in the products or services it offers, has access to them, and has the economic capacity to purchase them. The larger the potential market, the greater the business opportunity. There are many people who have no access to particular products or services due to factors such as age, gender, build and capability. Design for All tries to make the lives of all potential users or buyers of a product or service easier, resulting in increased sales.

The aim is to improve the company's results, offering consumers positive experiences based on respect for the individual, security, health, functionality, ease of use and aesthetic appeal. The company could seek to achieve this by improving its product or service, innovating, improving its reputation, or expanding or improving customer loyalty.

Each company will have a different set of objectives for improvement, as well as different opportunities that the HUMBLES method will offer to achieve them. What opportunities does the method offer? Let us analyse them one by one.

Increasing the Number of Consumers

As we will see in Chapter 2, human diversity can confound expectations – each of us is similar to other people in some respects, but very different in others.

If a consumer perceives that a product or service is easy to use, affordable and convenient, that it respects his or her own creed and lifestyle and generates satisfaction, then the consumer will enter a relationship with that product or service, as well as with the brand and the company it represents. Beyond that, a satisfied consumer will talk about his or her positive experiences (How many times have you recommended a restaurant?) and influence others' view of a product or service. On the other hand, many people have negative experiences with products or services from certain companies, which triggers the opposite effect.

If their products and services are addressed to a wide-ranging population, companies that do not pay attention to ease of use, reliability or respect towards their potential consumers' creeds and habits could be losing as much as 70 per cent of their potential clients.

> *The case of Oxo Enterprises, founded in 1990 with the mission statement "a company focused to provide innovative consumer products that make everyday life easier", provides a very clear example of this first stage of the HUMBLES method.*
>
> *Nowadays, it offers more than 850 products for both young consumers, who prefer them because they are more intelligent, efficient and funny than competitors' offerings, and older consumers or consumers with limited dexterity, because these products are easier to use, convenient and are also used by the youngest and fittest population. As a result of taking this human diversity and its characteristics into account, between 1991 and 2008 the composite annual index in sales growth for Oxo exceeded 27 per cent. (For more information, see Chapter 8.)*

Market research is too often focused on the average user or on ranks of users. We tend to rely on this paradigm in order to simplify matters, but it means that we lose the essence of what is relevant for each consumer. On too many occasions, products are designed with a user type in mind which is believed to represent the whole of a chosen segment. It is easy to miss the key point: each individual consumer wants a satisfying experience while consuming a product or service.

Pause for a moment and consider whether your company fully satisfies its consumers, regardless of their build, age, intellectual abilities, visual abilities, religious beliefs, type of family, gender, and so on. If it does not, your company has fewer consumers than it could have: this is why Design for All should interest you.

Increasing the Number of Clients

Despite their differences, most buyers have something in common: they want to be treated like your most valued client. Some people may be less demanding, or may be used to being treated badly, and may be content with being treated as a "normal client". However, any client will be positively surprised when made to feel especially valued, because everyone likes to feel that a product or service has been designed with him or her in mind.

Remember that the client is the person paying for your services, but on many occasions he or she is not the final consumer. Your client may live with other people who he or she loves and respects, and who in many cases share his or her values. For example, a person responsible for buying the furniture in a law firm will not want to become the target of criticism from his or her bosses because of the wrong choice of chairs.

Have you never felt awful when the toy you gave a child as a birthday present broke within a couple of hours? Do you have the name of the maker and the shop where you bought it etched on your memory, mentally crossed off your list of providers?

Simon is an international company that makes switches, plugs and products for technical installations at home and in the office. Its regular clients are installers, builders and estate agents of homes and buildings, to which it sells through specialized distribution channels.

The final user is rarely the client, except in some cases of home redecoration and DIY. In the design of switches and plugs, Simon has always taken into account all the factors involved in the process. The devices are easy to fit and easy to use. Switches are readily identified by their design and the size of their buttons. Installers can assemble the devices with minimum time and effort. Users, regardless of their age and height, can easily locate and use the switches. Simon also supplies luminous switches for children's bedrooms.

Today, the company trades in all the European Union countries, Russia, Ukraine, Turkey, China, India, Morocco, Brazil, Mexico and Argentina, and in each country products are designed according to clients' and users' specific needs and expectations.

We suggest you pause again at this point, close your eyes and consider these questions:

- Do our products and services appear to be sufficiently respectful of human diversity?
- Are we making clients think twice about their purchasing decisions?

Confirming the Strategy of the Company with Potential and Real Clients and Consumers

Even today, many companies maintain an attitude of superiority towards their clients. Such companies decide how to make the best products for their clients then inform them what is best for them, telling clients whatever serves the company's purposes, making offers when they consider it necessary, and distributing products through the most convenient channels for the company. However, consumers are no longer willing to be subjected to this sort of paternalism.

To stand out among the huge range of available bidders, your concern should be to ensure that clients know your company exists, that they can find it via the channels they monitor regularly, that they like your brands emotionally and for the relationship established with them, and that you are offering your clients something different that, if they like or want it, is worth sharing with whoever they wish.

Thus, if you want your company to be successful, you will have to strive to meet every consumer's demands, and the only way to do this is to learn about them, to get to know your current and potential clients and consumers – and with this in mind, you need to ensure constant redesigning of your company's strategy to satisfy and even exceed your public's expectations.

Each year, Fujitsu organizes The Fujitsu Forum to display the different innovative aspects of the company's work, in which Design for All (in Japan called Universal Design) plays an important role. The main objective behind organizing this forum is to give the company an opportunity to get to know at first hand the reactions and opinions of its potential and current consumers.

Ten thousand people participated in the Tokyo 2007 forum, where it was made clear that Design for All leads to innovation, based on current social trends, renovation of the workplace and favouring expansion of the business. In this way, Fujitsu not only manages to improve its reputation and gain benefits for the company, but also contributes benefits to society and the environment.

The way to achieve this, according to Kimitaka Kato, General Manager of the Fujitsu Centre of Design, is:

Observing how businesses relate to their clients, offering solutions from an approach based on design and realizing the integration of people, processes and technology. The best example of it is Design for All, the result of exhaustive research into the ease of use of products, and an environmental solution that embodies these ideas and concepts in products. This is why Fujitsu offers the latest in comfort for the user and environmental compatibility, developing products that take into account aspects such as the five senses, the physical abilities of the user, cultural and individual sensitivities and the ease of use of the product. Likewise, it also offers a product that satisfies the highest environmental standards, by relying on digitized information that not only reaches everyone everywhere, but also saves on paper and materials.

All of this clearly contributes to attracting new customers, encouraging current ones to remain loyal, and expanding sales. Moreover, it also promotes social responsibility on the part of the company, since corporate sustainability, Design for All and environmental initiatives are recognized and well valued by society at large.

Preventing Problems

Knowing your clients and users in depth enables you to avoid possible conflicts stemming from unexpected or wrong usage of your products.

In an analysis of the use of the BIC ballpoint pen by a relatively small number of users, we discovered more than 50 different applications apart from the logical one of writing with it. One of the unexpected uses is where a child puts the top that protects the tip in his or her mouth and accidentally swallows it. With the previous design, where the tip was closed, the top blocked the entry of air to the lungs, making an urgent tracheotomy necessary to avoid a fatal ending.

This motivated the company to redesign the top to include a small hole in its end so that, in case of involuntary ingestion, it would let air flow to the lungs, allowing time to take the child to hospital and extract it without further injury.

The observation techniques and analysis that we propose with the HUMBLES method will enable you to discover unexpected – and sometimes unfortunate – uses of your products and services before marketing them, which means that you will not only prevent accidents or mistakes in the use of your products or systems, but also the moral and legal ramifications that may result. Apart from this, it will also help you prevent failures in launching your products. Do you remember that birthday present that broke?

Selling in Other Countries

No matter what prestige a company may have, when it intends to sell in other countries, it has to worry about more than just translating manuals into other languages and finding dealers. To avoid failure, it is essential to develop an in-depth knowledge of the culture of the country where the product or service is going to be sold.

Who decides in most cases to buy a woman's perfume in Greece? Which is the best flavour for a sparkling wine in England? Which accessories are most necessary for a vehicle in Illinois? Which are the most wanted? In how many languages is it convenient to display the menus of a computer program in Spain or in South Vietnam? The ideal is to deal with users individually.

The strategy of the Nespresso company is based on three pillars: a very high-quality coffee supplied in individual aluminium capsules that are 100 per cent recyclable, technologically very advanced coffee machines with a great design, and an individual service that goes beyond conventional distribution channels, co-ordinated by the CRC (Centre of Relationship with the Client)

The consumer can choose from a wide variety of coffees. Nespresso is not interested in offering just four brands of coffee. Nespresso asks its clients what type of coffee they like, takes this into account, then makes management and distribution of the product easier for the client (you can call for free 24 hours a day and Nespresso will deliver your order wherever you want within 48 hours).

Furthermore, if the client has a problem with his or her machine, he or she just needs to call Nespresso and its Customer Service Department will supply a replacement machine until it is repaired, within at most one week. Thus, the client can still have his or her coffee and Nespresso has been able to ensure that the service offered is five-star.

Nespresso has six million consumers; it knows the precise profile of each (what type of coffee they like, whether or not they consume decaffeinated varieties, and so on), and a central database allows users to tell when they have made more than 600 cups of coffee and their machine needs to be decalcified. (For more information, see Chapter 10.)

While it is true that this book focuses on success stories, we could write another one full of anecdotes of boycotts, manifest or silent (or even unconscious), of imported products because they have not been tailored to the culture of a territory.

Design for All and the user participation methods that we propose can help you answer all the questions related to adapting to a new territory, ensuring the success of your expansion efforts.

Selling More in the Tourist Sector

A similar situation to selling in other countries occurs with the tourist sector. If it is true that tourists generally travel to get to know other cultures and exotic places, it is also true that in some ways they also want to "feel at home", or at least not to forgo their basic needs and customs.

Thus, for example if they have mobility problems due to their age or other causes, they need to move around their hotel room, and also around their surroundings, without encountering barriers that make the use of a scooter or wheelchair difficult or impossible.

This not only affects those who have a direct problem of temporary or permanent limitation – as we mentioned above when talking about increasing the number of clients, a family with a member who has mobility difficulties will not travel to a place which does not take this into account, so all the family members will be lost as customers.

It is also necessary to respect – and to *show* respect for – different habits and beliefs. For instance, if your restaurant's cellar includes kosher wine (wine manufactured following procedures dictated by the Jewish religion), not only you will be able to offer it to Jewish customers, but others will very likely gain the impression that the restaurant's management is anxious to satisfy all their wishes and needs.

Generally, what almost all tourists want above all is *reliability* in information about means of transport and during their visit, *confidence* in information about their destination and the quality and prices of services, *security* in the streets or in the natural environment, and *reliability* in terms of complementary services (such as medical assistance or local transport). Basically, everyone expects to receive what they have been promised, and to rest assured that in case of any incident, they will be able to communicate with a responsive representative.

If your company operates within this sector, are you convinced that your clients will find all these needs met in their tourist destination? Even if your company describes your offer in all necessary languages and in great detail, who assures your customers that they will enjoy security during their holiday?

The methods of implementation of Design for All also contemplate the establishment of co-operative networks between enterprises and administrations with a common objective.

Sol Meliá, one of the biggest hotel chains in the world, acknowledged that one of the challenges of the Design for All was co-ordinating its efforts with those of the public administration. This is because if a hotel company attempts to implement accessibility and Design for All in a hotel whose surroundings are inaccessible and the services that the town or city offers do not take into account all people, its efforts will have been in vain. (For more information, see Chapter 10.)

Improving the External Reputation

If users and clients are satisfied, it is because they have been offered something that meets or exceeds their expectations and respects their individuality. Companies have their reputations called into doubt when they show a lack of respect towards people. Indeed, we can all think of companies that still have a bad reputation after actions carried out against a certain group of people ten or twenty years ago.

If a company is appreciated by its clients and consumers due to its sensitivity and its respect for human diversity, this will easily spread to their circles of acquaintances. This will contribute to an exponential increase in the number of prescriptors and approval by society at large.

Axel Hotels is a small chain with establishments in Barcelona, Buenos Aires and Berlin catering for the homosexual market, but without excluding anybody. Its official slogan is "Axel, the heterofriendly hotel".
Axel's management focused on offering a good service to a sector of the population who had been unable to find an attractive offer that met their expectations and whom no one else was catering for. This change in vision has led to several awards and acknowledgments because of Axel's defence of equality for all people, as well as expanding its business from its first hotel in Barcelona and increasing its number of customers. (For more information, see Chapter 10.)

Improving the Internal Reputation

From what has been said in the previous section, we can gather that employees and providers have a social motivation as well as an economic and corporative one to insist that the products and services they produce, apart from being high-quality, also respect human diversity (which should also be reflected in the company's human resources policies) and the environment. This way, whatever position you hold in your firm, you will sleep better because the company will improve in reaching its goals, you will keep or improve your job, and you will be collaborating in building a better society.

The experience of developing working methods in a socially responsible company increases self-esteem and has a positive effect on the workplace atmosphere, but we also need to add that employee satisfaction is intrinsically linked to that of the clients.

Sears Roebuck, the big store chain, found that an increase of 5 per cent in employee satisfaction led to an increase of 1 per cent in client satisfaction, which led to an increase in profits of 0.5 per cent, reaching $23.6 billion in 2001: employee and client satisfaction increased profits by $11.8 million.

Furthermore, a study we carried out for the global temporary job recruitment agency Manpower proved that the company's clients valued temporary job recruitment agencies that offered the best treatment and training to their collaborators. The clients felt that employees who had good training and were satisfied with the recruiting agency were more efficient within the company that offered them temporary employment.

Anticipating Trends

This factor is one of the top ten keys to innovation in a company. In some sectors, such as fashion, companies hire observers of trends to detect changes in consumer preferences.

Following the reasoning we have been developing in this chapter, if your company applies the HUMBLES method and as a result you listen to your clients and consumers in the process of product development, you are inevitably interested in the local culture of the countries where your product or service is sold and you maintain a relationship with your clients and consumers. To foresee market trends, you merely need to identify who among them are the most innovative. If you read the situation correctly, what your consumers tell you about their lifestyles, preferences, emerging needs or new products launched by your competition will allow you to anticipate societal trends.

Don't you feel the world's pulse every time you watch TV, read a newspaper, talk to friends or listen to a taxi driver's comments? If so, you will certainly find it appropriate to ask your clients and users about the position of your company in society and what they expect from both of these.

Fiat understands the importance of knowing the most current needs and wishes of its clients, taking into account the rapid changes that are taking place in present-day society, as well as the new social and environmental concerns that are emerging. This is why it took a chance by letting the conception of the model of its brand-new urban car be inspired by users via the Internet.

Continuing the celebration of its thirty-year presence in Brazil, the auto maker encouraged consumers to take part in developing the new Fiat Mio (FCC I Concept Car) model, which is positioned as a car for the new generation.

The festive advertising campaign included the "Fiat 30 Years, Inviting You to Think about the Future" project, launched in 2006, in which Fiat asked Internet users to explain via text, video or audio messages how they saw the brand evolving over the next three decades.

Guided by these perceptions, the Centre of Style/Design of Fiat Brasil developed the FCC I (Concept Car Fiat 1). Following this, they came up with the FCC LL, an environmentally friendly car, and finally, the company started making a third model that includes all the previous ideas and developments.

According to the company's description, "the Fiat Concept Car III is the result of the interpretation of our designers, engineers and researchers, based on all the discussions, suggestions and analyses given by the 14,000 registered participants". In developing the concept, the team processed suggestions submitted by people from more than 40 countries.

The end result is, according to Fiat, "an agile, safe, comfortable compact car with new solutions for inner-city traffic, with a pollutant-free engine and the capacity for updates, personalization and configuration changes with a cutting-edge interface between the cars and its users".

Creating Loyal Clients and Consumers

With the HUMBLES method, we can develop strategies to get to know our users and clients better and maintain constant feedback about their interests, motivations and degrees of satisfaction. The relationship with the client does not end with the purchase of the product – this is just the beginning of a bond that must continue and develop over time.

How many companies devote a huge amount of effort to winning new clients without worrying at all about those who have already purchased a product or service? Let us remember that a satisfied client is the best prescriptor, whose perception of the company has a multiplying effect. According to the American Consumer Association, the cost of obtaining a new client is 5–20 times greater than that of retaining an existing one.

Curiously, on many occasions when companies do recognize existing clients' potential as prescriptors, instead of trying to establish a long-lasting win–win relationship, they overstep the mark, for instance by sending them a form letter asking for their friends' contact details in exchange for free coffee machines.

Clients and consumers are loyal when a relationship of trust based on satisfaction has been established. If this trust is sustained only by the quality and price of your product, any element that unbalances this relationship, or even the appearance of new competition in the market, will endanger your company. However, maintaining a dialogue with your clients will lead to their loyalty being based on something much more solid.

Do you think that by improving the process of developing loyal clients, your company could obtain benefits?

Again, the Nespresso example is eloquent. As Vincent Termote, Managing Director of Nestlé Nespresso Iberia, explained:

"All the activities we carry out are based on one model: to win clients, welcome them and transform them into 'fans'. The Nespresso model is based on the fact that our consumers are our best ambassadors – what more can we ask for? It is because of this that over the past five years we have been talking more about experience. I think Nespresso has managed to change a consumer article, a coffee – the second most consumed product after petrol – into a unique experience. I always say that before now, luxury was confined to 'the few lucky ones'; now Nespresso has created a luxury with a new equilibrium – a luxury for all."

We also find this predisposition in the Ferrocarrils de la Generalitat de Catalunya (FGC).

FGC is a public rail company that runs some inter-city lines in Barcelona as well as other minor trunk lines in other regions. It has a reputation and for high quality and a strict policy on Design for All.

For years it has used two concepts to measure the quality of its services: expected quality (the level it hoped to attain) and programmed quality (the level it has committed to provide), without overlooking transparency in its management at all levels of the company. FGC wants people to explain to it what exactly has happened, what went wrong, and what it can do to prevent it from happening again.

Thus, FGC distinguishes itself through its culture based on quality of service, reflected in details such as design, signage, cleaning standards and the friendliness of its staff. All this is very highly valued by the users of its service, and is monitored annually by means of a survey in which the company obtains an Index of Client Satisfaction, considered "a thermometer of what people think about their service". (For more information, see Chapter 10.)

Cutting Costs in the Medium Term

Nowadays, many books about bringing down costs feature in the top ten lists of bestsellers. All businesses are looking to reduce costs in order to improve their competitiveness. These reductions are sought mainly in administration and production departments, but only too rarely does the idea crop up that creating loyal clients can be an important source of savings.

There are companies in some sectors that have managed to almost eliminate their marketing expenses because their clients themselves call them when they need their products or services. Why? Because they have managed to be perceived by their clients as a "solution" to their needs – they have reached a level of trust based on transparency and flexibility in adapting to their clients' demands and consumers' needs, so they know who to contact when such a wish or need arises.

If concerted efforts are made to maintain contact with clients and users, focusing on creating and strengthening the bond with them, marketing expenses can be reduced radically, as the Nespresso example shows.

Since 1999, Nespresso has developed a network of boutique-style shops, so that clients can "see the face of the brand". For the company, these shops are very important because they serve three purposes:

1. *They build up the brand because they convey its identity (the values being elegance, quality, perception of luxury, and so on); on entering the Nespresso world, you perceive a different experience – it's not just a coffee, it's a lot more than that.*
2. *They establish a direct relationship with the consumer.*
3. *They serve as a distribution channel for the sale of coffee capsules, machines and accessories.*

The boutique expansion has taken place bearing in mind the individual characteristics of the countries where they are located. At an international level, the boutiques represent 35 per cent of turnover; in some countries like Spain it reaches almost 50 per cent. Some countries are very Internet-oriented, like the USA, whereas others are less so, like Spain. In some countries Nespresso has developed what it calls "boutique bars", because they allow it to appeal to people in markets where Nespresso has not yet established a strong base.

Nespresso has managed to become a "loved" brand due to this marketing strategy, and specifically the focus on communication and design as an integrated whole: the boutiques, mailings, Internet outreach, communication in appliance shops – everything is harmonized to achieve 360-degree communication. (For more information, see Chapter 10.)

If you believe that your company can develop its methods for creating loyal clients as a marketing tool, then you have another reason to apply Design for All.

Innovating in Products and Services

Innovation is obviously a creative process. To achieve commercial success, it is essential to innovate in order to meet the consumer's wishes or needs better than competitors do, or to create new desires or needs. In any case, these wishes or needs originate from the users.

Companies often resort to improving their products in technical terms, changing the image of their services or hiring renowned designers to apply their creative abilities to improving the aesthetics and functionality of their offerings – even in some cases coming up with completely new products. Since the target of the innovations is the users, in all their diversity, it is essential to take into account their wishes, needs and views when developing new products or services. This is the basis of *user-centred design* – a method adopted by a number of leading companies.

> *Volvo is an automobile company whose focus on safety has made it famous. The company's innovations have always been based on making people's safety a basic priority. It has also other values, as the development of "Your Concept Car" (YCC) has shown.*
>
> *One study showed that in the USA, the most important car market in the world, no fewer than 54 per cent of Volvo's clients were women, so the company committed to the idea of YCC, a prototype created by a team made up entirely of women, bringing a breath of fresh air to the world of car-making with solutions based on simple everyday life concerns.*
>
> *The design for YCC was really surprising. The team focused on three areas: ergonomics, storage and comfort.*
>
> *Although the car was designed by a group of women, this did not imply that this was a communication strategy aimed at conquering the female market. What it really aimed to do was increase the profile of women working within the company, and in this way to keep innovating by promoting the social responsibility politics of Volvo, nominating women to occupy up to 25 per cent of the company's management positions by 2005.*

According to accepted wisdom, these processes slow down the design process, and given the tight deadlines currently involved in launching a product, user participation is not feasible. However, the HUMBLES method suggests various formulas to make it possible without lengthening the processes of innovation.

Transforming Products into Services

Not all innovations concentrate exclusively on technological development or industrial design. Some companies that make and sell products have managed to transform these through a chain of services. We only have to remember, for example, the step taken by Nestlé when it went from selling coffee using traditional distribution channels to developing the Nespresso concept with its own boutiques, maintenance service, and so on.

In addition to this, if the company is able to keep abreast of its consumers' diversity, the opportunities multiply. This is the case with IKEA, in the words of its Communication Managing Director:

> *"We must look at several different aspects. One of them is the development of the product. We don't just sell products; we are also selling a way of furnishing their home, informing people about how to live in their home, and this kind of information*

is free; it is something customers can find for themselves in the stores. So the idea is that we don't sell products; we sell solutions to improve home life. Thus, our idea is to convey this kind of recommendation via the Web, the catalogue and the stores. And we are doing this for everybody."

In the case of IKEA, it has evolved from the business model of a "furniture shop" into the IKEA concept, which includes transport and assembly services, coffee bars, decorative objects and in-house grocery shops, but also nurseries, design assistance, preferential parking and loyalty cards as values added to the purchase.

Do you think this is the right approach for your company?

Focusing the Company on the Client or User

Transforming the culture of an organization from "We offer this and we have to convince our clients to buy it" to "We are going to try to satisfy consumers' diversity with our abilities" is a gigantic step forward.

Santa & Cole, an editing design company with international scope, put Design for All into practice when it considered that its focus was not only individuals, but the whole planet.

The idea of Design for All – Universal Design, design without exclusion – was a prime consideration for the company when it evolved from designing for people to designing for cities, or even for the planet. In the words of Javier Nieto Santa, founder and CEO of Santa & Cole: "If you then go on to design with the planet in mind, you include everybody and you exclude no one."

Design for All has become a lot more than a business opportunity for the company. (For more information, see Chapter 10.)

Changing an organization and replacing one model with another is a prodigious task – it doesn't just involve a change of strategy, but a transformation of the entire business model.

The HUMBLES method does not seek to guide companies through this process. It aims only to establish in-depth knowledge of users' and clients' wishes and needs, and to take them into account while making this transition between models.

Finding New Business Lines

When establishing innovative processes, you may often find that apart from information that is relevant to developing the intended line of products and services, unexpected elements will appear that will open up new possibilities for innovation that were totally unexpected. Once they have learnt at first hand their users' expectations, many companies have decided to start up new lines of products and services.

We have followed with interest how one robotics software company successfully opened up a new arm devoted to producing touchscreen software for vending machines and public information displays. Another company developed mobile phone accessories for noisy environments and enabling users to listen to music underwater, which was triggered by its aim of enabling the use of phones by people with hearing difficulties. We could carry on with a long list of examples of new product lines that originated from collaborative design processes with users. To achieve, this you only need to devote some effort and use the right methods.

> *IDEO, a design services company, obtained a major contract from Bank of America to study its clients' behaviour. Traditionally, many American families saved the small change from their everyday purchases, eventually amounting to a small savings account. Payment by credit card made that custom obsolete.*
>
> *Thanks to the IDEO project, the bank offered a system that rounded up the amounts paid by credit card and lodged them automatically in a savings account. In less than a year, Bank of America opened 700,000 new bank accounts and a million new savings accounts.*

Consolidating the Ethical Principles of the Company

Very often, large companies draw up a code of ethics or declare their principles from the highest levels of the company's executive board. However, ensuring that these ethical principles penetrate the whole structure and culture of the company and are finally reflected in its relationship with society involves a long and complex process that rarely takes place in a completely satisfactory way. One of the main reasons for this is the perception that there is little relationship between these principles and everyday work. Fortunately, there are occasions when these principles are well rooted in the culture of the company and are evident at all levels.

> *IKEA started looking for people who shared the founder's values (a sense of fraternity, respect, simplicity, cost-awareness, and so on) with the idea that they would become ambassadors for the company's philosophy. One of its managers commented:*
>
> *The IKEA philosophy refers to the idea that we are aiming at the majority of people, to help them find ways of improving their home life, and in order to do that, accessibility is a very important concept. Accessibility in all senses – price or functionality – is definitely part of this company's value system.*
>
> *And according to the company's Corporate Social Responsibility Policy:*
>
> *At the IKEA Group, we believe that taking responsibility for people and the environment is a prerequisite for doing good business. IKEA works actively to reduce our impact on climate change, and IKEA products must be produced under acceptable working conditions at suppliers that take responsibility for the environment. (For more information, see Chapter 10.)*

One of the objectives of Design for All is to ensure that these principles of respect towards human diversity and the environment are reflected in the products and services offered by the company. The HUMBLES method develops tools that enable everyone involved in the administration process of the company and in the design, manufacture and marketing of its products and services to integrate those ethical values into their everyday work.

All of this makes ethical principles compatible with corporative objectives, promoting development of the company while serving as an engine for social improvement.

Increasing the Company's Prestige

This is the last, but not least important, reason to apply Design for All in your company.

Companies must ensure visibility in their immediate surroundings and in society as a whole by promoting a positive image.

Axel Hotels didn't rely on conventional advertising, but undertook a major initiative to generate positive news coverage. One of the basic objectives of its press office was to obtain considerable media coverage through articles, interviews and advertising.

It was very important to convey to the media and society in general that the destinations that the Axel Hotels chain offers are not conventional, but vibrant and dynamic places: cornerstones of the gay scene in each of the cities where they are located, but with a "heterofriendly" philosophy that welcomes everybody. The Axel atmosphere, the excellent service, the great loyalty of its cosmopolitan and very demanding clients, as well as an excellent quality–price relationship, mean that the future for Axel Hotels looks very rosy. (For more information, see Chapter 10.)

Any of these reasons to apply the HUMBLES method and each of the phases are potential generators of a great quantity of "good news" that society around you and the media will welcome with open arms if they are the result of a transparent and honest process.

In the past, the vast majority of publicity that could make or break companies or organizations relied on conventional media. Nowadays, means of social communication are available to all citizens, such as Twitter, Facebook and YouTube, so consumers can play a direct role in granting your company the prestige it deserves for its efforts to satisfy them and share their values, potentially enhancing respect towards your company and its reputation, both among your consumers and the general public.

Which Companies are Most Likely to Benefit from the HUMBLES Method?

HUMBLES is mainly geared to companies whose products or services will directly interact with their final clients or consumers and that wish to establish a strong bond between those customers and their brand. This includes manufacturers of all types of consumer products – electronic gadgets, appliances, publications, vehicles, toys, buildings, furniture, distribution and retail services, virtual shops, multimedia products, communication and distribution services, tourism and restoration, health or transport – all can expect to benefit from new opportunities.

However, HUMBLES can also be of great benefit to companies that do not have direct contact with the public, for example:

- **companies that provide public administration** – since they usually values aspects like ethics and respect towards citizens;
- **manufacturers of products that are integrated into another product** – for instance, manufacturers of seats for transport vehicles, iron fittings for furniture, elements for construction or packaging, to name only a few;
- **companies whose clients value their codes of ethics** – you must not forget that your company can potentially arouse the sympathy of friends and families of people who may face marginalization; and
- **companies concerned with innovation and/or the constant improvement of quality** – for instance, any company that cares about its clients' values, that explores trends in an effort to respond to its clients' expectations and whose business model is based on the development of new concepts to satisfy emerging needs in the market; this group of companies includes consultants for innovation and professionals in the field of design in the widest sense of the term, such as those working in software, architecture, graphic, fashion and industrial design.

To help you understand the opportunities HUMBLES could generate for your company, we suggest that you complete a brief exercise. In the middle column of the table below, mark with dense shading those opportunities you consider fundamental, with less dense shading those that, while important, are not essential, and leave blank those that are not relevant to your company. On the right-hand side of the table we have laid out the aspects you will have to focus your energy on when it comes to implementing the HUMBLES method.

Design for All (DfA) opportunities table

Opportunities of Design for All	Degree of interest	Main aspects to bear in mind
Increasing consumers		✓ Functional diversity and age of users/clients ✓ Cultural diversity
Increasing clients		✓ Functional diversity and age of users/clients ✓ Cultural diversity
Winning loyal clients and consumers		✓ Cultural diversity ✓ Observation of final user and that user's participation in design processes
Reducing costs in the medium term		✓ Observation of final user and that user's participation in design processes ✓ External communication of DfA ✓ Integration of values of DfA in the organization of the company
Selling in other countries		✓ Functional diversity and age of users/clients ✓ Cultural diversity
Selling in the tourist sector		✓ Functional diversity and age of users/clients ✓ Cultural diversity
Preventing problems		✓ Functional diversity and age of users/clients ✓ Cultural diversity ✓ Observation of final user and that user's participation in design processes
Confirming the company's strategy		✓ Observation of final user and that user's participation in design processes ✓ Integration of values of DfA in the organization of the company
Foreseeing trends		✓ Cultural diversity ✓ Observation of final user and that user's participation in design processes ✓ Integration of values of DfA in the organization of the company
Being innovative in products and services		✓ Observation of final user and that user's participation in design processes ✓ Integration of values of DfA in the organization of the company
Transforming products into services		✓ Observation of final user and that user's participation in design processes ✓ Integration of values of DfA in the organization of the company
Focusing the company on the client/user		✓ Observation of final user and that user's participation in design processes ✓ Integration of values of DfA in the organization of the company

Opportunities of Design for All	Degree of interest	Main aspects to bear in mind
Finding new business lines		✓ Cultural diversity ✓ Observation of final user and that user's participation in design processes
Improving the external reputation		✓ Cultural diversity ✓ External communication of DfA ✓ Integration of values of DfA in the organization of the company
Consolidating the company's Code of Ethics		✓ External communication of DfA ✓ Integration of values of DfA in the organization of the company
Improving the internal reputation		✓ Integration of values of DfA in the organization of the company
Increasing the company's prestige		✓ Functional diversity and age of users/clients ✓ Cultural diversity ✓ Observation of final user and that user's participation in design processes ✓ External communication of DfA ✓ Integration of values of DfA in the organization of the company

Once you have completed this exercise, you should have a clear idea of the opportunities that the HUMBLES method can generate for your company.

To illustrate the HUMBLES process, we will end each chapter in this part of the book with an episode of a story about a fictional company, Sweetme Ltd, and various characters that draws together many of the insights, procedures, anecdotes and results of the HUMBLES method that we have observed in real business management environments.

Peter Kwan's Story

Peter Kwan had finished his marketing studies many years ago, and since then had developed his career in two major distribution and retail companies. About two years ago, the opportunity he had been waiting for arose – the position of Marketing Director in a company with a smaller turnover than the chain he had been working in, but with a truly international market. As its name suggests, Sweetme Ltd manufactured sweets. Although Peter did not have a deep knowledge of this market, he was thrilled by the challenge of developing the company's marketing strategies.

During his first months with the company, Peter assimilated a large amount of knowledge about the history of the company, which had made the same successful product since 1969, including its manufacturing processes, distribution networks, geographical penetration across five continents and its human resources, and obviously he had studied in depth everything involved in his new responsibilities.

Peter had landed the job because the business owner was retiring and could not consolidate a second generation of his family to run the business, and had therefore decided to sell it to an investment fund. The fund hired a new CEO, Frank Wright, who analysed the sustained decrease in sales over recent years and decided the organization needed new blood.

Peter immediately spotted several aspects in the areas of distribution and advertising that were frankly desperate for improvement.

One day, driving home in his new car, he listened to an interview that caught his attention. Someone was talking about improving company results by improving consumers' experiences – pretty obvious, he thought. However, when he started listening to the data the interviewee was citing about consumers that companies unintentionally excluded, he started taking a greater interest in the interview and wondered whether any of this information could be applied to Sweetme.

When he arrived home, he decided that to avoid forgetting all about it, he would visit the website mentioned by interviewee. There he found a description of a method called HUMBLES that he had heard about in the interview. He also found that just a week later, a seminar to introduce the method was going to be held in his home city.

The following day in his office, he checked the information available about HUMBLES on the Internet, and decided to sign up for the seminar. He told Frank about his intention, giving him an overall explanation of the seminar programme and arguing that it would be very interesting to develop their knowledge of their consumers, since the only such data currently available had been gathered for advertising campaign briefings some time ago.

At the seminar, as always happens in these situations, the consultant who was introducing the seven-stage HUMBLES method described with enthusiasm cases of companies that had succeeded because they were consumer-oriented. He also set out the benefits just waiting to be claimed. He talked about Design for All and the ethical aspects this philosophy entailed. Near the end, in a bit of a hurry, he handed out a folder of tables and a book, explaining very superficially how to use them to start applying the method in participants' own companies.

On the way home, Peter kept thinking over that day's experiences. "You get the feeling that the developers of every method think that it will sort out all a company's problems," he thought. "The amount of work I have in my department, now that I'm familiar with the company, and these people want me to spend my time filling out tables! And very likely all the time devoted will be wasted on paper exercises. Papers are all very well, but once you have to turn theoretical ideas into reality ...."

Arriving home, he decided to forget about the whole thing and focus on his family. He took the seminar folder to his home office, and after hesitating a little, decided to leave the book on his night table. Peter liked reading in bed, but usually fiction, especially science fiction. However, he found what he'd been reading recently very boring, and thought he might skim through the new book instead.

The following day, while having a coffee with Frank Wright and Fiona Belsem, the Finance Director, Frank asked him about the seminar. Despite not being at all sure whether it had been worthwhile, Peter talked to them about it with a degree of enthusiasm, to make clear that it had not been a total waste of time.

Back in his office, he thought that on reflection, the seminar hadn't been so bad.

One night three days later, reading in bed, an unforgivable mistake in the plot of the boring science fiction novel he was reading made him throw it aside in disgust and he started to riffle through the book from the seminar.

When he reached the table about "Opportunities of Design for All", he thought about which ones could apply to Sweetme. Next morning, he completed the exercise and captured them on paper.

Opportunities of Design for All	Degree of interest	Main aspects to bear in mind
Increasing consumers		✓ Functional diversity and age of users/clients ✓ Cultural diversity
Increasing clients		✓ Functional diversity and age of users/clients ✓ Cultural diversity
Winning loyal clients and consumers		✓ Cultural diversity ✓ Observation of final user and that user's participation in design processes

Opportunities of Design for All	Degree of interest	Main aspects to bear in mind
Reducing costs in the medium term		✓ Observation of final user and that user's participation in design processes ✓ External communication of DfA ✓ Integration of values of DfA in the organization of the company
Selling in other countries		✓ Functional diversity and age of users/clients ✓ Cultural diversity
Selling in the tourist sector		✓ Functional diversity and age of users/clients ✓ Cultural diversity
Preventing problems		✓ Functional diversity and age of users/clients ✓ Cultural diversity ✓ Observation of final user and that user's participation in design processes
Confirming the company's strategy		✓ Observation of final user and that user's participation in design processes ✓ Integration of values of DfA in the organization of the company
Foreseeing trends		✓ Cultural diversity ✓ Observation of final user and that user's participation in design processes ✓ Integration of values of DfA in the organization of the company
Being innovative in products and services		✓ Observation of final user and that user's participation in design processes ✓ Integration of values of DfA in the organization of the company
Transforming products into services		✓ Observation of final user and that user's participation in design processes ✓ Integration of values of DfA in the organization of the company
Focusing the company on the client/user		✓ Observation of final user and that user's participation in design processes ✓ Integration of values of DfA in the organization of the company
Finding new business lines		✓ Cultural diversity ✓ Observation of final user and that user's participation in design processes
Improving the external reputation		✓ Cultural diversity ✓ External communication of DfA ✓ Integration of values of DfA in the organization of the company
Consolidating the company's Code of Ethics		✓ External communication of DfA ✓ Integration of values of DfA in the organization of the company

Opportunities of Design for All	Degree of interest	Main aspects to bear in mind
Improving the internal reputation		✓ Integration of values of DfA in the organization of the company
Increasing the company's prestige		✓ Functional diversity and age of users/clients ✓ Cultural diversity ✓ Observation of final user and that user's participation in design processes ✓ External communication of DfA ✓ Integration of values of DfA in the organization of the company

"OK," he thought, "I wish it were true that these aspects could be improved. Tonight I'll continue reading the book, but I have a hunch that this approach may involve expensive and complicated techniques."

To be continued ...

2 User Identification

One of the main marketing principles is the concept of segmentation and the segmentation strategies companies must follow. It stems from a simple statement: the market is made up of people, and these vary greatly. This means that it is impossible for a single offer to satisfy all potential customers. Efficient and effective companies encourage people to choose their products or services because the companies adapt to their customers and offer what they need.

The first step is to get to know the market your company is addressing and the features of the people it comprises. Faced with the obvious difficulty of getting to know them all, companies try to group customers together according to common characteristics. These are known as *segments*.

There is no unique formula to divide a market into segments. The variables can very diverse, depending on the product, the consumers, and even the creativity of the company in coming up with original ways to group the segments. The traditional variables are gender, age, build, purchasing power, and so on – variables that depend on tangible characteristics of the individual. There are psychological values, such as lifestyle or the attitude towards a product, that are more difficult to measure, although useful for some offers. In short, confronted with the general impossibility of satisfying everybody, the aim is for the company to select those segments in which it is more likely to succeed, and to tailor its offers to cater for these. This is known as a *concentrated segmentation strategy* if addressed to just one segment, or a *differential segmentation strategy* if addressed to several segments through different offers. The offers can be distinguished by differentiation of the product or differentiation of other aspects, such as distribution, prices or communication methods.

This idea of segmentation as a tool for achieving efficiency is not at all contrary to the philosophy of Design for All. On the one hand, Design for All tries not to lose any potential consumer within the company's chosen segment, and on the other hand, it bears in mind that people belonging to other segments than the chosen one can also be clients/users who share the product with the chosen consumer type.

We must also bear in mind that the market has been moving from a situation where companies used to tell consumers what they needed to the present-day one where consumers choose what is suitable for them and compare offers.

This is their priority option, and they do not care whether or not this is part of the marketing mix that your company has designed.

Would you reject anyone who might like to buy your product?

Who are the Hidden Clients and Consumers?

As we mentioned at the beginning of this chapter, market research tends to identify an average client as a target. However, such average clients do not exist.

It is very common to attribute specific characteristics to a given age group. For instance, someone can generalize that youngsters are non-conformist, and such non-conformity is expressed through their clothing, the music they listen to and their limited dialogue with the adults who have some authority over them. It could also be said that these youngsters, born into a highly technological world, have created new languages such as textspeak, and that parallel to this, their oral and written abilities have decreased. Thus, someone could state: "Youngsters are like this."

However, many young people study and play classical instruments, others win literary awards before the age of 20, and others are absolutely convinced that their parents are the model to follow and have never questioned their authority – they may even dress as formally as their parents do.

Why, then, do advertisements for small cars, supposedly aimed at youngsters, feature rock music, non-conformist-looking youngsters and provocative messages? Do these advertisements appeal to youngsters who do not comply with the stereotype? The answer is that since it is impossible to produce an advertisement that fits the tastes and preferences of each of the young potential clients, the campaign is geared to what is thought to be the majority group. This may rule out as much as 35–45 per cent of potential customers.

Now let's look to the other extreme: the elderly. Are they really keen on ballroom dancing and board games, or is this simply a stereotype? When is someone classed as old – when they are 55, 65 or 80? People generally consider someone old if they are 10 or 15 years older than they are. Because of this, when we look at ourselves in a mirror, we may find it hard to accept that the person reflected is us, since we may feel a lot younger than the physical aspects of the person in the reflection.

How many people older than 100 drive their own car? How many social volunteers older than 80 devote a great deal of their day to helping others? How many people older than 70 serve as political, religious or entrepreneurial leaders?

Despite the evidence, the market tends to behave as if the elderly are constantly practising ballroom dancing and macramé, thus neglecting to offer adequate services to the group in society which happens to have the highest purchasing power.

We could talk about other stereotypes, but the aim of this chapter is to encourage you to think about human diversity and the all too common mistake of basing marketing strategies on stereotypes and prejudices. We must consider human diversity in all its aspects when it comes to designing and marketing products and services aimed at clients and users.

Aspects of Human Diversity

AGE

Many everyday products may be chosen by adults or the elderly, but be used or consumed by children. The choice between one product and another may be based on their nutritional qualities, the ease of opening and using them, or how well they fit in the larder. However, children will be more likely to focus on flavour, any associated gifts or the colour of the packaging, as well as ease of use.

Another aspect to take into account is that some products and services are addressed to wide age ranges: hotels and other accommodation, vending machines for transportation tickets – the list could go on and on. All of them seek to offer safety, comfort, functionality, respect, attractiveness and clarity, regardless of the user's age.

In the most developed societies, children constitute 17 per cent of the population, while the elderly currently make up only 16 per cent. As we mentioned above, demographic trends predict a major increase in the elderly sector of the population, and by 2050, in the most developed countries, 40 per cent of the total population will be over 65.

LATERALITY

How well we can use our hands depends on our age, but mainly on laterality. Between 8 and 13 per cent of the population are left-handed (13 per cent of men, 9 per cent of women), while another 5 per cent show crossed laterality, where the laterality of the most skilled hand does not coincide with that of the most skilled eye or leg.

Despite the fact that left-handed people are a very important sector of the population, a large number of products that require manual ability have been designed exclusively for right-handed people. Examples include scissors and knives or some models of computer mouse.

DIMENSIONAL DIVERSITY

It is common in schools to find chairs and tables designed for average age group heights that were standard many years ago. Especially during adolescence, this can mean that some students cannot put their feet on the ground while others have their legs literally jammed between the table and the floor.

We have all experienced the uncomfortable situation in a cinema of sitting behind someone who prevents our seeing the screen properly. Obviously, it is not the person's fault that they are of a certain height or build, but that of the cinema theatre designer for failing to consider this issue.

Let us consider the unfair overpayment that a very tall person who does not have a high income must face in buying clothing, shoes and special-size beds, let alone the risk of banging his or her head against door lintels, sleeping with legs folded in hotels and countless other inconveniences.

Similar considerations apply to short people. Difficulty finding suitable clothing in shops, being unable to reach lift buttons or the card slot on ATMs – these are just a few examples of the many inconveniences they can face.

Another aspect of dimensional diversity is build and obesity, which may compel people to buy special clothing, or mean that they cannot fit in standard armchairs or that they have to buy two plane tickets in order to have something approaching a comfortable journey. On the other hand, very thin adults may have to buy clothes made for adolescents in order to get clothing in their size.

An estimated 20 per cent of the population have dimensions that companies do not usually take into account.

FUNCTIONAL LIMITATIONS

Functional limitations include restricted ranges of body movement, sight, hearing or balance problems, as well as limited reasoning abilities or difficulties understanding the environment where we manage our lives.

We may notice how useful one of our fingers can be and its key roles in our daily activities when, due to a small accident, we have had to bandage or immobilize it. Throughout our lives, there are many circumstances in which, due to a deficit in our abilities or an unfriendly environment, we may experience problems with communication, mobility or perception. For example, people who wear spectacles have their lenses mist up when they open the top of a pressure cooker, and they also see distorted images when, on a rainy day, raindrops fall on their lenses. A slight stiff neck or lumbago can make many of our everyday movements difficult. When we are in a country whose language we don't know, we may find ourselves lost, and if we are within a group that speaks a language we don't know, we may feel isolated and vulnerable.

All of these are small changes in our life whose memory will eventually fade because they are fleeting situations. However, when we grow old, we face on a daily basis text that is too small to read without aids, messages we cannot understand if the speaker does not vocalize clearly and situations that demand a speed of reaction that is beyond us.

We should not forget that a significant number of people – whether due to accident or illness – cannot walk, or perceive colours, or hear well, or make logical deductions, or use their hands or practise any other ability that we take for granted. Around 20 per cent of the population in developed countries cannot go up stairs unaided, and 20–25 per cent face situations in which it is difficult to move without assistance.

In Europe, one in four families has a member with disabilities. Offering products or services that marginalize such people means that the company renounces 25 per cent of its potential market.

In considering functional diversity and cultural habits, we find a wide range of factors that make it difficult for some people to read or understand written messages, or to communicate with their social environment. Dementia, lack of knowledge of the local language, mental disability, a low level of education or dyslexia are some of the factors that we need to take into account.

RELIGIOUS AND CULTURAL HABITS

Each of us is born into a culture based on values, beliefs and traditions passed down from generation to generation. Despite the fact that globalization frequently puts us in contact with unfamiliar traditions and cultural values, and despite the fact that in some locations such traditions are fading away, our ways of thinking and behaving are totally imbued with aspects of the civilization we belong to. For instance, while it is true that in Europe and North America, eating sushi or ostrich or kangaroo meat has become more widely accepted, this is not the case with dog meat or insects.

Likewise, some religions impose restrictions on some nutritional habits and promote periods of fasting, seclusion or celebration that are different from those we are used to. Over the years, successive migrations have transferred these habits and beliefs to areas of the planet where they were not customary. To grasp this diversity, it is worth bearing in mind that the world's population includes 2.1 billion Christians, 1.5 billion Muslims, 900 billion Hindus, 376 million Buddhists and 15 million Jews, to name just a few religions.

However, not only religious habits must be considered. We also need to bear in mind that together with habits and beliefs that are typical of each civilization, some people decide, as a group or individually, to adopt a set of values or habits with the aim of feeling healthier or more balanced – for example, vegetarians, athletes or those who practise meditation.

With every passing year, due to economic factors and ease of travel, cultural diversity at the core of our societies is growing. We can no longer regard France as a country made up of white Catholic French-speaking people. Nowadays, people of all sorts of races and creeds live together, speaking a large number of languages. What would be extraordinary nowadays would be to find a place in the world with a culturally homogeneous population. We need to bear all these factors in mind when trying to place our products in the market.

FAMILY STRUCTURE

While all cultures consist of one type of family arrangement or another, whether extended or nuclear, in the most industrialized countries several sociological and cultural factors have contributed to the disintegration of the family unit. In the United States, for instance, only 20 per cent of homes are inhabited by what might be considered a typical family structure, with a father, mother and biological children. The rest are inhabited by family units with a wide variety of compositions. In countries like Germany or Denmark, 40 per cent of the population – mostly the elderly – live on their own. Nevertheless, family movies and advertising keep being addressed mainly to particular – clearly minority – family clichés.

The situation is similar with many of the products offered on the market. Some food products are sold in packs that it would take one person a year to consume. On the other hand, in Europe, three- or four-bedroom apartments are advertised, whereas the use of these rooms will usually be two bedrooms, a home office and a storage room or room for ironing and/or storage.

ILLNESSES AND ALLERGIES

It seems that one of the consequences of our highly developed societies is that allergies are increasingly common. In Europe, one in three inhabitants is allergic to some element in the environment (dust, animal hair or foods, for instance). In the United States, an estimated 4 per cent of its inhabitants are allergic to some types of dried fruit or fish. On the one hand, scientists have observed that the prevalence of allergies has increased in parallel with the level of development. On the other hand, genetic changes are also becoming more frequent; it becoming commonplace to encounter children and adults who are intolerant to gluten, lactose, nuts, fish or other foodstuffs.

Psychological ailments are also having a bigger impact in modern societies, where we find frequent cases of depression, claustrophobia or agoraphobia, not to mention organic illnesses related to work and consumerism, such as hypertension, obesity, stress or muscular and skeletal problems.

All these factors must be taken into consideration when it comes to the design of buildings, products and services.

SEXUAL ORIENTATION

In addition to the considerations above – and aside from any moral judgements any of us may make – there are sexual orientations like bisexuality or homosexuality that are part of the way of life of very important segments of the population, to the extent that that some tourist destinations and companies focus on catering for consumers with minority sexual preferences.

DIFFERENT ECONOMIC RESOURCES

This is one of the few aspects of human diversity that companies have studied in depth so far. Before launching a product into the market, it is common to analyse the population's purchasing power and consumption habits, with the intention of placing the product successfully among its competitors. Some companies even manage to place several brands in the market with different qualities and pricing in order to achieve the widest population coverage.

We should not forget, however, that even people with the highest incomes use everyday basic products (often it is an employee who purchases them), and that people with more modest incomes may decide to celebrate special events in very expensive ways. In Europe, for instance, a Gypsy wedding can mobilize hundreds or thousands of people to gather in a celebration full of luxury and spectacle.

While bearing in mind the fact that there are old people, numerous types of families, left- and right-handed people, people with a wide range of abilities and practitioners of different religions, we must remember that, in general, each of these persons is unique and may not conform to a group stereotype, and that each brings his or her individual values to society, and because of this, needs individual attention to his or her needs and wishes.

We cannot forget, either, that each of these people has a family and/or a close social circle of friends and acquaintances who share love and respect, and that they will feel offended if someone marginalizes or mistreats a loved one. Neglecting this could have very negative consequences for your company.

For instance, the owner of a hotel oriented to holding conventions may decide that, given the low percentage of wheelchair users, it is not profitable to invest in ensuring the hotel is accessible for this sector of the population. By taking this decision, the owner may have made a conscious decision to forgo the opportunity to sell services or products to these people, but perhaps not realize that the decision will also deter any groups of family members or friends that include a wheelchair user, or regular clients who, because of an accident or ageing, begin to use a wheelchair, and will also lose the opportunity to host any convention where wheelchair users are expected to participate. In addition, the owner may not realize that the modifications needed to make the premises accessible for wheelchair users would make it a more comfortable hotel for all customers.

PUTTING YOURSELF IN SOMEONE ELSE'S PLACE

A very widespread assumption is that clients will appreciate the values and quality we offer as much as we do. However, only rarely do companies try to step into their clients' shoes and find out how their offer is perceived from the perspective of customers' value systems, abilities and social circumstances. Even when this exercise is attempted, it is usually conducted based not on reality, but on false clichés stemming from preconceived ideas about what it means to be an old person, a Muslim, a homosexual, a tall person, a Hispanic person, and so forth.

Putting yourself in someone else's shoes relies on open-minded communication with a wide variety of people. You need to set aside preconceptions and explore wherever you intend to market your products or services, sharing views with people you would probably never otherwise meet. This means that you need to get out on the street if you want to get to know your potential consumers, and not do it alone – take with you directors who are usually office-bound, escape from the pages of market reports, and venture out into the real world to test and change your ideas and opinions about those who consume your product or service. Only in this way – by asking questions, listening to people and learning – will you be able to begin to take a proper look at your consumers' world and see it as it truly is.

Who are Our Current Users and Clients, and Who Do We Want them to Be?

Many companies do not gather any data about their client's characteristics; others gather such data, but never analyse the results. Some analyse certain clients' data, but fail to do so for data from their end consumers. In general, companies do not have access to sufficient data to guide them in how to communicate and what they should offer to their clients and consumers.

If this is true in your case, what can you do to improve the situation?

First, you need to establish who is buying and using your products and who you need to reach out to with your communication methods. Depending on the resources available and whether you decide to make an initial superficial analysis or tackle the subject in a more scientific way, the methods used will need to be more or less sophisticated in order to obtain more or less accurate data.

Whichever option you choose, the aim is to narrow down who the company's message is addressed to, who buys its products, or who uses them. You also need to establish who should *not* receive your message, who should *not* purchase your products or services and who should *not* use them. It may initially seem absurd to limit your range of clients and consumers in this way, but it is obvious that children should not drive cars or buy medications.

Finally, your research should answer the most important question: which clients and users have not been taken into account when it comes to offering and using the company's products, and therefore, which sectors of the population are potential clients that are currently being neglected.

In order to achieve this, you can draw up a User Map, tailoring its complexity and extent to your own needs, ensuring that your company adapts to its types of activities and reality without neglecting any aspect of human diversity. The sample layout we give tries to cover most (though not all) of the aspects of human diversity. You can simply use our version as a template to draw one up that reflects the diversity of your company's users.

With the results of the User Map, you can start answering interesting questions such as these:

- If you are in communication with various age groups, why do only some of them buy or use your products?
- Had you never thought that there could be left-handed people amongst your consumers?
- If you use Arabic on the packaging of your products, is the dialect in general use in the country where you are selling?

According to the experiences gathered by the Design for All Foundation regarding products and services that respect human diversity:

- Ten per cent of users urgently need companies to improve their products and services in order to be able to use them.
- Forty per cent of them consider the improvements very necessary.
- Almost 100 per cent of the population will welcome these changes.

Once you have completed this phase, you will be in a better position to establish who your clients and users are and where to address your attention when you observe them interacting with your products and services.

User Map

You can use colour or a shading code (for example, green, yellow and red, or three grey tones) to indicate whether products are satisfactory, problematic or unsatisfactory.

	Current clients/users			Potential clients/users			Should not be clients/users			Approx. % users
	Communication	Sale	Usage	Communication	Sale	Usage	Communication	Sale	Usage	
Male										
Female										
Age and gender groups										
Create age groups depending on the situation, e.g.:										
27–40 years — F										
27–40 years — M										
90+ years — F										
90+ years — M										
Sexual orientation										
(Heterosexual, homosexual, bisexual, etc.)										

	Current clients/users			Potential clients/users			Should not be clients/users			Approx. % users
	Communication	Sale	Usage	Communication	Sale	Usage	Communication	Sale	Usage	
Laterality										
(left- or right-handed)										
Body dimensions										
(thin, short, etc.)										
Transfer of goods										
(ability to cope with weight)										
Grasping objects										
(can use both hands, only one, difficulty with manipulation)										
Vision										
(good/poor, blind)										

	Current clients/users			Potential clients/users			Should not be clients/users			Approx. % users
	Communication	Sale	Usage	Communication	Sale	Usage	Communication	Sale	Usage	
Hearing										
(good, poor, deaf)										
Movement										
(can walk with difficulty, can't walk)										
Orientation										
(good/bad)										
Intellectual capacity or knowledge of local language										
(literacy, able to understand long texts, complex words)										

	Current clients/users			Potential clients/users			Should not be clients/users			Approx. % users
	Communication	**Sale**	**Usage**	**Communication**	**Sale**	**Usage**	**Communication**	**Sale**	**Usage**	
Level of studies										
(basic, graduate, etc.)										
Religion										
(Christian, Muslim, Buddhist, agnostic, etc.)										
Use of technologies										
(Internet, mobile phone, etc.)										
Habits										
(sporty/sedentary)										
Values										
(environmentalist, progressive, vegetarian, etc.)										

	Current clients/users			Potential clients/users			Should not be clients/users			Approx. % users
	Communication	Sale	Usage	Communication	Sale	Usage	Communication	Sale	Usage	
Type of family unit										
(traditional/single-parent)										
Allergies										
(gluten, pollen, tobacco, etc.)										
Territory or geographical origin										
(from Western Europe, South or Central Asia, China, etc.)										
Income/economic resources										
(low/medium/high)										

In order to establish the approximate percentage of users that need to be taken into account in your decisions, you can gather a great deal of data from sources available in the Internet. As an example, we will provide you with some information obtained from bodies such as the Migrations International Organization (MIO), the World Health Organisation (WHO), the Department of Finance and Social Affairs of the United Nations, and Etnologue (*The Encyclopaedia of World Languages*).

The world population in 2009 was 6.907 billion people, of which 3.482 billion (51 per cent) were male and 3.425 billion (49 per cent) were female. The age composition was as follows:

* 0–4 years – 9.3 per cent
* 0–14 years – 26.9 per cent
* 15–24 years –17.6 per cent
* 15–59 years – 62.1 per cent
* 60+ – 11 per cent
* 65+ – 7.6 per cent
* 80+ – 1.5 per cent.

In terms of sexual orientation, the proportions were: 89 per cent heterosexual and 11 per cent homosexual (males 4.2 per cent, females 6.8 per cent).

According to the MIO, there are 214 million international migrants, representing 3.1 per cent of world's population, of which 49 per cent are women.

According to WHO estimates in 2005, there were 194 million people with diabetes, and this is projected to rise to 366 million by 2030. There were 314 million people with visual disabilities and 45 million who were blind; 4 million people were deaf; 400 million people were classed as obese, projected to increase to 700 million by 2015.

In terms of religion, the figures for 2007 were:

* Christians – 2.199 billion
  - Catholics – 1.121 billion
  - Protestants – 381 million
  - Orthodox – 233 million
  - Anglican – 82 million
* Muslims – 1.387 billion
* agnostics – 1.071 billion
* Hindus – 879 million
* Buddhists – 385 million
* atheists – 262 million
* Sikhs – 23 million
* Jews – 25 million.

Several studies point out that there are 5,000 languages in the world; 94 per cent of world's population speaks 389 languages, and the remaining 6 per cent (approximately 4,000 languages) are spoken by less than 1 million people each. Another interesting fact is the ranking of languages according to the number of people who speak them and in how many countries:

- Chinese – 213 million people in 31 countries
- Spanish – 329 million people in 44 countries
- English – 328 million people in 112 countries
- Arabic – 221 million people in 57 countries
- Hindi – 182 million people in 20 countries
- Japanese – 122 million people in 25 countries
- German – 90.3 million people in 43 countries
- French – 67.8 million people in 60 countries.

Peter Kwan's Story

Peter read the book over a couple of nights, revising the information given in the seminar, but also discovered that the consultant had left many things unsaid.

A few days later, Frank Wright called him in for a meeting. He tackled the subject at hand directly: he was worried about the constant decrease in sales in almost all the territories where the company traded. He asked Peter, "How are we going to reverse this trend?"

For days, Peter had been waiting for Frank to pose this question. He answered in a hoarse voice, "The product is almost the same as it was when the company was established in 1969. During the early years, the range of flavours was increased. In 1981, the company marketed a new product, a whistle sweet, but this wasn't very successful and was withdrawn from the market. I think a local competitor still markets it in one country, but with modest success."

Clearing his throat, Peter continued: "The decrease began in 1993. As you know, three years ago we developed a new line of sweet with a plastic toy incorporated, but it didn't change the trend, although the margin saw an increase. What I have observed by analysing our sales data per country confirms a hunch I had: in many cases there has been a slight recovery which coincided with the implementation of anti-tobacco laws. Quite possibly, the fact that our sweet has a stick means that ex-smokers can use it as a cigarette replacement. Drawing on my previous experience in retail, the truth is, Frank, that the market is more and more crowded with competitors, many of them Oriental or manufacturing in China, driving prices down. I have a feeling that consumers are considering price more than before. Furthermore, we have now the 'light' food fashion, and every now and then some doctor crops up stating how bad sugar is."

"Yes, but ...", interjected Frank.

Peter anticipated his objection: "Sure, Frank, we have to develop a strategy to reverse the trend. Could you give me a few days – a week – to finish refining a proposal I have in mind?"

"OK, Peter, a week. The owners understand that it will take us a while to increase profitability. At the moment they aren't pressuring me, but we can't fall asleep at the wheel."

Peter felt that the meeting had not gone so badly. He had already met staff from the company's main advertising agency, in order to get to know them. They had confirmed his opinion: the product was widely known and the brand was a prestigious one. They had also showed him the restyling of the brand logo and packaging, along with displays from recent years. However, due to the growth in the number of competitors, some of them with a clear dominant position in the world of sweets, the market was subject to price wars, and Sweetme was having a tough time competing.

Peter had the feeling that an increase in advertising or a minor restyling of the product would not be enough to improve the situation. They had to do something innovative – but what? He had just taken up his position with the company, and he couldn't start suggesting dramatic changes that meant large investments, or risk making a mistake with the strategy and triggering a larger drop in sales.

He decided to study what his competitors were doing. After hours and hours in front of his computer visiting websites, reading reports about exports and watching videos about advertising campaigns, two things drew his attention. The worldwide leader in the sector, Mars, had a rapidly growing diversification strategy, and on its main page – unlike its competitors, which merely displayed their brands and products – Mars talked about its principles and ethical commitment.

"The tendency to be more and more transparent to the consumer is spreading really quickly," he observed.

With tired eyes and stiff shoulders after spending so long in front of his computer, he remembered that somewhere in the HUMBLES method book there was a section aimed at company managers. The advice was that they should spend more time learning about their consumers – at least 25 per cent of their time! "How crazy!" he thought, smiling. Still, it was the perfect excuse to escape the office. He would get out there, and in addition, he would have a look at how and where the retailers he encountered on his travels were displaying Sweetme products.

He walked for a long while and noticed his shoulders had loosened up. With the excuse of buying a newspaper, he went into a newsagents that had a Sweetme display, but on a shelf behind the counter. "It would be better if it was placed closer to the customers," he thought.

When the shop assistant was giving him his change, he dared to ask, "Do you sell a lot of sweets?"

"Which ones?"

"Sweetme."

"Oh! Well, yes."

"And who buys them?"

"Sorry?"

"I mean, are they children, elderly people, men, women?"

Recovering her smile after a surprised grimace, the girl replied, "Oh! I don't know … children … Sometimes they ask their mum when they see it, I think, because of the toy that's included."

"No one else?"

"Well, there is a man who works nearby and buys lots – he seems to smoke them!"

"Thanks," grinned Peter, "have a nice day."

"This doesn't really add up to a lot of information," he thought. "If sales were like this in all shops, we'd go out of business in no time."

Feeling a bit depressed, he decided to get on a bus and return to the office.

Life can be full of coincidences – at the next stop, a child with a woman who looked like she was his granny had a Sweetme in his hand. They got into the bus and sat down beside Peter. The child started to unwrap the packaging.

How awful – he couldn't do it! He first tried with his fingers, then with his nails, and finally he started biting one of the edges of the plastic wrapper until he managed to break his way in. Of course, by now the packaging was full of saliva. His granny took a white tissue from her bag and wrapped the discarded plastic in it, then started wiping the child's fingers and mouth, which made him protest.

"Is this always the case?" Peter asked himself, "Does it mean we have a manufacturing problem that makes some of our packaging too firmly stuck together?"

When he arrived at his office, he went straight to the sample display and started trying to open the wrapper of a sweet. It was very difficult! Fiona Belsem was leaving her office at that moment.

"Hey, Fiona, is unwrapping a Sweetme always so hard?" Peter called over.

"Huh? No idea. Sorry, I have a taxi waiting for me downstairs. I'll see you tomorrow."

Gripped by a sudden obsession, Peter started to ask people in the office whether they found the sweets as difficult to unwrap as he did. Most didn't know what he was talking about. Gloria, the switchboard operative, told him, "Well, it is a bit difficult – you do it like this with your nails." Peter copied her and eventually managed to break open a corner of the wrapping after three tries.

Gloria put the sweet in her mouth and added with a smile, "They *are* tasty, though, aren't they?"

Peter went into his office, collapsed into the armchair, and with the still fresh images of the competition's products dancing before his eyes, told himself, "This can't continue. How are we going to sell more if when someone tries to eat a Sweetme, the first thing they encounter is a problem?"

On the spur of the moment, he decided that maybe the HUMBLES method could come in handy. He took the User Map from the folder he'd been given at the seminar and began to go through it in detail.

He devoted all the following day to drawing up a User Map related to Sweetme. This is what it looked like.

Poor display visibility

Mars says that they do not address their ads to children under 12 years old

		Current clients/users			Potential clients/users			Should not be clients/users			Approx. % users
		Communication	Sale	Usage	Communication	Sale	Usage	Communication	Sale	Usage	
Male		✓	✓	✓							
Female		✓	✓	✓							
Age and gender groups											
0–5 years	F			?			The decision must be made by their parents				
	M										
5–12 years	F			?							
	M										
12–20 years	F	✓	✓	✓							
	M										
20–50 years	F		✓	✓	✓	More	More				
	M										
50–70 years	F		✓	✓	?	More	More				
	M										
70+ years	F		For grand-children?	✓	?	More	More				
	M										
Sexual orientation											
(Heterosexual, homosexual, bisexual, etc.)l			✓	✓	Is there any difference?						

How many more?

	Current clients/users			Potential clients/users			Should not be clients/users			Approx. % users
	Communication	Sale	Usage	Communication	Sale	Usage	Communication	Sale	Usage	
Laterality	*Indifferent*									
(left- or right-handed)		✓	✓							
Body dimensions	*We should be careful with obesity, especially children*									
(thin, short, etc.)		✓	✓			*Light?*				
Transfer of goods										
(ability to cope with weight)										
Grasping objects										
(can use both hands, only one, difficulty with manipulation)				*People with arthritis or a broken arm. How can they unwrap?*						
Vision										
(good/poor, blind)		?	?	*Can see the display?* *Radio ads?*	✓	✓				

	Current clients/users			Potential clients/users			Should not be clients/users			Approx. % users
	Communication	Sale	Usage	Communication	Sale	Usage	Communication	Sale	Usage	
Hearing										
(good, poor, deaf)	?	?	?		✓	✓				
Movement										
(can walk with difficulty, can't walk)		✓	✓							
Orientation										
(good/bad)		✓	✓							
Intellectual capacity or knowledge of local language	Review campaigns	?	?		✓	✓				
(literacy, able to understand long texts, complex words)	Speak with the advertising company	?	?		✓	✓				

	Current clients/users			Potential clients/users			Should not be clients/users			Approx. % users
	Communication	Sale	Usage	Communication	Sale	Usage	Communication	Sale	Usage	
Level of studies										
(basic, graduate, etc.)		✓	✓							
Religion	✓	✓	✓							
(Christian, Muslim, Buddhist, agnostic, etc.)	*Is there any religion that forbids eating sweets? No idea*				✓	✓				
Use of technologies										
(Internet, mobile phone, etc.)										
Habits										
(sporty/sedentary)				*If they are concerned about calories*	✓	✓				
Values										
(environmentalist, progressive, vegetarian, etc.)										

	Current clients/users			Potential clients/users			Should not be clients/users			Approx. % users
	Communication	Sale	Usage	Communication	Sale	Usage	Communication	Sale	Usage	
Type of family unit										
(traditional/single-parent)		✓	✓							
Allergies										
(gluten, pollen, tobacco, etc.)				*Sweetme contains gluten? What about diabetics?*	✓	✓				
Territory or geographical origin					✓	✓				
(from Western Europe, South or Central Asia, China, etc.)		✓	✓	*Bigger penetration in Asia, South America, Africa: opportunity*						
Income/economic resources		✓	✓							
(low/medium/high)										

Realizing that he needed to draw up a clean draft, Peter decided it was about time to start structuring the proposal he was going to hand in to Frank.

On his way home, stuck in a small traffic jam, he thought over his experiences out on the street and decided that tomorrow he would try travelling to work by public transport. He hadn't used it since his student days, but he'd give it another go.

To be continued …

CHAPTER 3 Monitor Interaction

In order to establish a deep knowledge of your customers' needs and wishes, it is necessary to get to know, listen to and observe them. From this observation, you will obtain the necessary inspiration to improve your products and services.

Companies' marketing and communication departments are quite used to dealing with consumers, but design departments do not usually have this kind of direct interaction. Some designers, since they lack the training and the tools to gather users' opinions, shy away from contact with customers for fear they will interfere with the "creative process" and seek to amend their designs – a prospect they obviously find horrifying. It is the task of marketing department to conduct surveys and interpret interviews, filtering and analysing the results to translate its vision of users' needs to the design department.

A frequent mistake is to rely on a literal interpretation of consumers' observations, following the maxim that "the client is always right". However, we all know that consumers often express a wish for things they do not need or that would only make their life more complicated, with subsequent feelings of rejection towards the resulting product.

For instance, in Southern Europe it is common to buy all-terrain vehicles, although these are generally only used to move around cities and well-paved roads, and the same is the case in countries where snow is virtually non-existent. However, some consumers still feel the need to buy such vehicles in anticipation of the thrill of adventures in mountainous terrain. After a while, the novelty palls in the face of reality: these types of vehicles use more fuel, are more expensive to tax and are more difficult to park, and the feelings of disappointment and rejection become impossible to ignore.

On the other hand, in market research aimed at elderly people who lived at home and were in good health, when they were asked what type of home improvements they would consider to prepare for future deterioration in their abilities, most replied that even if such alterations would cost them nothing, they would not change anything in their homes except, maybe, the entrance steps. One conclusion from this study might be that people give little thought to the deterioration associated with growing old because they are reluctant to face the prospect of their situation worsening.

Learning about your client's needs is not an easy task. For instance, the end consumer is crucial for Sol Meliá. It conducts regular quality surveys because it considers the client's perception of the company very important.

The customer is our raison d'être, the company's soul, the end user. We are absolutely clear about this. For example, in these times of budget cuts, the most important thing is that the customer is not aware of them. I mean, we can make budget cuts in other areas, but not when it comes to customer service and quality of service.

Sol Meliá is aware of how advances in technology have affected its industry. Customers now interact directly with the company, making all their reservations via the company website, whereas in the past such interactions were not direct, but through travel agencies. Sol Meliá's Corporate Social Responsibility Department, is working on issues involving new, more demanding customers:

It is difficult because it is a mature segment, so it is very hard to surprise the client. You have to be constantly innovating and looking for new sensations.

In order to obtain information about clients and users, we can use many different methods. We don't intend to offer a comprehensive description of them all, but rather a brief description of those that stand out as the most useful when it comes to discovering both current trends and the different aspects of human diversity.

The methods are grouped according to their aim:

- monitoring usage, wishes and needs
- monitoring complaints
- monitoring reputation and satisfaction.

The goal of all of them is to obtain the most accurate information possible about which aspects of products are open to improvement, what they lack, and what opportunities exist for the development of new products within or outside the same range. Some companies take on this task in-house, while others prefer to hire experts who, in some cases, may speed up the process of analysis by combining their observations with pre-existing data.

In any case, it is desirable for at least 25 per cent of the working time of the company's board of directors to be devoted to observing, listening to and understanding customers' actions, wishes and motivations, both regarding the product itself and other areas.

This process of observation should also be used to develop the "analytical eye" that allows us to discern what is relevant and what is not, discovering indications of new trends as well as the causes of frustration. In developing this "analytical eye", you should focus on the following aspects:

- interest
- curiosity
- the ability to analyse

- the ability to listen
- the ability to understand people's values and emotions
- lack of inhibition
- empathy with the customer
- the study of details
- the avoidance of prejudices
- the ability to describe objectively what has been observed
- intuition.

Our advice is that you get out into the street and observe, or perhaps follow your clients' blogs, for instance – we are sure you will be surprised.

Monitoring Usage, Wishes and Needs

It is important to take into account that when we talk of "usage", we mean all the aspects involved in the relationship between the product or service and various people outside the company (prescriptors, distributors, installers, consumers) from the moment they learn about the product or service until the end of the relationship regarding the service or when the product finally sells out or is discontinued.

If we imagine, for instance, the case of monitoring the use of microwave ovens, we must bear in mind the distributors, transporters, installers, buyers and the different users in the household environment. This gives rise to a number of questions:

- Is your advertising really addressed to all the sectors of the population we defined as potential buyers in Chapter 2?
- Is your website attractive and easy to use for all these sectors, as well as for the distributors that need to fulfil their orders?
- Do the design and packaging help distributors to handle the product with ease and display it simply and comfortably in a visible location?
- Does the packaging design help transporters to handle of the product without damaging it, and also without damaging the packaging itself, which will diminish its attractiveness?
- Are there any problems with such basic things as the length of the flex?
- Is the user manual easy to understand?
- Is the product easy and intuitive to handle for all potential users – even with just one hand, while wearing gloves, without being able to hear or see, without being able to make rotatory wrist movements, and so on?
- If someone makes a mistake with the product or uses it wrongly, can fatal consequences occur? Does the accompanying literature warn users of the dangers?
- If problems arise, can the customer consult a website or after-sales service?
- If the product breaks down, is it easy to find out where it can be repaired? Can the user be provided with a temporary replacement?

- When the consumer finally decides to dispose of the product, who will deal with this? Is the information on how to dispose of it clear?

If we manage a service business, what questions should we ask ourselves? Let's take the case of a hotel:

- Is the website easy to understand and navigate for all users, even if they are not expert in the use of computers?
- Is the website easy to consult on small screens such as those of mobile phones?
- Does the website carry adequate descriptions of the details and dimensions of the rooms so that people of extreme build or wheelchair users can form a clear idea of any possible problems?

At the front desk:

- Are the staff friendly and efficient?
- Do they know all the languages that clients may use, along with their cultural habits?
- Do they know how to interact with a blind or deaf person?
- Is the front desk a convenient height for people of all heights?

In the hotel area itself:

- Is there relevant written information (restaurant menus, weather forecasts, events diaries, locations of toilets, and so on) accompanied by appropriate icons and in the languages customers may speak?

At the restaurant and bar:

- Do they offer sufficient variety to cater for the needs of people with allergies, particular religious habits or followers of certain types of diet?
- If so, are staff well trained to convey this information?

Considering the organization of the accommodation:

- Are rooms grouped in such a way that a client's habits or needs will not conflict with your other clients – for instance, couples with babies, early risers, night owls?

About the rooms themselves:

- Has anybody checked that the each and every element and accessory in a room (soap packaging, curtains, and so on) is comfortable and easy to use whether or not the customer has the use both hands, is right- or left-handed, or is tall or short?
- Is there sufficient storage space and are there enough hangers to cater for long stays?

- Is it possible to avoid rooms suitable for clients in wheelchairs resembling hospital rooms? If they look like that, other clients who might occupy them may reject them.

We have all had the experience of finding a customer satisfaction questionnaire in our hotel room. If you have read some, you will know that the only thing they are able to measure is your emotional attitude towards several types of services. If you have filled one of them out, it is probably because you were greatly satisfied or deeply unsatisfied with the services that were provided. Do you really believe that you can obtain practical ideas about those things that could be improved from these questionnaires? Other types of strategies can be more effective.

OBSERVING CLIENTS (AND USERS, WHEN POSSIBLE)

Getting to know the real and potential clients and users we have identified in the previous stage means you are in a better position to find out how they interact with your products and services. In order to do this, we can use several techniques that we will not describe in depth here, since they are discussed extensively in other publications. You need to choose the most suitable ones depending on the activities of your company and its resources.

Which stages of using your products or services present problems for customers because of their personal characteristics? Who has problems doing what? What does it depend on – for instance, age, build, complexity?

This technique is most suitable in environments with a large number of visitors and open to the public, such as amusement parks or large shopping centres.

Despite the fact that you can hire professionals to carry out research based on observation, we must emphasize strongly that it will be very enlightening for yourself and your board directors to observe in person what people do with your products or services.

INTERNET MONITORING

Nowadays, more and more consumers express their views about companies and their products and services through blogs, opinion forums, Facebook, Twitter, YouTube and a wide range of other social participation means via the Internet.

If your company or your products are widely available, you will be able to discover what Internet users think of them. What is more, you will find out what uses they make of your products, what aspects they consider problematic, and possibly discover some applications your company has not foreseen.

Such media can also be very useful in discovering users' attitudes towards your competitors and their services and products.

MYSTERY CLIENT

In this technique, someone completely unknown to the employees plays the client's role and notes down aspects of the service that need to be improved. It works best in companies offering services, such as hotels or companies working in the field of passenger transport.

The mystery client may be a professional in this type of analysis with specific characteristics (size, physical abilities, appearance, gender, and so on) who is engaged to test the systems and report on his or her experiences afterwards.

EXPERT ASSESSMENT

When tackling very specific aspects of human diversity – food allergies, signage, disabled access, environmental improvements, customer care – it is not unusual to engage companies or organizations that are expert in this field to highlight specific areas for improvement.

If you delegate the assessment to outside organizations, it is important to ensure that it will be objective and that they have previous experience of the issues you wish to focus on.

FOCUS GROUPS

This technique consists of holding a meeting with a group of people who are believed to be more or less representative of current or potential clients or users. Participants are normally chosen because they belong to a specific consumer sector (for example, aged 30–40, middle-class, with high purchasing power), but a common mistake is to assume that this sample truly and unequivocally represents that sector. It is important not to forget that each person is unique and is rarely typical of the majority. If you are not convinced of this, ask yourself whether you are completely representative of any market segment.

During the meeting, you can obtain a variety of data, depending on your aims. You can seek information about their wishes and expectations, about aspects that could be improved, or their opinions about a new concept or a prototype.

As we mentioned earlier, it is important to remember that while wishes are easy to establish, needs will not always be reflected accurately in the opinions you gather.

In Chapter 8 we will describe the experience of Oxo and how it uses focus groups to study aspects for improvement.

INTERVIEWS

Depending on the group or the theme, a person may be shy about offering opinions, or feel inhibited by peer group pressure. One way to overcome this is to conduct personal interviews. While they take longer, they usually allow you to delve deeper into particular aspects.

It is important to establish a series of ground rules to avoid biasing the interviewee's opinion. The interviewer must know how to listen, ask the appropriate questions and pay attention to the interviewee's body language.

WRITTEN OR PHONE-BASED QUESTIONNAIRES

This method allows you to cover very specific aspects of the use of your product or service, although it is often used to establish degree of satisfaction or frequency of use. One drawback with this technique is that it demands exhaustive sample selection and a large quantity of responses in order to ensure diversity among participants.

By using these or other techniques, you can start drawing up a list of the aspects of your products and services that can be improved in order to make them more satisfactory for current and future consumers.

Monitoring Complaints

Many companies still regard complaints negatively, considering them as attacks from neurotic individuals who enjoy nitpicking about a perfect system. However, a complaint can be a gift, as it can point out an opportunity for improvement.

A consumer who bothers to submit a complaint is very likely annoyed or upset. However, rather than taking this personally, it is important to realize that the details of the complaint reveal that what is being offered has not complied with the customer's expectations, giving your company a chance to revise the service or product according to firsthand user feedback. Obviously, the response to the complainer should include an apology, an explanation of the reasons behind the problem, and if possible, compensation in one form or other for any inconvenience.

However, it is within the company itself that the complaint can produce benefits. To secure these, it is important to study the characteristics of the person who complained, to establish the cause of the error or problem, to provide sufficient documentation, to study possible solutions in order to avoid the same thing happening again in future, and to communicate these to the departments that will put them into practice, as well those in charge of designing future products or services.

Clearly, the analysis of the complaint will enlarge the list of aspects to improve that has been created from monitoring the usage of the product.

In 2007, the company Transports Ciutat Comtal (TCC) – aware that the strategic challenge for the future lies in the ability to adapt to the market's needs and the continuous technological and social changes that are taking place, to increase the scope of its services in order to meet users' requirements – decided to appoint a User Ombudsman.

This service is managed by an organization outside the company – the Design for All Foundation (DfA Foundation) – since TCC wishes to guarantee rigour and independence in the analysis of complaints.

This has allowed complaints and suggestions to be treated effectively and objectively, with the DfA Foundation studying each case in order to produce management reports making recommendations about how to improve the services offered by TCC.

This approach to managing the complaints and suggestions process has enabled TCC to develop its corporate social responsibility policies, promoting economic growth and greater social cohesion, adopting the principles and values derived in order to continue to develop dialogue and initiatives for social change with its customers.

It is important to bear in mind that complaints are usually submitted by people who are annoyed with a service, and only occasionally by customers who believe that their contributions will help improve the system. If you review your own personal experience, you will no doubt recall more than one occasion when you felt furious at treatment you received, but felt it was not worth the effort to make a formal complaint.

Any company that discourages user feedback or makes it difficult for customers to complain or has no formal systems to monitor customer satisfaction is in a perilous situation: it may be generating dissatisfaction among its customers without understanding why. Such a company's days are probably numbered.

To avoid this, it is sometimes useful to establish contact with consumer groups. The example of FGC illustrates how to deal with a complex problem by working closely with such a group.

FGC's focus on Design for All increased with the publication in 1991 of a law in the Catalonian parliament[1] and the signing of an accord with the CRID (Personal Autonomy Documentation and Resource Consortium) that provided advice on an action plan and acted as an advocate for groups of people with limitations on their activities.

Thanks to FGC's collaboration with CRID, for the past seven or eight years, and currently as an accredited company of the DfA Foundation, it has developed its projects taking into account Design for All, adapting all its stations and trains to suit the diversity of its users, as well as implementing Design for All within the company itself.

Oriol Juncadella, Operations Manager of TCC, said:

---

1   Spanish Act 20/1991 of 25 November promoting accessibility and barrier-free architecture.

"The process is continuous one. Sometimes groups we had not considered before, such as people with hearing difficulties, come in and tell us that we are doing a good job, but are not paying attention to them. In that case, we reply, 'OK, let's talk and see what we can do.'"

Monitoring Reputation and Satisfaction

Since one of the objectives we established in the first stage of the HUMBLES method was to improve the company's reputation and create loyal customers, it is obvious that we need some tools to find out what clients think about the company. Likewise, the company needs to establish the attitude of society as a whole towards it. These tools can include questionnaires, short interviews and customer satisfaction surveys.

One of the techniques that proved very useful for us in our efforts to learn about the image of a very well-known company was called "I have never been there", and involved choosing a sample of people who had used the company's services or facilities, plus a second sample who had no prior experience of these.

The first sample were asked to answer some questions about specific aspects of the service: personal care, standards of cleanliness, quality, and so on. The second sample, who had never had any experience of the service, were asked to imagine what these factors would be like. When the results of both groups were compared, it was easy to establish whether the public image of the company was better or worse than the service it actually offered.

This technique is especially suitable for companies that offer public services, tourist destinations or well-known companies.

The results obtained about the company's reputation and client satisfaction will complete the list of aspects that need to be improved in your product or service. In addition, contributions from different employees and company departments (marketing, sales, production, design, billing) can add to the value of what will very likely be a long list.

Depending on the aspects to be analysed, each company will choose the techniques that offer the most detailed results in order to gather information about which aspects of a product or service need improvement. Based on our experience, some methods provide more information at lower cost, as shown in Figure 3.1.

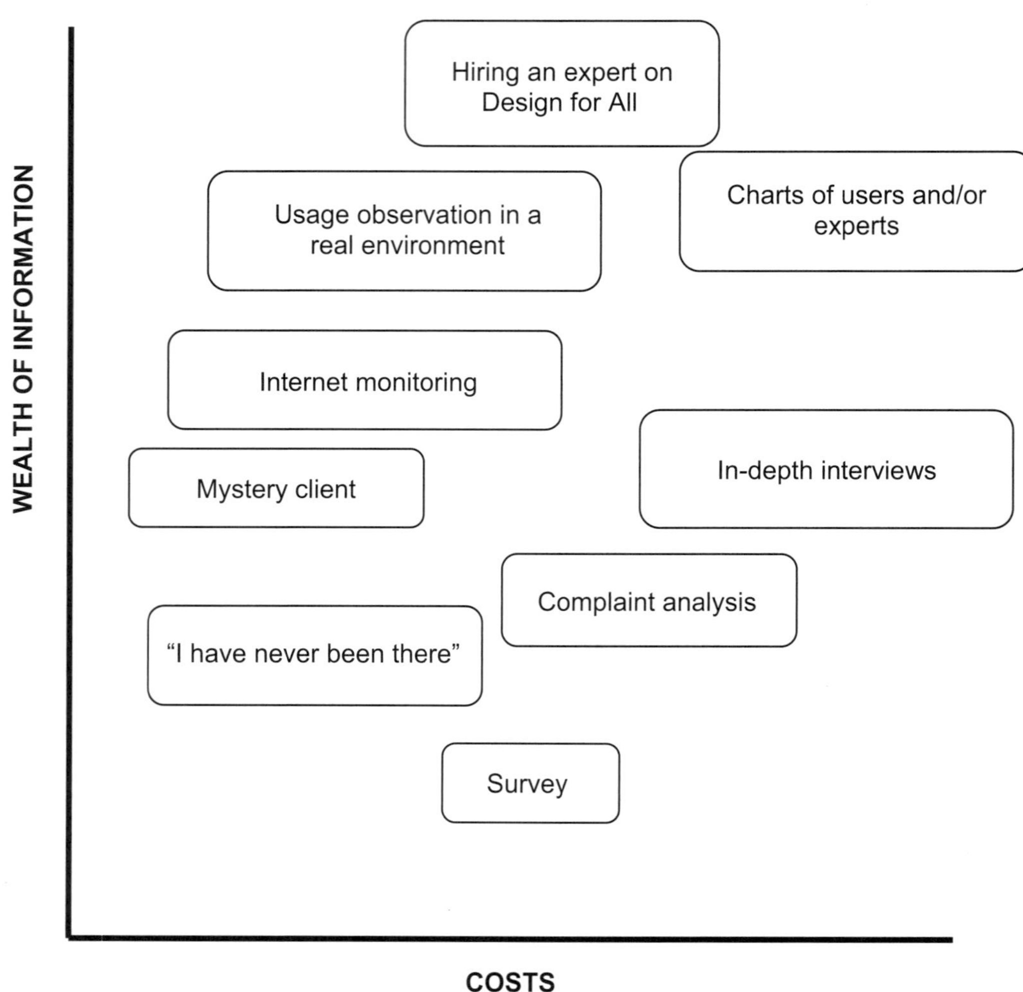

Figure 3.1   Relationship between costs and wealth of information obtained

Beware: Do Not Make Your Clients Work for Free!

Almost all the techniques we have mentioned rely on voluntary and motivated participation by clients, users or unknown citizens. It is a good idea to offer compensation or rewards that are proportional to the effort required, but it is important to bear in mind that this may bias the answers.

Gathering Data

Once interaction with the customer, complaints and company reputation have been analysed, you will have at your disposal a longer list than you may have expected concerning the aspects of your products, services or company that require improvement.

To help you structure your notes on these improvable aspects we suggest you continue to use the User Map, transforming it into an Improvements Map that clarifies the relationship between existing and potential customers to the areas where these improvements can be made. In general, these will be:

- advertising
- information
- distribution and presentation
- packaging and transport
- sales
- price
- usage
- technical assistance and maintenance
- returns and recycling
- methods to register complaints, suggestions and user satisfaction
- reputation.

To increase the richness of this information, we suggest you focus on the six most critical aspects to guarantee appropriate use and acceptance of your product or service by your customers. We will deal with these next.

In order to be sufficiently flexible to adapt to the needs and wishes of most consumers, the product or service must be:

- **Respectful** – It should respect the diversity of users, so no one feels marginalized.
- **Safe** – It must avoid risky situations for users. Thus, all elements must be designed with an emphasis on safety.
- **Healthy** – It must not constitute a health risk or cause inconvenience to those who suffer from illnesses or allergies. In addition, it should promote the healthy use of locations and products.
- **Functional** – It must be designed in such a way that it can fulfil its function without posing problems or difficulties.
- **Understandable** – Any user must be able to understand what it is, how it works, how to use it, and so on.
- **Attractive** – This is important since it encourages acceptance by customers (but always bearing in mind the previous five points).

Once you have drawn up your Improvements Map, you can start to write down in the corresponding boxes your conclusions, using whatever monitoring techniques you have decided to apply.

Considerations of space mean that the Improvements Map we provide below is not full-size, merely illustrating its structure. In order to use it, we recommend you draw up your own version based on the User Map from Chapter 2 and print it out in at least A3 format, to allow sufficient space for your comments.

Don't worry – the longer your list, the more opportunities there are to improve your product or service.

This list is essential to the next stage of the HUMBLES method. Once you have filled it out, we recommend you use it to revise your User Map, because what you have learnt by monitoring users will allow you to refine your predictions about potential users and how to grow your market.

Improvements Map

	Male	Female	Age and gender groups	Sexual orientation	Laterality	Body dimensions	Goods transfer	Grasping objects	Vision
Reputation									
Complaint, suggestion & satisfaction capture									
Refusal and recycling									
Technical assistance & maintenance									
Usage — Attractive									
Usage — Understandable									
Usage — Functional									
Usage — Healthy									
Usage — Safe									
Usage — Respectful									
Price									
Sales									
Packaging & transport									
Distribution & display									
Information									
Advertising									

	Hearing	Intellectual ability or knowledge of local language	Religion	Level of studies	Use of technologies	Habits	Values	Type of family unit	Allergies	Territory or geographical origin	Income/economic resources
Reputation											
Complaint, suggestion & satisfaction capture											
Refusal and recycling											
Technical assistance & maintenance											
Usage — Attractive											
Usage — Understandable											
Usage — Functional											
Usage — Healthy											
Usage — Safe											
Usage — Respectful											
Price											
Sales											
Packaging & transport											
Distribution & display											
Information											
Advertising											

Peter Kwan's Story

At home, Peter's wife Kumi and their children Alex, Monika and Jan were waiting for him to take them to their friend Anna's birthday party.

Kumi had bought a turquoise ceramic necklace as a birthday present. When they arrived at Anna's home and presented her with it, she wanted to try it on immediately. Peter noticed that she was finding it difficult to close the clip, and Laura, Anna's partner, had to help her. Peter smiled to himself – was he starting to get obsessed with handling problems?

They had not seen each other for a long time, and Anna was interested in Peter's new job. While he was answering her questions, he thought that he couldn't understand why Anna, an attractive and kind woman, lived with Laura, who was somewhat older than Anna and more of the sarcastic type. His train of thought was interrupted when Laura broke in abruptly: "So, you're doing well in your new job in that refined calorie factory, yeah?"

"What do you mean?" asked Peter, used to her almost constant abrasive attitude. "No wonder you're a tax inspector!"

"Well, the refined sugars that are used in confectionery are very bad for the brain, not to mention how fattening they are. People who can't go without constant snacks would be better off eating celery sticks – they're a lot healthier."

Peter was a bit annoyed at this comment, and they started arguing until Kumi and Anna changed the subject.

On their way home, Jan, Peter's youngest child, only 11, asked, "Dad, is it true that sugar is bad for the brain?"

"No!" answered Peter tersely, but he asked himself, "Or is it? The truth is, I don't know."

He qualified his answer, "Look, Jan, everything is bad if taken in excess." "Even celery," he mused to himself.

Later on, when he went to bed, Peter found it hard to sleep. "Why is something as simple as Sweetme, that existed even before I was born, beginning to look so complicated?"

The next day at work, he filled out the Improvements Map as shown below.

Improvements Map

I= improvable
S= study
L.D.= lack data
OK?=make sure

	Advertising	Information	Distribution & display	Packaging & transport	Sales	Price	Usage						Technical assistance & maintenance	Refusal and recycling	Complaint, suggestion & satisfaction capture	Reputation
							Respectful	Safe	Healthy	Functional	Understandable	Attractive				
Male	I	I	I	L. D.		OK?	OK?	S	L. D.	I	OK?	OK?		S	S	OK?
Female	I	I	I	L. D.		OK?	OK?	S	L. D.	I	OK?	OK?		S	S	OK?
Age and gender groups	I need to define them						S	S	S	I	S	OK?				
Sexual orientation																
Laterality	OK?	OK?	OK?													
Body dimensions																
Goods transfer																
Grasping objects																
Vision																

	Hearing	Intellectual ability or knowledge of local language	Religion	Level of studies	Use of technologies	Habits	Values	Type of family unit	Allergies	Territory or geographical origin	Income/economic resources
Reputation											
Complaint, suggestion & satisfaction capture											
Refusal and recycling											
Technical assistance & maintenance											
Usage — Respectful											
Usage — Safe											
Usage — Healthy											
Usage — Functional											
Usage — Understandable											
Usage — Attractive											
Price											
Sales											
Packaging & transport											
Distribution & display											
Information											
Advertising											

Is there any link between the lower sales in countries antagonistic towards USA and our name being in English?

Peter was starting to realize that he didn't understand many aspects of the product. Was there anybody in the company who did? He didn't have much data, there were many aspects to be analysed, and Frank was beginning to pressurize him to submit a proposal. "Damn seminar! I knew it was going to complicate my life," he thought.

After a coffee break that calmed him down, he opened up the book to look for some inspiration about how to compile all the information in a short time. After riffling through it for a while, he decided that the phone, factory employees and his own experience in the food business would be the most efficient tools to obtain some initial data on which to base his proposal.

He called the company's distributors in a number of countries, his dentist, a doctor friend, associations offering support to those with coeliac disease and diabetes, a gerontologist, a sports doctor and a nutritionist a friend had recommended. He then spent a whole day in the factory talking to everybody.

His first stop was the Claims Department. "Do you get many complaints?" he asked.

"Yes, of course we get some. For instance, some outlets may receive a broken display or find that some sweets are missing, because in some countries they do go missing, you know?"

"But what about complaints from customers?"

"None that I know of. Oh, wait – a couple of years ago there was a crazy woman who wanted to get some cash out of us because she said her son had hurt himself with the stick, or something like that. We passed it on to our lawyer, and I don't know how the matter ended. There are so many odd people in the world."

Peter kept his opinion to himself and thanked her for her time.

The rest of the day he spent talking to shopfloor employees, after asking for permission from the Production Manager, of course. He spoke with new workers and others who had been with the company since it was founded. He listened to anecdotes, compared criticisms, noted some unease about the change of ownership, and so on.

The following day, he sat down to expand his notes into a list of findings and conclusions.

- The company launched a good product, convinced users to buy it, and this has continued for more than forty years.
- We know little or nothing about our consumers.
- Our campaigns are aimed only at youngsters.
- Neither our product nor our displays give nutritional information – what little information there is appears in a tiny typeface.

- Our website doesn't give this information either, nor does it feature a complaints section. It is designed for young people.
- We sell only one product with a wide range of flavours, and a variant that includes a plastic toy that we buy from China.
- Refined sugar gets a bad press.
- Gluten is an ingredient of some of our flavours but not others, but we do not indicate this on our packaging.
- Diabetic people could consume our products safely, depending on the type of sugar we used.
- Unwrapping the sweet is difficult.
- Children could damage their throats if they fell over with the stick in their mouth. Some children chew the stick, which sometimes splinters, then the children eat the bits.
- Luckily, it is easier for a child to choke on a sweet without a stick than on a Sweetme.
- The wrapping and stick are not environmentally friendly.
- At Ramadan, Muslim people cannot place anything in their mouth during daytime.
- In Slavic countries, we mix our original logo in English with text in the local languages on our display, wrappings and advertisements.
- In China and Japan, we also change the language; in Singapore, they do speak English.
- We do not label or advertise in regional languages (such as Gaelic, Flemish, Welsh, Catalan, Basque or Quechan).
- In India, all our materials are in English.
- Our nutritional experts are located in the factory.
- We have never had a panel of users, though our advertising agency has occasionally checked our campaigns with young people.
- Hard sweets are better than soft ones for children who wear dental braces and for people with false teeth.
- Sucrose is more likely to cause caries.
- Sweets must be avoided during a child's first dentition.
- The problem is not occasional consumption, but daily persistence.
- Eating sweets is recommended when engaged in sports like mountain climbing, when driving on long journeys (sweets with caffeine?) and to reduce anxiety while quitting smoking (sweets with a stick).
- People are less likely to eat non-chewable sweets compulsively (it looks like a better option than chewing gum).
- Some people I have been speaking to regard the product as "having been there forever", traditional, old-fashioned. We'll have to study this.
- The consumption of sweets worldwide breaks down as 40 per cent hard sweets, 40 per cent soft and 20 per cent chewing gum.
- The company does not have a code of ethics, nor a set of behavioural norms, nor does it set out a social memory.
- Coeliac associations frequently include some of the ingredients in our products in their lists of foods to avoid.
- According to the HUMBLES method, if we eliminate or reduce these problems, we can increase sales by 20–30 per cent.

Was it really true that improving these aspects would lead to improved sales? Even if this was the case, it would take months, perhaps even more than a year, to improve all this. Would the owners be willing to be so patient?

Peter started preparing the material he wanted to hand in to Frank within his three-day deadline. He asked for data about sales, advertising and promotional campaigns for each country. With the data he was able to gather, he established comparisons with similar products from competitors. He drew up a fresh, clean version of the User Table and the list of notes he had been writing. Pulling all this together, he prepared a printed presentation titled "Towards a Market Strategy Focused on the Consumer", understanding the risks it implied.

To be continued ...

4 Breakthrough Options

The main objective in this stage of the HUMBLES method is to select from the vast number of options for improvement you have identified in the previous stage those that will generate opportunities while being easy to adapt to the culture and capacity of your company. This entails prioritizing the improvements according to the individual features of your company, weighing the advantages you will obtain against the difficulties that might be involved in putting them into practice. In general, we believe these are the main aspects a company should take into account:

- the potential increase in clients and users, and other objectives of Design for All
- reconciling improvements with the general strategy of the company
- gauging the investment effort required
- promoting a sense of opportunity
- the capacity for development and implementation of improvements
- the capacity to manage the project.

The Potential Increase in Clients and Users, and Other Objectives of Design for All

Identifying your current and potential users and the aspects of the interaction between them and your product or service that can be improved will make it easier to establish which sectors of the population are experiencing difficulties or inconvenience. With this in mind, you can calculate the increase in your market niche if you solve the problems you have detected. Thus, if you determine how intensely each interaction problem affects each sector of the population, you will be able to determine the potential increase in customers that will result from each improvement you implement.

The analysis we suggest can also be carried out on other aspects described in Chapter 1, such as preventing problems, selling in other countries or selling in the tourist sector. In this way, you can obtain a general idea of the impact each of the improvements will have on your market.

We must say that our experience shows that the resulting estimates are always understatements, since we can calculate the percentage of the population that will benefit from an improvement, but it is harder to estimate the number of consumers for whom the improvement may not be essential but who will choose the new product because they find it more practical and convenient.

Reconciling Improvements with the General Strategy of the Company

It is obvious that not all improvements will be compatible with the direction established by your company, and because of this, you must decide which improvements to forgo or which aspects of the your company strategy to change. For instance, if your company markets high-quality dairy products, how will you deal with customers who are allergic to lactose? Will you ignore them? How will this affect your brand's image?

It is necessary to answer all these questions in order to ensure that your improvement proposals are compatible with your company's long-term strategy.

Gauging the Investment Effort Required

This entails carrying out the cost–benefit analysis required when taking any kind of commercial decision.

You may be surprised to discover the number of improvements that can be implemented without much effort: increasing the font size of a manual, improving the functionality of a hotel when undertaking a large-scale refurbishment project or including Design for All criteria in the design process of a new product demands minimal investment. On the other hand, changing your packaging systems or the design of elements produced in large runs could have a major impact if they demand investment in new machinery.

It is also possible that introducing an improvement may not lead to great direct benefits in terms of increased sales, but may have a meaningful positive impact on your company's reputation, thus increasing its value.

Promoting a Sense of Opportunity

This is a sense every board of directors should encourage. It is obvious that any improvement process is likely to be difficult to manage when a company is going through a rough period, although sometimes this offers the best opportunities to reverse the situation.

It is a very bad idea to entrust the design and implementation of any improvement programme to employees who are already overloaded with work.

We must admit that there is little general advice that we can offer about how to instil the sense of opportunity. However, our experience has shown that it is easier to integrate the implementation of the criteria of Design for All at the beginning of the process rather than later on. For instance, it is easier to create a website that relates to users' needs and wishes during a renovation programme of your online presence, rather than simply adding such features to an existing site design.

In short, you and your company will have to determine what to improve now, and what to leave for the future.

The Capacity for Development and Implementation of Improvements

Each company has its own characteristics and work methods. Some companies are clearly resistant to change and to all developments in their environment. Our opinion is that unless these companies have a captive market, they have very limited prospects for progress. Nevertheless, perhaps they will find that the HUMBLES method can serve as a trigger for innovation.

In any case, a degree of commitment towards improvement and innovation must be evident before setting out to design solutions.

The Capacity to Manage the Project

Up to this point in the implementation of the stages of the HUMBLES method, we have offered a wide range of information on potential areas for improvement. If the improvements you want to introduce are obvious, low in cost and your company is relatively small, you can begin the process and monitor it directly, then analyse the results later. However, if this is not so, from now on, the application of the HUMBLES method will require the concerted involvement of many departments in your company, so the decision about which aspects should be targeted for improvement must be achieved by consensus among your company's departments, or at least among those that will be directly involved.

Beginning the improvement process demands the design of a project or projects that will allow your company to achieve its desired objectives and innovations. To guide you in the design of these, we have adapted the method of execution set out in the publication *ECA for Administrations 2008*,[1] which describes what we call the "Seven Interdependent Success Factors" that we feel must be planned and managed in a co-ordinated manner and without underestimating any of

---

1   Francesc Aragall, Peter Neumann and Silvio Sagramola, *ECA for Administrations 2008*, Luxembourg: EuCAN, 2008, http://www.eca.lu/index.php?option=com_docman&task=cat_view&gid=13&Itemid=26.

them in order to guarantee success in the development of any project. These seven factors are:

1. executive support and leadership
2. existence of an executive manager
3. co-ordination and co-operation among all those involved
4. strategic planning
5. the resources required
6. knowledge management
7. internal and external marketing.

The tasks to be carried out regarding these seven factors will vary depending on the level of maturity of the project – whether it is at the initial, development or consolidation stage. The factors can be plotted against the stages as shown in the table below.

	Initial stage	Development stage	Consolidation stage	Comments
Executive support and leadership				
Existence of an executive manager				
Co-ordination and co-operation				
Strategic planning				
Resources required				
Knowledge management				
Internal and external marketing				

If you find this model interesting, you can test its efficiency by using it to analyse a failed project and one that has been successful. In all likelihood, you will confirm that in the case of the project that did not turn out as expected, some of the checkboxes will remain blank, since the activity required for that factor was not undertaken. On the other hand, in the case of the successful project, all the factors will have been taken into account in one way or another.

The Seven Interdependent Success Factors

EXECUTIVE SUPPORT AND LEADERSHIP

When you are about to commence a process of innovation, your company's management should not only tacitly assume the reasons for adopting Design for All as a company strategy, but also explicitly promote them. It is essential for this to be communicated internally and externally, since this alone will have a positive impact on your company's reputation.

If you are a decision maker in your company, go ahead! If not, you will probably have to discuss with your management the opportunities that will arise from the project, drawing on the analysis work you have carried out earlier.

EXISTENCE OF AN EXECUTIVE MANAGER

The role of the executive manager is essential to promote the project, motivate staff and to follow up all the activities involved. We like to compare this role to a juggler who keeps a number of plates continually spinning on sticks, because if the juggler stops, they fall on the floor and break. You may already have guessed that the plates represent the other six factors.

The executive manager's mission includes taking responsibility for strategic planning, gathering, organizing and distributing knowledge, obtaining the resources required, involving everyone who can contribute and convincing the executive board to pursue the project.

While this role demands a lot of effort, the rewards are usually high, as it contributes significantly to the company's success. We know of at least two cases where taking on this role led to the person being promoted to a general executive management position in the company.

CO-ORDINATION AND CO-OPERATION AMONG ALL THOSE INVOLVED

This does not involve creating a committee, but detecting and involving at the right moment all the actors who must contribute to launching and consolidating the product in the market. This includes the executive management team, the design, marketing and advertising departments, suppliers, users who have participated in the process, and the media. All of them have a role to fulfil that will be set out in the strategic plan, and they all need to share this knowledge and develop a common language regarding the HUMBLES method and Design for All.

According to Subramanian Ramadorai, Executive Manager and CEO of Tata Consultancy Services (TCS), "sharing what has been learnt is the main tactic of our business strategy". In order to do this, TCS uses a platform called the Participation Network, made up of more than 36,000 employees in over thirty countries, to share good practices and innovative solutions. To avoid losing its position in the market, this approach draws together talent from all over the world.

The executive manager's aim must be to call on each actor to participate at the right time, getting the best out of everyone and avoiding confrontations between groups with conflicting interests.

One of the key results that must be obtained through this networking process is a consensus about the improvements that must be tackled and the company's goals. This will overcome inertia and help to ensure that the project is shared by all.

Do not forget to involve clients, suppliers and final users, and even your competition if possible, to confirm the feasibility and the potential for success of the improvements you have set in train.

STRATEGIC PLANNING

Every action that must be carried should be planned in advance, and you need to develop indicators to measure the degree of fulfilment of partial objectives. Depending on the size and complexity of your company and the scope of the project you are undertaking, this process can be very simple or very complex, but it must always be realistic.

To do this, it is necessary to identify clearly your general objectives, the development phases, the milestones and indicators you will use to measure the project's evolution and partial results, the human, technical and economic resources involved, as well as timing.

THE RESOURCES REQUIRED

These must be taken into account in your strategic planning, since they represent the investment in terms of time and money required to launch the product successfully.

However, although it is normal to use the company's own human and technical resources, as well as its own capacity for investment, do not undervalue the roles that suppliers, clients, users, the media and so on can play in your project, producing a greater effect than money or time alone can give you.

KNOWLEDGE MANAGEMENT

Your executive director, as well as your marketing and design departments, must be familiar with the principles of the Design for All approach. They must be convinced about its efficacy before getting deeply involved in the project. On the other hand, your company should be able to identify shortcomings in its internal knowledge and decide when to hire external experts if that becomes necessary. You also need to plan all the actions required to develop the necessary knowledge within your organization.

You should also take into account that all the previous phases of the HUMBLES method will generate a large amount of knowledge about your customers and products or services. You need to maintained and distribute this internally to contribute towards the culture of change to the Design for All strategy in the company, thus transforming it into practical ideas to generate value.

However, it is important to exercise caution – many of the things you will discover when applying this method may be of great interest to your competitors, although they can also form the basis for creating some strategic alliances.

INTERNAL AND EXTERNAL MARKETING

From the very beginning of the project, it is necessary to start promoting within your company the opportunities that will open up through implementing the HUMBLES method. Doing this can multiply the beneficial effects if you spread the idea that being more responsive to customers' needs will improve your relationships with them. Likewise, inviting your employees and suppliers to communicate the potential improvements and convey the proposals can make a useful contribution.

Do not forget to value and be grateful for the contributions and efforts of each of your team members.

Since 1996, Nestlé Spain has been running Nestlé Innova, a programme run by its Market Intelligence Manager designed to get the whole company, including retired employees, involved in the innovation process by coming up with ideas. The company has a suggestion box on its intranet which everyone can use. A committee selects which ideas to adopt according to their degree of innovation, and the best idea each year is rewarded with a weekend trip for two to any city in Europe.

Since the programme was set up, more than 5,000 ideas have been submitted, of which 9 per cent have been developed. At present, more than 10 per cent of Nestlé Spain's sales are accounted for by products that have been on the market for less than three years.

From the moment you receive the go-ahead to start up the project, you should also consider whether it might be worthwhile to communicate externally certain aspects of the project. This will contribute to an atmosphere of expectancy about the innovations proposed.

Once familiar with the Seven Interdependent Success Factors, we suggest you draw up a table like the one below for each of the projects you have decided to undertake, to define your objectives, your strategies, the people or organizations involved and the timing.

PROJECT						
Responsible					**Date**	
	Objectives	**Strategies**	**People involved**	**Timing**	**Indicators**	**Observations**
Executive support and leadership						
Existence of an executive manager						
Co-ordination and co-operation						
Strategic planning						
Resources required						
Knowledge management						
Internal and external marketing						

Once you have designed the structure of the project and defined its objectives, establishing the support and resources required, you will be ready to move on to the next stage.

Peter Kwan's Story

At 10 a.m. on the day of the meeting, Frank Wright welcomed Peter into his office and closed the door. "Bad omen," Peter thought. He knew that Frank only did this on rare occasions.

"Well, I hope you're bringing me something interesting," Frank began. "The Production Department Manager told me you've been talking to everybody over there. Are you going to suggest incorporating our workers into the Marketing Department, or are you organizing a trade union?"

Peter smiled, as it sounded like a joke, but Frank didn't.

"Well … see … I needed to obtain some historical data, and I thought that the most senior production staff could maybe …"

"OK. Have you brought something to show me?"

"Yes, of course," Peter replied. "It's not a finalized project, but it outlines what I think we should do."

"*We* should? I thought it was your responsibility and you were in charge of it all."

"Yes, sure, but there are some aspects – not many – that could affect other departments. If you want, I'll begin," Peter said, handing Frank his bound report.

For about forty minutes he explained to Frank the lack of orientation of the company towards its consumers, the need to introduce innovation as a constant element, and so on. The whole time, Frank sat there like a statue. He didn't say a word, which made Peter very nervous since he couldn't tell whether he was being understood by his boss, or whether he liked the proposal or thought it was stupid.

"This is pretty much all I have at the moment," concluded Peter.

"If I've understood you correctly, you've just explained to me that our product is a disaster, our company is badly organized, our sector gets bad press, and our marketing campaigns are wrongly oriented. By chance you attended a seminar last week. Someone who has possibly never set foot in a company shows you the way, and a voice that comes out of a burning bush in the shape of a lollipop tells you that if we turn the company inside out as if it were a sock, doing nothing else for the next year or so, maybe – maybe! – we'll increase sales by 20 per cent. Is this, to sum up, what you've explained to me, Peter?"

"See … it's not so …," Peter tried to argue, but Frank cut across him.

"Absurd? – Is that what you want to say? Sweetme has been sold for over forty years without major problems. I ask you to plan something to address a slight annual market downturn and you suggest that the remedy is to demolish the company!"

Peter was upset. This was the first time since he'd joined the company that Frank had spoken so harshly to him, and he was surprised. Luckily, he'd had enough experiences with tough bosses in the past that he didn't let it intimidate him.

"I'm not suggesting that we change everything at once. What I'm suggesting is that little by little we re-orient ourselves towards the consumer. Times keep changing, and so do consumers' motivations. For example, did you know that our sales in non-USA-friendly countries fall every time international relations deteriorate?" added Peter, making a point he hadn't explained in the report. "We're a multinational – the name of our company being in English and our being a multinational leads some people to wrongly assume that ours is an American product. The same sort of thing applies to many other considerations. The other day, someone told me that I was working in a refined calories factory, and that we would do better if we worked on marketing celery sticks!"

Peter paused to draw breath, then continued. "Look, Frank, maybe I've explained it to you a bit dramatically, but we must start adapting to the current times, and I'm not saying we should do it all at once – we can take it one step at a time. And by the way, the seminar has nothing to do with it. It simply served as a reminder that every now and then we need to look at things from a different perspective."

"OK, OK," Frank sighed, "Maybe I was a bit too harsh, but the thing is … either we make a profit, or the group's going to sell us at knockdown price to who knows whom, and then we might as well start packing up."

"Frank, if you agree, I'll get down to elaborating a plan of action taking into account your objections, modifying things little by little. I want to have enough time to adapt if I get it wrong. I promise to keep to the budget and keep the advertising campaigns going."

"OK," replied Frank, "I'm not saying that I don't like taking risks, but you know what's at stake here, so be sensible."

The phone rang. Frank picked it up and bade Peter goodbye with a gesture.

Leaving Frank's office, Peter felt like his shirt collar was far too tight. He knew what he had to do. He understood his boss's reluctance, and understood the personal risk he himself was taking – especially now, with his three young children and a mortgage, this wasn't the best time to lose his job.

He started to write down some notes for his plan of action:

- What to do?
- Re-orienting communication
- Increase information on the product
- Could we change the website?
- About the product:
    - Segmentation children/adults?
    - A light/healthy line? For ex-smokers? Gourmet?

- Improve wrapping
- Make the product more "eco-friendly"
- If we make changes, we need to emphasize them changing the product's appearance
- Language, stickers
- Composition
- Preventing accidents
- General:
  - Code of Ethics?
  - Frank's support
  - External support or recommendations
- User involvement:
  - Build up a panel?
- Resources and time:
  - Re-orienting communication with same budget
  - Design costs – Who is designing for us? How long does it take them?
  - Reformulating the product – Can the factory chemists do this?
  - How much would it cost it to create a new website?

"Maybe Frank's got a point," Peter thought, his mind racing, "this is going to take a long time. What's the main concept? What attributes must the product have? Is it an indulgence for oneself, or something to offer to someone else – family, parents, children? No one wants to pass around something that might damage a loved one's health. Respecting sensitivities – what are they? Creating a user panel? An expert panel? A survey on the Internet? Commission a study?"

Now he was really a mess. He left the office, caught the bus and went to the gym.

Next day, his mind a little clearer, he remembered the HUMBLES table setting out how to plan projects, and he filled it out provisionally.

Ideal situation in 9 months

	Initial stage	**Development stage**	**Consolidation stage**	**Comments**
Executive support and leadership	*Need to fully convince Frank*	*Frank supports because he is starting to see results*		
Existence of an executive manager	*To make things go smoothly with the system*	*I need to co-ordinate with everyone without driving them mad.* *Talk to Frank about moving the Claims Department into my area.*		
Co-ordination and co-operation	*Define partners*	*All internal and external partner defined*		
Strategic planning	*The plan we decide and management approves*	*Plan follow-up*		
Resources required	*I think that they will be*	*If we obtain results, there will not be a problem*		
Knowledge management	*Start systematizing information*	*Start orienting staff towards the client/user*		
Internal and external marketing	*Internal Inter-personal* *External not yet*	*Campaign of the prearranged line*	*Idea: Turn retailers in Prescriptors*	

This time, it was Peter who asked for a meeting with Frank. Peter brought up a long list of approachable objectives, but wanted to avoid disrupting the organization.

"I'd like you to call another meeting with all heads of department to figure out what we can deal with during the next twelve months," Peter said.

Frank thought for a minute, then gave his opinion. "Peter, last time there was a meeting of all heads of department it was to introduce me and to let my predecessor communicate the change in ownership. I think your idea of seeking a consensus about any changes with all the areas involved is a good one, but I think it would be much better if you spoke with each of them individually about what will affect them, and then present me with the plan. Is that OK?"

"No problem – I'll do that," Peter replied. "How different this meeting has been from the previous one," he thought.

The following two weeks were a whirlwind. Production, Sales, Human Resources, Finance, Distribution – all the departments expressed resistance to change, a fear of giving away some of their power.

For example, after listening to Mr Martin, Production Manager for the past twenty-five years, explain that he had to find the woman in charge of the Claims Department other work to do because complaints were not providing enough work, Peter raised the possibility that this department be moved to another area. Mr Martín was furious. He finally grudgingly accepted the solution when Peter promised his support in convincing Frank to invest in a new machine.

Two weeks later, Peter held another a meeting with Frank to try to persuade him to accept his proposal.

"Have a look at this, Frank. On the first page there is a summary of the topics that I think we can tackle, and on the following ones, the plan for each of them."

"Are you sure that this isn't excessive?" Frank commented when he saw the long list. "Have you talked about this with all the department heads, and do they agree?"

"Yes."

"Are you telling me that Mr Martin has agreed to renounce to his Claims Department?" asked Frank, slightly aghast.

"Yes."

Frank was suspicious. "And what have you promised in exchange?"

"He seems to be very interested in a new sealing machine for boxes. It's not a significant investment. I told him I'd mention it to you."

"I see, I see. So you're plotting," smiled Frank.

"I think the investment is a good idea – at the moment we seal boxes with the standard brown packing tape, and the new machine would allow us to use tape with our logo and print the Quick Response code on it – from what he says, that would pay off quickly."

"Peter, have you ever thought of selling fridges to Eskimos?"

In a more relaxed atmosphere, they went through all the proposed innovations one by one. After arguing, negotiating, discussing and editing the list of actions to undertake, they came up with the following plan:

- Redesign the website, incorporating, among other things, complaints, suggestions, user participation, detailed descriptions of products, nutritional information, promotional elements and a code of ethics regarding the responsible purchase of raw materials, responsible advertising and our environmental policy.
- Problem-solving:
  - wrapping
  - allergies and illnesses
  - languages
  - the stick.
- Launch three new lines of the product (pending studies that confirm feasibility):
  - Sweetme Earth – an ecological product, without additives, using natural ingredients
  - Sweetme Energy – a Sweetme version of an energy drink
  - a Sweetme Gourmet line to follow later if these two are successful.
- Start up new strategies for user participation:
  - campaign validation
  - product validation
  - adapting new ideas?

When Frank was ready to draw the meeting to a close, Peter asked him, "By the way, Frank, is there a designer we usually work with?"

"Isn't that the job of the advertising agency?"

"I'm talking about a product designer."

"I don't think we've ever hired anybody directly. Ask the agency – they may know."

To be continued ...

5 Lay Out Solutions

Once you have clearly defined the direction for your innovations and set up the work team, it will be important to make sure this team has all the information its needs for the task, along with the strategy for the new product or service and its planning and development.

Both proactive and reactive strategies may achieve success, as long as design plays an important and innovative role. In any case, planning the process is necessary to reduce the time to market – the time from the development of the product until it is launched.

Planning a project concerning a new product relies on teamwork, where all the departments of your company, especially marketing and design, play a very important role. The design of a product and the development process are very reiterative and non-sequential processes, often moving backwards and forwards.

Figure 5.1 sets out the main phases and different but complementary focusing methods adopted by design and marketing managers. The diagram compares the marketing and design functions linked to the process of development of the product, divided into five main phases:

1. investigation
2. exploration
3. development
4. execution
5. evaluation.

It is obvious that the draft will vary, functions are approximate and no phase is the exclusive domain of one discipline or other. In fact, it may be useful to share many of these functions.

Ideally, in the investigation phase, the Marketing Department should be responsible for leading the generation and selection of ideas, particularly the sales network, which should be given the mission of contributing ideas obtained from direct contact with the market, as we explained in Chapters 2 and 3. As we explained in Chapter 4, the selection if ideas must conform to the criteria set out in the strategy for the new product or service.

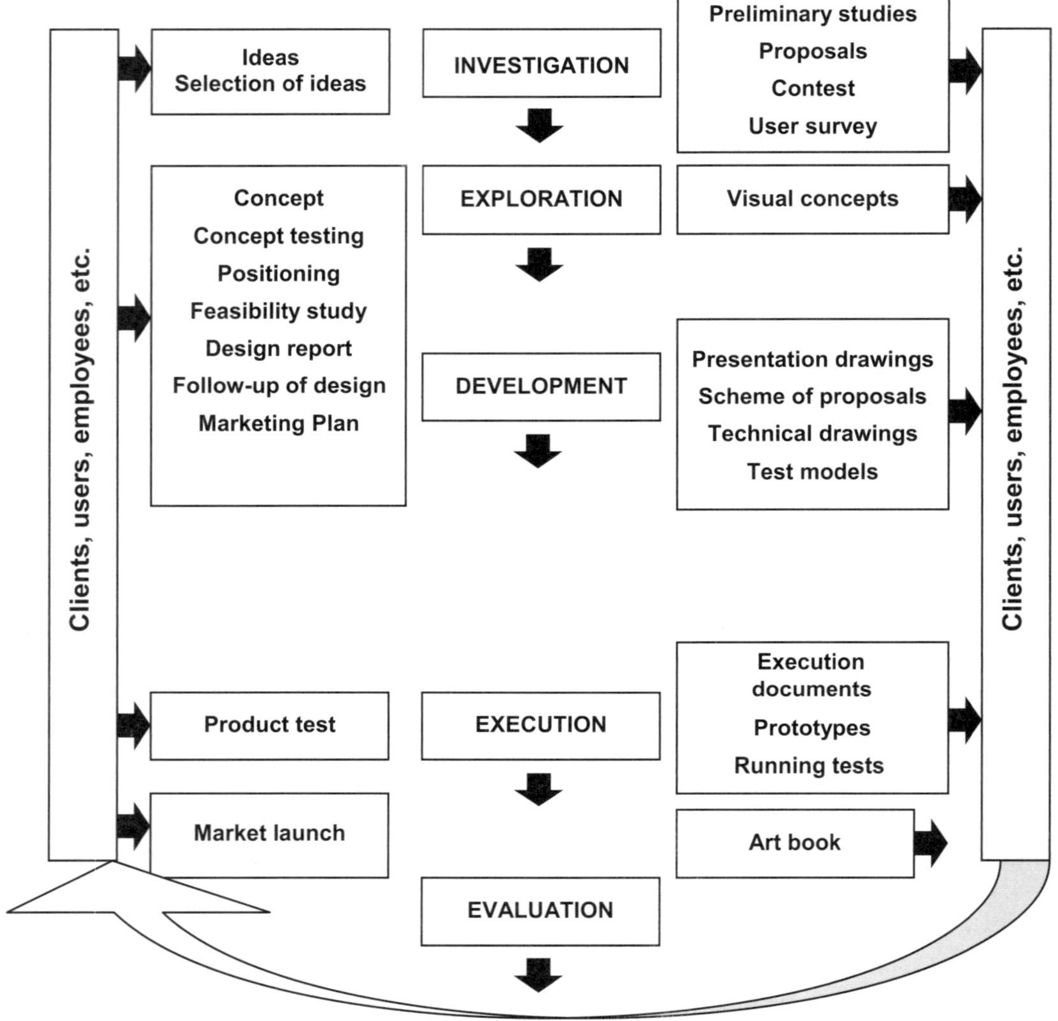

Figure 5.1   Outline for developing a new product project

In this phase, the designer must also carry out preliminary studies to identify possible new products or modifications to current ones, based on market data or your company's internal information, as well as on the analysis of the products of competitors and the reaction of different consumer profiles towards the product.

Designers will have their own methods to develop ideas and concepts: creative teamwork, research into limitations and restrictions, studies about future scenarios, and so on. However, the ability to visualize ideas and concepts is especially important.

The phase of conceptualizing the product or service is crucial to its subsequent design. The concept is basically a message to the consumer: a promise by the product to satisfy unsatisfied needs, the reasons why it will satisfy these needs, and information about the aspects that will affect the perception of the product. The designers are responsible for transforming these verbal concepts into concepts capable of being apprehended through the senses. These sensorial concepts in two or three dimensions often come together with experimental models, making it easier to try out concepts and decide which to incorporate into the development process.

The development phase varies to a large extent from one product to another, but basically relies on the Marketing Department defining the position and main attributes that will later be developed, analysing the financial feasibility of the project and drafting the design report which will define requirements. This report is the cornerstone of the design process, and an essential factor in facilitating communication between the company and designer. The design process then continues by paying special attention to important targets defined in the project calendar. Meanwhile, managers can begin to draw up the marketing plan for the product or service and the launch.

Meanwhile, the Design Department will create successive drafts of the chosen concept to firm up proposals, possibly with several alternatives. After approval of the most suitable concept, technical plans are drawn up and experimental models created to test the product – tasks which are normally carried out by the Marketing Department with users' involvement. This phase can consist of a series of tests, or one test with several judges, to measure understanding, identification, handling and ease of use. Ease of use and identification are the responsibility of the Marketing Department, but handling and understanding are the responsibility of the engineers and designers, although the opinion of the Marketing Department will also be important, of course.

If the results are positive, the Design Department will then commence work with the Production Department, which will already have been part of the development phase, to define the execution documents, prototypes, conduct tests, and so on.

A well-integrated Design Department should bear in mind the visual aspects of a product, from the packaging to printed material like instructions, communication material and point-of-sale material, if necessary. This work would have begun with the design of communication graphics at the same time as the marketing plans, and the resulting materials will be distributed in their final format with the prototypes.

Production will begin in a co-ordinated manner before the launch of the product in the market to ensure that it is already in distribution channels when the sales, promotion or advertising campaigns begin. However, the process does not end here: a follow-up is required to determine whether the product has been a success.

The process we have presented here is necessarily generalized, and each company must adapt it to its own circumstances and to the type of service or product it has decided to develop. Nevertheless, it is essential to ensure that the following ten steps are taken into account:

1. Conduct a thorough study of each of the aspects to be improved.
2. Avoid reinventing the wheel.
3. Identify the scope for innovation.
4. Study feasible solutions.
5. Consult clients and users about the possible solutions.
6. Ensure flexibility in the course of action.
7. Draw up an exhaustive briefing.
8. Design the prototype.
9. Test the prototype.
10. Test the resulting product or service.

Naturally, it is a very different matter to design improvements in an after-sale service rather than a kitchen tool, which is why we are not more specific in our recommendations. Your company will have to determine the specific methods for following these steps.

Conduct a Thorough Study of Each of the Aspects to be Improved

The "Monitor Interaction" phase set out in Chapter 3 should have allowed your company to identify problems with interaction or aspects that could be improved and decide which of them to address. Now is the time to analyse each of these aspects in depth. It is possible, for instance, that what might be a problem for one group of users could be considered a positive factor by others, or that what some consider a slight setback, others may describe as their main reason for deciding not to buy the product.

If the product is widely known, you could check what opinions people have expressed on various social media on the Internet. On the other hand, by using the Improvements Map from Chapter 3, you can focus on a detailed analysis of the aspects to improve, ensuring that the improvements will make your products more respectful, safe, healthy, functional, understandable and attractive to all the consumers you have decided to target. It will also be very useful at this stage to check your findings through in-depth interviews of critical users and subject experts. These can prove a valuable source of inspiration.

When your company has developed a solid reputation among its clients, it can then decide to create a section on its website to receive suggestions. You may be surprised how creative users can be.

Avoid Reinventing the Wheel

Look around you, at your competition and their similar products and services (in your own country and others). Check whether similar problems have been encountered in the past and how they have been dealt with.

If it is possible in your sector, collaborate with other companies within the same field, or with user associations, to develop solutions. Sharing is always enriching.

Identify the Scope for Innovation

Once you have decided on which aspects to improve, armed with knowledge about what others have done, it is time to decide how to bring innovation to your company.

Do you have the knowledge, economic support and technical resources required? Can you hire external professionals, co-ordinated by your company's Design Manager? Do you have access to support from public funds for innovation?

Given the problem of lack of human resources devoted to innovation that small and medium-sized enterprises and public administrations face, in collaboration with several universities and companies i2CAT and the Design for All Foundation have developed iCell – Cells of Innovation,

For each iCell group, three to six students from a postgraduate course on technology, business and design are selected to work in teams in a specific territory and field of innovation.

These teams constitute the nucleus of iCell, with support from specialized tutors, selected companies with the capacity to work synergistically, and in each case, local administrations with common interests and potential clients and users of the innovation.

In a highly monitored process over about ten months, the teams develop prototypes of business models, the nature of the participation of each of the agents involved varying from project to project.

It is very likely that if you do not make the right decisions based on honest self-analysis, the results will not be as good as expected. If your company decides to undertake a project such as this without much financial support or access to external resources, go ahead, but make sure that the person who will lead the process will be able to call on expert support when needed.

Study Feasible Solutions

Improvement can be approached from a wide variety of perspectives. Depending on the improvement sought and the product or service in question, you can tackle the problem using six different strategies:

1. **Trying to ensure that a single product is suitable for all potential users** – This strategy is appropriate in architecture or the design of specific websites, for instance.
2. **Creating an array of products adapted to people's different characteristics** – This approach has traditionally been adopted for items such as clothing or shoes, providing different lengths and sizes of the same design, but has also been applied to cars, mobile phones, many canned commodities or designing hotel rooms.
3. **Creating a product that can be adjusted or configured by the user** – Two examples of this are office chairs and desktop computers.
4. **Ensuring your product or service is compatible with others your clients use** – Examples include public address systems in airports or theatres which include induction loops to communicate with people with hearing aids, or boarding card codes that some airlines send to travellers' mobile phones to simplify the boarding process.
5. **Associating your product or service with a particular service for clients who have specific needs** – Examples include providing facilities for people with limited mobility in airports, or a repair shop providing courtesy vehicles to customers while their cars are being repaired.
6. **Personalizing the product or service** – This is a very common approach for consultants (for instance, lawyers) or in handcrafts (personalizing clothing or vehicles, and so on). We could also include consideration of the specific needs of some minority groups in this category, such as making available kosher wine or gluten-free bread in a restaurant, or wheelchairs in a museum in case someone gets tired of walking or is injured.

   We could also include consideration of the specific needs of some minority groups in this category, such as making available kosher wine or gluten-free bread in a restaurant, or wheelchairs in a museum in case someone gets tired of walking or is injured.

Depending on your situation, you will have to decide which of these strategies to choose as a basis for the creative development of the realistic solutions that must be conceived.

Consult Clients and Users about the Possible Solutions

Don't restrict your research to your customers, but also include your employees, colleagues and friends, and listen, listen, listen …

However, it is important not just to listen yourself – those involved in the design process must be direct witnesses of what customers consider important.

Ensure Flexibility in the Course of Action

As we commented when describing the design phase, this is not a linear process – in many cases it is necessary to return to earlier stages to revise approaches or confirm hypotheses. If certain courses of action have been identified in the "Breakthrough Options" phase set out in Chapter 4, it is advisable to remain flexible and to reconsider these in the light of findings that may emerge in the "Lay Out Solutions" phase.

Draw Up an Exhaustive Briefing

It is essential to compile a very detailed list of all the functional, emotional, perceptive, communicative, economic and ecological aspects of the product or service once it has been subject to innovation. The priority is to define the diversity of the population to which it is addressed, and decide whether there is a sector that you wish to exclude (drawing on the User Map from Chapter 2).

You should ensure that the preparation of this report draws together participation from all the key agents, then revise it with employees, managers, clients, suppliers, family members and friends – and above all, with individuals from those sectors of the population you wish to retain or win as clients and users. The wider the diversity, the more guarantee you will have of the validity of the briefing.

Design the Prototype

Whether you are dealing with a product or a service, it is possible that you have already used drafts or graphics to consult users about possible solutions. Now is the time to capture in two or three dimensions the ideas that have arisen during the process.

Test the Prototype

Often, the prototype manufactured must be fully functional to enable users to test all the possible details of interaction. Obviously, the scale of investment in this stage will depend on the cost of the product or service, how widely it is distributed and how long its lifecycle will be.

It is normal, for instance, to build 1:1 scale models of train carriages to allow users to test them. However, we have always found it very curious that while houses may cost just as much or more and their lifecycles will be much longer, they are never tested in this way by users.

This phase will be much more illuminating for industrial products than for services, which, since they are easy to adapt, will be better addressed in the testing phase.

Test the Resulting Product or Service

Prior to market launch and advertising campaigns, is usual to test the final product or service. Software is often released in beta versions that allow developers to identify and remedy flaws that may be detectable only through feedback from many respondents over an extended period of use.

It would be so much better for users if more companies put into practice the concept of beta versions. We will analyse how to do this in the next phase.

Peter Kwan's Story

Kumi, Peter's wife, was a bit worried because in all the years they had been together she had never seen him so obsessed with his job, but on the other hand, she was happy to see in him again that spark and drive he had when they first met. He was often late getting home from work, and she frequently had to remind him that he had a family and household chores to share.

One night, in bed, Kumi brought up the subject of his preoccupation with his job and his high spirits. Peter replied, "This is the first time in my entire life that my job is giving me more than just a way to earn a living. Many people have no idea, but what we're going to do with Sweetme will help to improve some things in our society a little."

"Are you going to hand out Sweetmes at the UN?" joked Kumi.

At this, Peter, with that look in his eyes she'd seen before, started to explain to her about Fair Trade, environmentally friendly products, people with coeliac disease and diabetes, and so forth. Kumi kissed him and Peter stopped talking, but it took a long time for them both to fall asleep. "If only Sweetme Energy already existed ...," he joked to himself.

Peter's work time was taken up with a frantic round of polishing projects, designing the user panels, and holding meetings with website design companies and advertising agencies.

The topic of design was one of his main concerns. Up to now, the advertising agency had been almost solely responsible for deciding campaign targets, whether to update the logo or the design for new displays. Despite their initial reluctance, the agency staff finally understood that Peter wanted to run the design process himself. What they didn't manage to grasp fully was his obsession with complicating matters by getting users involved. With all the experience they had in setting up user panels for different displays or campaigns, what was the point in involving the consumers, associations and all kinds of other entities? Still, they were comforted when Peter assured them that he wanted to launch another advertising campaign soon and he was counting on their input.

Peter knew that the design was a critical aspect, so he wanted a good result, which led him to define the steps to be taken in this stage meticulously. First, they had to select a designer with sensitivity towards and experience of the topics he wanted to tackle. They would then have to create a user panel made up of people with characteristics and values related to the topics they had decided to deal with. Finally, he wanted to ensure that the problems identified were being addressed satisfactorily, so he wanted to consult a long list of NGOs, regulatory organizations and administrations, to avoid mistakes.

To his surprise, choosing a designer was not an easy task. Only a few had experience with food products, and even fewer worked from a Design for All perspective. None of them had the slightest clue about the HUMBLES method.

After holding interviews with several designers, Peter opted for Xavier Foix because from the beginning there had been a good chemistry between them, and when Peter mentioned HUMBLES, Xavier had written down the URL, the book references and the consultant's name. In short, he was a professional, keen on all kinds of knowledge – this was an excellent quality to incorporate into Peter's team.

Peter realized that his current excitement made him open to options and challenges that he had never though of before. He liked that. For example, when he was drawing up an outline of the makeup of the user panel, he thought of their friend Laura. If Sweetme could convince her to eat one of their products, it would be quite a triumph!

Full of self-confidence, he gave her a call and suggested having lunch together. It took a while to persuade her, but she finally agreed. "Peter inviting me to a vegetarian restaurant – what does he want?" Laura asked herself.

A couple of days later, at the restaurant, Laura could not believe what she was hearing. "You want me to participate in a user panel for Sweetme?" – her roars of laughter made all the other diners look over at their table.

After listening to a long litany of swear words about multinationals, transgenic foods, additives, capital stock and suchlike, Peter commented, "You see – you're perfect! Your critical faculties will surely enable you to detect any Machiavellian strategies we can come up with to manipulate citizens as you say we do. Just sitting there criticizing is easy. Now you have an opportunity to devote your critical abilities to something constructive. Or are you scared?"

Peter knew this last sentence would have a galvanizing effect.

"Scared? What do you mean 'scared'?" snapped Laura. "At the first sign that you're pulling my leg, I'll quit the panel!"

"Does that mean you're in?"

"Yes! I accept the mission of watching you very closely and hitting you where it hurts most at the first sign that you're trying to manipulate gullible citizens with your marketing techniques."

"Thanks, Laura," Peter smiled, satisfied at having won a small battle among the many he was setting himself at this point.

Within a few days the first panel began, where they started defining the new product lines. It would take another two months before Peter presented Frank with the precise definition of the characteristics of the three new lines they had decided to pursue. This was the design summary:

- The sweet is to keep its traditional shape and appearance.
- All plastic elements will be replaced by bio-plastic made from cornstarch. The stick will be slightly flexible.
- The new shape and wrapping material will allow consumers to unwrap Sweetme easily, regardless of their manual abilities.
- All flavours will be suitable for those with coeliac disease, diabetes, and those allergic to dry fruits or dairy products.
- The Sweetme Energy line will have a range of flavours that is more intense, even spicy. The coffee-flavour one will also include the minerals the others contain, and offer three times the calories of Sweetme Classic.
- The Sweetme Earth line will group together the most varied flavours made of natural extracts of fruit, honey and medicinal herbs. This line includes a new tea flavour that has surprised everyone by its popularity among adults. This flavour is actually a mixture of tea and the Argentinean mate herb (a highly creative contribution from the South American distributor), and contains only a third of the calories of Sweetme Classic.
- Sweetme Classic will remain much the same, but its flavours will be adjusted according to more refined evaluations in user tests. It will contain 70 Kcal per sweet (3 per cent of the recommended daily intake).
- Each line will be differentiated from the others by the colour of the stick – wood colour for Sweetme Classic, a more intense shade for Sweetme Energy and pastel colours for Sweetme Earth.
- There has been concerted work with distributors and retailers to establish their needs regarding displays, and these have been redesigned.
- New five- and ten-unit packaging has been designed for the shelves of large stores, service stations, airports, and so on.
- The process of adaptation to local languages is almost complete.
- In total, the process's cost has amounted to 15 per cent of what the company normally pays for a standard national advertising campaign.

Frank gave the go-ahead for production of a beta series to test the new lines with consumers from different countries.

And Laura … Laura was becoming an addict of Sweetme Earth tea flavour!

The production cost of the new product was 5.7 per cent greater than the current one, but with the expected increase in sales and the differential in price for Sweetme Earth and Sweetme Energy, the gross market was set to increase.

All the participants in the design process felt that things were proceeding too quickly for comfort, but Peter himself was working full out, considering that along with his role in these developments he was co-ordinating the design for the launch campaign and the new website.

To be continued …

6 Efficient Communication

Once the design of solutions has been tackled, the next task is to conduct an in-depth analysis of your communication with clients and users. We could recount many examples of how excellent products and companies have failed because of poor communication.

As in previous chapters, we will illustrate our argument with practical examples. We will address the challenges of communication under the following headings:

- flexibility
- avoiding stigmatization
- sincerity and honesty
- simplicity
- receptivity
- permeability.

Flexibility

As explained in Chapter 2 with the User Map, it is desirable for your company's message to reach a wide range of clients and users. Thus, the first step is to establish which media and channels of information they prefer. Once more, instead of making decisions based on assumptions, it will be necessary to consult those addressed via your communications to find out which channels or media they actually use.

For instance, we know that 500 million people have a profile on Facebook, which is the second most visited website in the world, and that a percentage of them update it several times a week, while others only access it when they receive a "friend" invitation; others never access it at all. This shows that while your company may feel it necessary to set up a Facebook presence, you should bear in mind that this tool will not reach all users or prospective users.

Your company needs to open up a wide range of channels of communication, since customers and potential users will have their own preferences about which to use to obtain information about your company and its products. In addition, you must also bear in mind users' personal characteristics, and seek to minimize any obstacles to your message reaching them. For example, if you advertise your products on television, make sure, among other aspects, that:

- the timbre of the voices featured allows people with hearing difficulties to understand them easily, and that the voices are not obscured by background music;
- any relevant text is also narrated, unless you want to exclude blind consumers;
- images do not change too suddenly, since otherwise, many viewers may miss your message.

If, on the other hand, we are talking about your corporate website, apart from guaranteeing that it is attractive and friendly for your users, you should ensure you comply with the WAI (Web Access Initiative) guidelines, which will help to ensure, among other things, that:

- it is compatible with a variety of browser software;
- blind people can also navigate your site;
- it complies with different countries' legal requirements;
- users do not lose their way within the site.

In short, as we have been explaining throughout this book, your company must make a constant effort to adapt to its users' wishes and communication needs. There are two important reasons for this:

1. Your client will only make an effort to adapt to you if there is no alternative.
2. Your competitors are already doing it.

Other aspects to bear in mind about this flexibility are linked to the culture of the target territory and its inhabitants – for instance, using your consumers' first language or adapting to their habits and manners.

Once more, we remind you that you should not take anything for granted; instead, observe, ask and analyse. For example, many assume that blind people rely on Braille to read, and that they cannot use computers since they are unable to see the screen. However, the reality is very different: in the most advanced countries, only 12–17 per cent of blind people know Braille, and more and more blind people are using computers by means of speech synthesis software that describes and reads the screen; those who know Braille can use hardware such as *Braille Line*.

Do Not Stigmatize

Muñecas Llorens is a Spanish toy company that has invested a great deal of time and effort in designing its "Dolls for All" range. Its aim was to develop a series of dolls that were as realistic as possible and were especially suitable for children with certain types of visual, motor or physical disabilities. With this in mind, it studied details such as hand shape, how easy it was to dress the doll, length of hair, lip profiles and eye movement. All of this entailed a huge effort involving consultants and users that was rewarded by the Design for All 2009 Award.

However, the social motivation of Muñecas Llorens's management and their certainty that this product was socially necessary led them to make a common mistake: conveying on the packaging of its dolls that they were appropriate for all children, but in particular those with visual or physical disabilities. Despite the good intentions behind this, these were some of the reactions from prospective customers:

"The doll is really beautiful, but my daughter is "normal" and doesn't need a special doll."

"My son has a physical disability, but it's minor, and I don't want him to have a 'special' toy."

For these reasons, an excellent product for all children suffered a setback in its market launch and did not achieve the anticipated sales.

This example emphasizes that no one likes being stigmatized by being associated with a group that may carry negative connotations in particular contexts. Words like "old", "disabled", "obese" or "short" have pejorative meanings, so it is best to avoid using them. In this case, it might have been better to describe the characteristics of the dolls with statements such as:."The lips are shaped so that they are easy for your child to locate even in total darkness, and the clothing has been designed so that no child will have a problem dressing or undressing the doll without a parent's help."

In the same vein, we advised the Sol Meliá hotel chain that it should modify the design and communications systems in its accessible rooms. Instead of furnishing the rooms with all the support features that were available, which often meant the accommodation resembled a hospital room, we suggested that it made the accessories available only if a guest requested them, according to his or her needs. In tandem with this, we advised Sol Meliá to produce literature describing in detail the dimensions and characteristics of these rooms and the accessories that were readily available on request.

We also suggested that Sol Meliá change the naming convention for its rooms – Standard, Suite, Junior and Accessible – and instead refer to them as Standard, Standard Plus, Suite Junior, Suite Junior Plus, Suite and Suite Plus – the "Plus" rooms allowed easy use of a wheelchair and were designed to accommodate the accessories. The results were that:

- guests with no functional limitations who would be likely to reject the Accessible rooms felt comfortable in Plus rooms since they were less cramped;
- guests with disabilities had the choice of several types of rooms and had at their disposal only those accessories they actually needed.

The important point here is that customers generally prefer to be treated as unique individuals, and not as a collective. With this in mind, when it comes to describing your product, try to describe its characteristics and functionality instead of to whom it is addressed.

If you are interested in an in-depth analysis of this facet in particular, we recommend you read the contribution from Alex Lee, Oxo's CEO, in Chapter 8.

Sincerity and Honesty

Do not make any promises you cannot fulfil. For example, have you ever felt hoodwinked when the pictures of the accommodation and surroundings on a hotel's website have not been borne out by reality? To safeguard your company's reputation, it is important to communicate with honesty its values and intentions, and to explain sincerely what it can and cannot offer.

Consumers are only too accustomed to companies (not to mention administrations) failing to fulfil their promises, and will look for independent confirmation of the validity of your offer. Certificates, links with NGOs and their testimonials about your company on the Internet will help you consolidate your image.

Simplicity

Els de Vries, an expert consultant in tourism and transport, showed us some years ago the importance of KISS – Keep it Simple, Stupid! There is no need to complicate matters.

Remember that even in your own country, many people may not have mastered the dominant language or may have difficulties with it or with complex processes. Therefore, try to make your messages simple and intuitive in style and language, using short sentences and icons, when appropriate. For instance, illustrations in instruction manuals should be very accurate drawings or high-quality photographs, to avoid confusion. How often have you been late for a date with friends because it took so long to program your video recorder?

As mentioned earlier, we recommend you never distribute a message, a set of instructions or the text on packaging without having trialled it beforehand with a sample of the users you wish to target.

The application of simplicity in communication is also necessary in automated phone services. Do not make your clients' interaction with these systems too complex or longwinded. The worst offenders force users to press numerous buttons to select options, and when they finally manage to talk to an operative, that person ends up running through the options all over again, deeply frustrating the caller.

An example of good practice in this field is the company Radio Taxi 033. Its system allows callers to make automatic reservations using previously registered personal details and to communicate with operatives via the telephone service, SMS or the Internet. The customer chooses which channel to use to make the reservation, obtaining the same service regardless of the means used.

Receptivity

This means focusing your communications on generating responses from the public and ensuring that these reach your company. In Chapter 3 we explained the importance of monitoring complaints, and we pointed out that when clients decide to complain, it is usually because they are very upset with your service or product. If they are not already in place, we suggest that you create tools to permanently capture your customers' opinions and wishes.

Give your customers a call every now and then, reward those who complete surveys with free entry in a draw for one of your products or services, go looking for them and observe how they live, organize feedback meetings or sessions. If you use methods like these to gather information about your customers, you will be able to foresee changes in the market at very early stages.

Permeability

The considerations above are valid for and applicable to all your company's communication methods: advertising messages, customer care, news, your online presence, conversations with suppliers, your relationship with the political administration or the local Chamber of Commerce – all these convey the values of your company, so it is very important that these approaches permeate the working style of your organization, its management, employees, suppliers, distributors, and so on.

Not only will this promote your company's values and products or services, it will help to ensure that all the people in your organization are attentive to feedback from your social environment.

Once we have ensured efficient communication of the improvements that will be introduced, we can proceed to the final stage of the HUMBLES method, where you will be able to judge whether you have achieved your objectives.

Peter Kwan's Story

The Web designers were a fantastic double act. It was quite something to see them in action at meetings. One of them kept saying, "We could do this, we could do that," and each time he suggested something he looked at his partner and in a low and very deep voice started to talk in jargon that Peter did not understand to establish with his partner whether the idea was feasible.

One problem was the content of the new website. There was no point in migrating everything from the old one and Peter didn't have time to do it all, so he decided to hire a Web content management consultancy to work in tandem with the designers. Luckily, they hit it off immediately.

Peter felt like he was the captain of a storm-tossed ship up to his neck in water. He urgently needed confirmation from someone else that he was making the right decisions. He knew that the website complied with the WAI guidelines, or at least that's what the designers told him.

Peter had checked the new product ingredients with allergy support groups, dieticians and doctors. The new environmentally friendly materials had been approved by several bodies, and some had even offered their congratulations. Despite all this, Peter needed some guidance about the process, so he called the consultant who had conducted the HUMBLES seminar.

He felt frustrated when the consultant told him that his speciality was holding seminars and that he had no experience with food products. Peter recalled what Frank had said about seminars. However, the consultant did give him contact details for the Design for All Foundation, saying that it would very likely be able to help him.

That was indeed the case. They organized a long video-conference, during which they congratulated him for his initiative and gave him the contact details of a consultant with experience in the food sector who would be able to review the process.

Peter's relationship with the advertising agency was more complex. In the past, the company had delegated all decision-making to the agency, so its staff now felt uneasy with a newcomer trying to teach them their trade. A number of their meetings ran very late without giving Peter the feeling that they were making any progress. Although he had decided to retain the same agency to avoid upheaval, he was ready to throw in the towel.

After one of these meetings, he arrived home around 11 p.m. to find the house silent and in darkness. "Oh well, the children must be in bed," he thought, making his way to their rooms to kiss them goodnight. After doing so, he went to his bedroom, but Kumi wasn't there. He heard a murmur from the bathroom, and crept to the doorway. There he found his wife ensconced in the bathtub, her eyes shut, around her four or five candles, with Elvis Presley as an almost inaudible soundtrack, singing "Love Me Tender".

He drew closer to kiss her. To his surprise, he found that he couldn't because her mouth was full of a Coffee Sweetme from the prototype series. He stroked her hair and she opened her eyes with a sleepy smile.

Once they had both gone to bed, Peter sleepily mulled over how some moments, fleeting images, stay with you throughout your life. He was sure that he would never forget the feeling of relaxation, beauty and harmony the image of Kumi in the bathtub conveyed, and fell asleep happy.

The following day brought another meeting with the advertising agency staff, and Peter decided that he was going to have to decide whether or not to persevere with them. He felt it was unforgivable that they had been incapable of conveying the pleasant, generous, friendly and peaceful image that he wanted the company to represent.

During the meeting, he closed his eyes for a moment and the image of Kumi came to mind. Despite his doubts about whether it was appropriate to share such an intimate image, he went for it. That image ended up becoming the catalyst for the television advertising campaign. "Sweetme tender, Sweetme for you," a vocalist sang over the music for "Love Me Tender", accompanying a series of images. Two young skaters crossed paths while exchanging a Sweetme Energy. In the version for Sweetme Classic, a five-year-old girl gave alternate licks of her Sweetme to her dog and her doll.

Fortunately, the bathtub image was never used, and Peter didn't dare to confess to Kumi that he had shared it until quite a while later.

To be continued …

CHAPTER 7

Success Evaluation

"What is not measured does not count. What is not evaluated gets devalued."

One way to measure success in implementing the HUMBLES method is to evaluate the quality of the final design. In this context, by "design" we mean both the processes involved in developing the innovation and all its results – the product or service itself, but also the communication campaign, packaging, instructions, after-sale service, and so on.

A quantitative investigation of a sample of companies we recently completed confirmed statistically that good design leads to good results – this bears out our previous research. This means that evaluating the quality of the design resulting from your Design for All strategy will give rise to an indirect evaluation of the far-reaching effects of this strategy on your company's results.

How can we measure the quality of the design? In our research, we evaluated the design of a company through the effectiveness of the design of its products, its corporate identity and its Web presence as a means of expression and communication, in which users have a central role. For each of these aspects of the design of the company, we applied three criteria:

- functionality
- expressivity
- credibility.

Functionality

As far as functionality is concerned, we considered the following aspects that take into account all possible users:

- Are the products easy to use?
- Do the products fulfil their purpose?
- Do the products satisfy customers' needs?
- Are the products innovative?
- Do the products comply with and exceed general safety standards?

In gauging the functionality of the corporate identity, we took the following into account in examining identity signifiers:

- Is the company's objective easy to understand in terms of its identity signifiers?
- Do the signifiers transmit a clear message about the company?
- Do the signifiers chime with the company's mission?

In terms of website design, we considered:

- Does it allow effective communication?
- Is it easy and quick to navigate?
- Does it offer a wide range of possibilities for interaction?
- Does it offer access to a depth of information?

Expressivity

We measured expressivity of products as follows:

- Are they attractive?
- Are they easy to understand?
- Do they project a positive image?
- Do they exhibit an effective relationship between shape, function and colour?

In terms of the expressivity of the corporate identity design, we analysed the following:

- Is it easy to recognize the company through its identity signifiers?
- Do they promote a positive image?
- Do they exhibit an effective relationship between shape, function and colour?

We evaluated the expressivity of the website design by taking into account the following aspects:

- Is browsing within the website easy?
- Is the website design attractive?

Credibility

Credibility was measured in the following ways.

- For the product:
    - Does the product project a positive image of the company?
    - Is the product's quality apparent?
    - Does the product appear to be original and different?
    - Does the product have a good price–quality relationship?
    - Is the product environmentally friendly?
- For corporate identity:
    - Do the identity signifiers promote the company's credibility?
    - Do they project the image of an original and different company?

- Do they give the impression of quality in the company's products and services?

Website design credibility was measured as follows:

- Does the website make users feel that the company is trustworthy?
- Does it promote the company's credibility?
- Does it clearly convey the company's intentions?

This scale was tested, and proved to be an effective tool to evaluate design. In terms of evaluating design, one good example is Philips:

"At Philips, we believe that good design is about creating products and solutions that satisfy people's needs, empower them and make them happier – all of this while respecting the environment in which we live. We integrate design and ergonomics into everything, from development and production to marketing."

For Philips, design is a creative force for innovation. Philips's Design Department knows that the company can only create meaningful and relevant solutions by having a deep understanding of people's needs and desires.

The list of items Philips considers in evaluating its design is as follows:

- satisfaction of consumer needs
- whether aesthetic elements (form, colour, textures, graphic information, and so on) are expressed and integrated in an appropriate manner;
- level of innovation
- ergonomics and intelligibility
- safety
- environmental friendliness
- efficiency in terms of energy consumption
- efficiency in terms of materials and production processes
- adaptation to the company's internal and external production processes
- consistency with other products of the company.

A very good designer, Victor Papanek, had this opinion about design that to some extent took into consideration the principles of Design for All: "Design has become the most powerful tool with which man shapes his tools and environments and, by extension, society and himself." And he added: "Much recent design has satisfied only evanescent wants and desires, while the genuine needs of men have been often neglected by the designer."

Another designer, Dieter Rams, gave us the Ten Commandments of good Design for All:

"Good design:

1. is innovative
2. makes a product useful
3. is aesthetic
4. helps to make the product understandable
5. is unobtrusive
6. is honest
7. has longevity
8. is consequent down to the last detail
9. is environmentally friendly
10. has as little design as possible.

Return to purity, return to simplicity."

Dieter Ram's design principles have been influential on Jonathan Ive, the designer of the Apple iMac, iPod and iPhone.

You as a manager don't have to be a designer, but you do have to evaluate the results of the application of your Design for All strategy. Ettore Sottssas offers a summary of how to do this:

"Take into consideration the Bauhaus principles about design: form follows function, less is more, use of simple geometric forms (square, circle and rectangle …). They are easy to accept and understandable for everybody.

Look for the perfect application of ergonomics for all the people that you want to cater to.

In the designs of your products and services, think in terms of meanings and metaphors. Design should evoke an emotional response beyond function. Design has to have poetry, personality and passion."

Apart from the evaluation of the design, you have at your disposal other tools to analyse objective data and compare them with previous results and with those you anticipate, which in turn will give you a measurement of the success of your Design for All strategy. We choose to focus on four basic indices to measure and compare with previous results:

1. sales growth
2. margin growth
3. growth in participation in the market
4. profitability growth.

Sales growth is an easy and cheap index to measure. It is very immediate, and results can be available almost in real time, which allows rapid responses. However, sales growth without margin growth can be very dangerous, so you must also keep an eye on this.

Participation in the market may be difficult to measure in sectors where there are no market research agencies based on panels of consumers or distributors. However, the importance of this index, even if the data are not entirely accurate, is crucial: if you want your company to grow, the increase in your sales must be above market growth, otherwise you are losing participation, and in the long run, competitiveness.

Finally, without profitability, growth is useless. Make sure that your company's profits also increase, or are at least stable. External influences may have an effect on companies, as the current economic climate shows, which will inevitably have an impact on the results of any Design for All strategy. In any case, we suggest a few more measures:

- economic impact, measured by return on investment
- growth in a certain group of customers
- growth in the number of repeat customers
- growth in satisfaction indices
- a decrease in complaints
- an increase in success in marketing new products
- creation of new lines of business
- new products and services linked to existing ones
- an increase in the company's share price.

There are also tools to analyse subjective and intangible data:

- presence in the media (the amount of media coverage)
- an increase in the company's public profile (the percentage of people who learn about the company spontaneously or by word of mouth)
- the company's image in the media (how positive or negative the coverage is)
- the company's image in social media on the Internet
- brand image and corporate reputation
- an increase in strategic alliance proposals
- improvement in the work environment
- greater involvement of suppliers.

It is important to bear in mind that many of these measures may be subject to variation due to external influences that may not be related to the application of the HUMBLES method. For this reason, we suggest that you use the "Table of Subjective Evaluation of Fulfilment of Objectives" below to carry out your own evaluation of the extent to which you have met the targets you set yourself.

Table of Subjective Evaluation of Fulfilment of Objectives

Opportunities of Design for All	Degree of interest	% of expectations met	Comments
Increasing consumers			
Increasing clients			
Creating loyal clients and consumers			
Reducing costs in the medium term			
Selling in other countries			
Selling in the tourist sector			
Preventing problems			
Confirming the company's strategy			
Foreseeing trends			
Being innovative in products and services			
Transforming products into services			
Focusing the company on the client/user			
Finding other lines of business			
Improving the external reputation			
Consolidating the company's Code of Ethics			
Improving the internal reputation			
Increasing the company's prestige			

Success in putting Design for All into practice may not show significant returns for your company in the short term, but it may prove a decisive factor in the long term.

The company TOTS instigated a project to develop accessible bathrooms that was presented at an international fair in 2007, where it received an award for technological innovation. Before that, it had already won recognition in the Access Awards for products facilitating accessibility.

In March 2009, the project reached the commercial launch phase, having suffered some delays as a result of TOTS's merger with another company, Altro. At this stage, it was being installed in schemes that had been designed eighteen months earlier. There were TOTS toilets in a conference centre, a sports centre, an auditorium and a nursery, TOTS was specified for the new Repsol Building in Madrid, and TOTS had orders for Terminal 4 at Barajas Airport. There had still been no concerted communication campaign, yet there was a great deal of interest. The project had led the company to change its approach to one of Design for All in its other projects. A spokesperson reported:

"Yes, I'd say it's made us change. It sparked us off thinking about design that doesn't exclude anybody, and has also given us a different sort of inner satisfaction. Perhaps before now we focused more on formal qualities – we ourselves had to be pleased with the products we made. But in this case we could see that we were actually 'helping', that we were making things easier for people who have a problem. When we presented it, we thought technical professionals would value it, but that it might go unnoticed by the public – but in fact that wasn't the case."

The TOTS bathroom is aimed at families in which several generations live together. At it says in the introduction to the catalogue: "In Europe there are approximately 100 million people over 65 years of age and 50 million with some form of disability, and with a little luck we'll all come to form part of this group." The product has the advantage that it avoids people with disabilities feeling that they are being discriminated against. The spokesperson explained:

"Yes, it's the idea of unperceived design – things being useful, having a bar to grab when you need it, but it doesn't have to be red, or some great hulking object that is a nuisance for most people and is only of any use to a minority. That's the angle. And ideas have popped up to make modules that might lead us to enter very different markets. For example, although it's only at the concept stage, we've developed a medical module which is intended for nursing homes for the elderly that have an in-house maintenance and control service. This module incorporates scales and an instrument to measure blood pressure, and all this can be connected in order to transmit the information to a central point. Different applications are included in the facilities depending on what they're going to be used for. There's another module, the pet module, allowing people to bath their dog – maybe for an elderly person so that he or she can bathe it in a standing position with all the equipment close at hand. This is the idea – that you can put together the bathroom you need, and even change it at any given moment. It's a product that's getting a very good reception. In this case, unlike our usual way of working, we thought more about the essence than the form – more about the system than the outside finish, which wasn't such a big concern for us."

Some companies' experiences show that their expectations of what Design for All could deliver were borne out in practice. For instance, Axel's initial concept of a "heterofriendly" hotel turned into a chain of hotels.

The Axel Hotel Berlin had 87 rooms, and in 2009 it was the largest Axel hotel. Following enlargement in April 2010, the Axel Hotel Barcelona had 102 rooms, making it the group's largest. The smallest was the Axel Hotel Buenos Aires with 50 rooms, although the company's Juan Juliá describes it as "spectacular": "The New York Times came to the opening ceremony on 31 October 2007," he says proudly. "They published an article that ranked the Axel Hotel Buenos Aires 26th in the top 50 places to stay in 2008. It really is amazing."

Likewise, FGC, aware of the long life of its infrastructure installations, designs them for the long term.

FGC had already used closed circuit TV in stations to conduct ad hoc studies to see how many people with pushchairs, wheelchairs, shopping trolleys or bicycles made use of the types of facility for the disabled it offered. It turned out that only 3 per cent of passengers used the facilities:

"But this means nothing to us. We know that 33 per cent of the population will take advantage of these facilities at some point in their life. We are working for the future, right? We are working towards a system that doesn't exclude anyone. That is our philosophy."

Implementing the Design for All philosophy means having a clear vision of the path towards your company's future, but it often implies creating unique business models that are hard to copy. For example, in 1998 (only three years after we coined the concept) the Stichting IKEA Foundation financed the publication of *Diseño para Todos – Un Conjunto de Instrumentos* ("Design for All – A Toolkit").[1] Could another company compete effectively with IKEA in terms of adopting Design for All? IKEA's is such a specific business model that large-scale direct competition is unlikely to arise. An IKEA spokesperson told us:

"We have a lot of competitors who are out to copy us, but they are not in direct competition because they are so much smaller. To be IKEA, you have to have IKEA's organization, which is incredible. We do have some local competition, but major European chains like Carrefour or Leroy Merlín may be able to compete in terms of one product or another, but not across the entire range. IKEA's strength is that it offers everything – absolutely everything – you need to furnish a house. We have competitors in specific product areas, such as textiles, for example, or sofas or chairs, but nobody else has the whole range."

Habitat could possibly be a competitor to a more limited degree, and using a different business model, resembling IKEA's, offering good design at comparatively low prices. Habitat was founded by Terence Conran in 1964 and eventually ran 80 stores across Europe. By 2008 it was part of the IKANO Group, owned by Ingvar Kamprad and the Kamprad family. The same IKEA spokesperson explained:

"Habitat is connected to IKEA; Ingvar Kamprad has shares in it. The prices are different because they work in different sectors. But there is, for example, a table in the Habitat catalogue designed by Ingvar Kamprad."

Ingvar Kamprad wanted to build an ownership structure and organization that could be maintained independently and had a long-term vision. Since 1982, the IKEA Group had belonged to the Stichting INGKA Foundation, which has its headquarters in Holland. In 1986, Ingvar Kamprad retired from management, but in 2008 he was still a consultant with INGKA Holding BV, the parent company of all the group's firms, which also has its headquarters in Holland. IKEA Services BV and IKEA Services AB, with nine units in Holland and Sweden, backs the work

---

1   Francesc Aragall, *Diseño para Todos – Un Conjunto de Instrumentos*, Barcelona: Design for All Foundation, 2001 (currently only available in Spanish), http://www.townsandcities.designforall.org/publico/index.php?opc=articulo&artic le=652&idioma_article=es.

of all the group's firms, from the industrial firm Swedwood to the property sales businesses of the stores in various countries:

"The company's main challenge is to stay true to its philosophy. It is a challenge, because expansion is connected to large numbers, which are connected to major impact, which means huge responsibility. Apart from this question, it has to be said that our objective is not only to be number one in Europe and the States, but also in China, Africa and South America ...

So the question is how we can be affordable for that kind of market. This is one of the questions about the future which is often asked, along with others which crop up during research into raw materials, about the goal of reducing CO_2 emissions. Basically, for IKEA, the whole thing is to remain true to its principles, to its values."

So far, we have offered techniques and approaches that allow you to analyse the success of the application of the HUMBLES method from different perspectives, all of them linked to the results and projections of your company. But another question to be considered is the contribution your company can make to social progress. This cannot be accounted for with figures, although is clear that reducing social exclusion, promoting equality and respecting diversity can serve as very positive values for your company and its team.

It is important to remember that success generates satisfaction, but not everything that generates satisfaction is linked to success. If you review your life up to now, you will probably find that its most satisfying moments have not always been linked to success, and on only a few occasions to money. Thus, to complete our description of the HUMBLES method, we suggest you evaluate your own satisfaction at following a process through which has led you to relate differently to the people around you, and has very likely developed your most creative – and at the same time most social – characteristics.

To conclude this part of the book, we suggest you also analyse your feelings in light of the fact that you have contributed to converting people who in the past did not have access to your company's products and services into satisfied customers who are certain of your respect.

Peter Kwan's Story

Five months after Frank Wright had asked Peter for a plan of action, Peter was ready to begin the advertising campaign and the process of distributing the new products in three countries.

Frank, who had grown more and more distant from Peter, absorbed the tension of holding back complaints and comments from the most inertia-bound elements of the company, but also those resulting from his having allowed this small revolution to take place without much guarantee of success. Despite the fact that Peter overwhelmed him with constant emails setting out data about favourable expectations from all the processes that were running in parallel, he was not fully convinced.

"Well," Frank consoled himself, "we're taking a risk in three countries, and I've vetoed this initiative in those where we are already market leaders. If we crash, the impact won't be that damaging."

From the very moment of the launch, Peter began going from department to department trying to gather any data or indicators about how customers were reacting. The first information he came across chilled him to the bone: orders for Sweetme Classic had decreased.

Nervous and dejected, it took him two hours to realize his mistake. "Of course orders for Classic are going down – retailers are probably distributing it along with the other two new lines now." It took him another hour to obtain data confirming his suspicions. He breathed a sigh of relief. Indeed, adding up the totals for the three lines, orders had in fact increased by about 4 per cent.

Within two days, he called some retailers with whom he had been in contact during the design of the displays. "Sales are quite normal," one told him, "It looks like people are taking a liking to this Sweetme Earth line," another commented, but no conclusive picture emerged.

After a month, people started breathing more easily. Sales were not as high as he had anticipated, but there was a clear upward trend.

After two months, sales in the pilot markets had increased by 18 per cent. Frank called Peter to a meeting in his office. Frank closed his door and sat down behind his desk stony-faced. Both looked at each other in silence for a few moments.

"Well," Frank began, "it looks like you got your way. Can you tell me your plans for the rest of the countries now?"

"Do you mean that you're approving the expansion, that you're giving the OK for the trial?" asked Peter excitedly.

"The figures don't lie, right? If we pay attention to developing sales in the light of the previous campaigns, they should even increase a little more."

"I'll start preparing an expansion proposal right away." Peter rose to leave.

"Peter, just a minute."

"Yes?"

"Listen, that HUMBLES method book – can I borrow it?"

"Of course!" answered Peter, thinking, "I'll give you one as a present inscribed with your favourite motto, 'Seeing is believing.'"

Six months after the launch in the pilot market and four months after the progressive expansion, Peter took out the Table of Subjective Implementation of Fulfilled Objectives and filled it out as below.

Opportunities of Design for All	Degree of interest	% of expectations met	Comments
Increasing consumers			
Increasing clients			
Creating loyal clients and consumers		?	*Too soon to say*
Reducing costs in the medium term		?	*Ditto*
Selling in other countries			*Issue of languages has been important*
Selling in the tourist sector			
Preventing problems			
Confirming the company's strategy			
Foreseeing trends			
Being innovative in products and services			*Let's see what we will do with the gourmet line*
Transforming products into services			
Focusing the company on the client/user			*Increasing interaction on the Web*
Finding other lines of business			*Need to think of something*
Improving the external reputation			
Consolidating the company's Code of Ethics			*We are on the right path*
Improving the internal reputation			*When they forget about the tension created*
Increasing the company's prestige			*Even Laura!*

Eight months after the beginning of the process, Charlie, a newcomer in the Marketing Department who had been brought in to maintain and update the website, went to look for Peter to show him something.

It was amazing – a teenage boy had sent in a picture of a 2.5-metre model of the Eiffel Tower with all sorts of details constructed entirely of Sweetme sticks! In the message accompanying it, he explained that it had taken him two years to build, asking his parents and friends to keep all their sticks for him. He wanted to know whether they could tell him how to apply for a Guinness World Record, and thanked them for changing the composition of the sticks, since the new versions could be bent with the help of a hair dryer without breaking.

Peter's brain, by now much more trained than before to link apparently disconnected information, started to mull this over. "The best way to recycle is to reuse. This boy has used our sticks – bio-plastic, of course – as assembly pieces."

"Yes!" Peter exclaimed.

"I'm sorry ...?" Charlie asked, puzzled.

"Nothing, an idea maybe ...."

"Hmm," Peter thought. "'Sweetme Architect' sounds good – contests, prizes, competitions between schools. Wasn't there a contest to design packaging that would allow you to throw an egg out of a window without breaking it? It could be something like that. Yes, we must work on this!"

Peter had now been with Sweetme Ltd for three years. The work atmosphere was pleasant, the change of owners forgotten. Sales figures were also good, and according to Frank, the group of investors was satisfied. It looked like the economic crisis had passed the company by.

Sweetme Architect was launched to market later that month in two formats: a small bag of parts that could be joined together that was sold through the same outlets where they sold their sweets, and a full construction set that was sold exclusively in an educational toy store chain. It had been a lot of work, but very rewarding.

That same day, Frank called Peter at his office. "Can we have lunch together today?"

"No problem," replied Peter, who lately had only had lunch with Frank every three or four weeks. He was pleasantly surprised to hear that Frank had made a reservation at an excellent restaurant they had never been to before.

During the meal, Frank came straight to the point. "The owners want me to step in as Strategy Director for the whole group, which is obviously a very attractive position, and I've accepted."

"Congratulations!" Peter replied sincerely. "Will you be starting straight away?"

"It depends on how long it takes them to find a replacement for my position. They want someone to take charge of expansion in this sector. They think it has great potential for the future and want to invest in it."

Frank took a sip from his wineglass, dabbed his mouth with his napkin, then continued.

"That's why I asked you out for lunch – would you be interested in ...?"

Experiences, Examples and Case Studies

8 Experiences

This chapter offers real-life examples of the application of Universal Design as an engine for constant improvement. We are grateful to Keiji Kawahara, Joan Torres i Carol, Alesandro Manetti and Alex Lee for their contributions.

Successful Examples of Universal Design in Japan

KEIJI KAWAHARA, Industrial Designer, Executive Director of the International Association for Universal Design and Professor at Nagoya University of Arts and Sciences

The International Association for Universal Design (IAUD), established in November 2003, has a membership of more than 130 corporations, including leading companies in the fields of automobile and electrical appliance manufacture, along with housing and construction. The member companies have developed a variety of Universal Design products and services which consumers greet with enthusiasm. Panasonic is one of these companies which devote notable efforts to Universal Design.

Kunio Nakamura was appointed President of Panasonic (then called Matsushita Electric Industrial) in 2000, at a time when the company was recording losses, with falling sales and profits and a dearth of best-selling products. Although the company posted substantial losses in excess of 50 billion yen in the second year of Nakamura's term, he accomplished a remarkable feat, described as "a miraculous V-shaped recovery", by turning the company around in the third year with increased sales and profits. After four straight years of increased sales and profits, he led the company in accomplishing its target of a 5 per cent increase in operating margins in 2006, and was promoted to company chairman. He poured his energies particularly into product development. He called groups of products that would contribute to the company's growth "V Products", and required the products to meet three conditions:

1. They should rely on distinctive "black-box" technology.
2. There should be a focus on Universal Design to allow everyone to use the products with ease.
3. A concern for environmental considerations should be evident in every aspect of product development.

His unwavering business philosophy of vigorously promoting new projects by acutely observing changes in the consumer mindset and his management style founded on a fierce determination to drive the company on at a time of crisis are legendary in the Japanese business world. He also exemplified the importance of management decision-making.

PANASONIC

Panasonic approaches Universal Design not by designing specific products to meet the individual needs of elderly people or those with disabilities, but by creating products that satisfy the widest range of consumers. A number of Universal Design products have arisen from the development and testing of a variety of ideas.

In November 2003, Panasonic marketed the "tilted-drum washer dryer machine", a novel type of washing machine where the drum is tilted by about 30 degrees (see Figures 8.1 and 8.2). The machine became a hit, selling 200,000 units in a year.

Figure 8.1 Panasonic tilted-drum washer dryer machine
Reproduced with permission

Figure 8.2 Panasonic tilted-drum washer dryer machine (cutaway),
Reproduced with permission

Up until then, three main types of washing machine vere in use throughout the world. In Europe, front-loading drum washing machines, which rotate a horizontally mounted drum, were the most common. Top-loading drum washing machines were also available. The drum design enables clothes to be washed with a minimal amount of water, while the tumbling action of clothes inside the drum is also efficient for drying. In the US, agitator washing machines were developed, which had a large agitator at the bottom of the tub. In Japan, pulsator washing machines were prevalent, which washed clothes in the swirling water generated by a pulsator at the bottom of the tub. These were popular for many years, mainly because of their compact size.

In terms of usability, front-loaders required the user to bend down to load and unload the clothes. Top-loaders attracted complaints about the difficulty of opening and closing the door. Meanwhile, agitator and pulsator washing machines required the user to bend over and reach into the darkness of the vertical tub to access the clothes. Each type of washing machine therefore had some shortcomings in usability. Panasonic analysed the strengths and weaknesses of each design, and eventually came up with a tilted-drum washing machine that would make it easier for people of any height, from children to the elderly as well as people in wheelchairs, to load and unload clothes.

During the summer, Japan experiences an almost subtropical climate with high temperatures and humidity, making room air conditioners an indispensable household appliance. Air conditioner filters need to be cleaned from time to time – an annoying and potentially dangerous activity, particularly if the air conditioner is installed overhead. Panasonic's Air Robo air conditioner (Figure 8.3) incorporates an automated cleaning system which cleans the filter whenever required, freeing people from the potentially hazardous task of using a ladder.

Figure 8.3   Panasonic Air Robo air conditioner
Reproduced with permission

Induction cooker technology means that unlike conventional gas burners, they do not use an open flame, making them safer, particularly for elderly and visually impaired users. However, some users find that the absence of flames makes it difficult to tell whether the cooker is on or off. In order to improve this, Panasonic integrated glowing rings into the hobs of most of its built-in and free-standing induction cookers (see Figure 8.4). These red lights indicate intuitively which cooker ring is on and where to place cooking vessels. The control panel uses touchpads that can be operated with one finger – much easier on the wrist than the "press and turn" knobs on gas burners, which means they are popular among those with arthritis, for instance.

Figure 8.4 Panasonic induction cooker
Reproduced with permission

TOTO

TOTO is another leading Japanese company, in this case devoted to innovations in bathroom equipment.

In the 1960s, a prototype of the first multifunctional bidet was developed in the USA as a medical accessory. TOTO primarily imported and sold the equipment to hospitals in Japan. In 1969, it started production of the bidet, remodelled it as a consumer product (see Figure 8.5), and eventually created its own market in Japan. In 1980, it registered Washlet, the brand name of its bidet, as a trademark. The word "washlet" subsequently became synonymous with the multifunctional bidet, and the company firmly established itself as the market leader, capturing about 60 per cent market share. By June 2005, it had sold 20 million units, with its operations also expanding into the North American market.

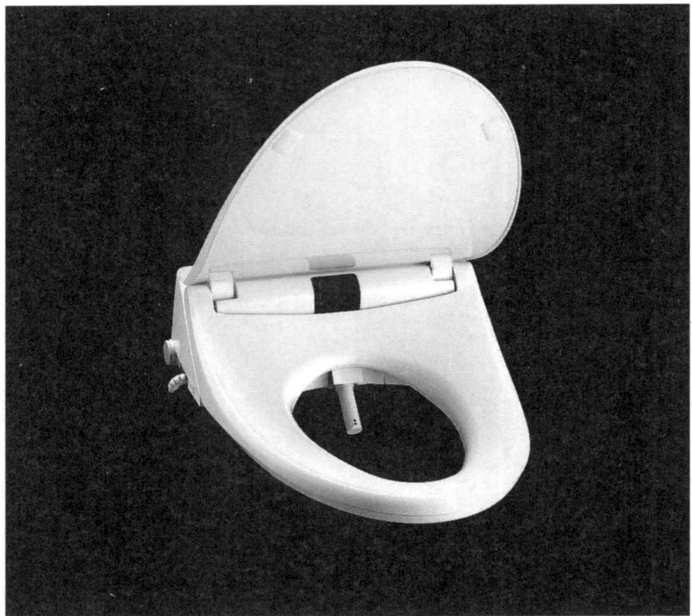

Figure 8.5   TOTO "Apricot" Washlet
Reproduced with permission

TOTO's Restpal SX is a toilet system consisting of a toilet, a small shelf, a washstand, a mirror, a toilet paper holder, a cabinet and a handrail. The toilet paper holder is designed to enable users to detach sheets of paper with just one hand. The shelf, which stands at 70 cm, doubles as a handrail, as it is at approximately armrest height when the user is seated on the toilet. The backrest provides support for the user's lower back, providing extra protection. Although most elderly people's leg joints become less flexible with age and extra effort is required for sitting and standing, many are reluctant to admit that they are getting old. Since they may find it objectionable to use the metallic handrails usually installed in such facilities, the shelf is invaluable as it provides physical support without making the user feel dependent on a handrail. The product's dual purpose is not obvious, and people may initially fail to notice the handrail function unless it is drawn to their attention. This kind of discreet attention to functional details is vital in applying Universal Design to personal and household items.

The above examples show that there are a number of common keys to successful Universal Design. First, it is necessary to systematically involve a diverse group of users and consumers throughout the product development process, in order to understand their lifestyle needs and identify problem areas. It is also necessary to develop new products and create new markets through breakthroughs in design and technological innovations. But of paramount importance is that management fully understands Universal Design concepts and promotes them.

This commitment should be apparent at each stage of the product development process, from planning and design to production and sales.

The Process of Integrating Accessibility into Services Offered by FGC

JOAN TORRES I CAROL, Chairman of the Board of Directors of FGC

Ferrocarrils de la Generalitat de Catalunya (FGC), a state-owned company operated by the Government of Catalunya, was set up on 5 September 1979 to run the railway lines which had recently been transferred to the Generalitat from the private sector. The infrastructure was significantly under-capitalized and obsolete as a result of long-term lack of investment.

From the outset, FGC's actions consisted of instigating important initiatives to renovate all its productive assets – the tracks, electrical power systems, signalling systems, stations and rolling stock. Once these installations had been updated, the company began designing a service focused on being competitive in every transportation market sector, in particular car owners.

In 2004, these objectives led FGC to formulate strategies aimed at increasing the value of the services it provides by improving clients' perception of the services and through a process of optimizing economic and social profitability, not neglecting the participation and commitment of everyone at FGC.

Today, FGC's main network is made up of two lines covering an area that spans from the city of Barcelona to the so-called "second crown" suburbs of the Metropolitan Region. The first of these, the Barcelona–Vallès line, is of international gauge, is 45 kilometres long and comprises 29 stations. It has a rolling stock of 42 trains, a service with two-minute frequency at peak time and an annual volume of nearly 60 million passengers. The second, the Llobregat–Anoia line, is of metric gauge and a length of 139 kilometres, comprising 43 stations. Service frequency on the Llobregat–Anoia line is one train every four minutes at peak time, and its annual volume is almost 22 million passengers.

The Design for All programme undertaken with the aim of making FGC installations accessible to all was seen from the outset as a pioneering initiative. The company not only anticipated social needs arising as a result of the ever-growing percentage of elderly and disabled people in the population (see Figures 8.6–9), it also introduced highly significant improvements in terms of quality. This has made the service more attractive and efficient as a result of measures being designed from an overall perspective, rather than for individual sectors or those with specific disabilities.

Figure 8.6   An FGC railway station with a level platform, allowing easy access to trains

Source: FGC Photographic Archives

Figure 8.7   A lift connecting platform and street level at an FGC station

Source: FGC Photographic Archives

Figure 8.8   A choice of lifts or stairs enables all users to access the platform easily
Source: FGC Photographic Archives

Figure 8.9   The level platform in use
Source: FGC Photographic Archives

As time goes by, it has become increasingly evident, thanks to specific examples from everyday life and accumulated experience, that improvements in accessibility eliminate not only physical but also psychological barriers in relation to the quality offered by public transport compared to its competitors. This is because Design for All's focus on ease of use, clarity and unhindered access makes it an ideal instrument to attract new types of customers.

The combination of all these factors has been taken into consideration as FGC has initiated new projects for its stations and trains. Nevertheless, a significant effort has also been made in recent years to renovate existing systems in order to improve their accessibility. This process is now almost complete, as the Llobregat–Anoia line has been fully accessible since June 2009 and only four stations await completion on the Barcelona–Vallès line, which are already in the project design phase. These works will have to be co-ordinated with the large-scale infrastructure for new interchange stations that are currently being built by the Autonomous Government.

FGC's work on improving accessibility has not ended there, however. Another major focus of the company has been customer care. FGC has led the way in implementing a new model for station management that entrusts ticket sales to machines designed using Design for All criteria (see Figure 8.10). This frees station staff from routine ticket office tasks and allows them to become more active agents, free to roam wherever customers require their assistance.

Figure 8.10 FGC's new ticket machines
Source: FGC Photographic Archives

Likewise, FGC's train drivers no longer simply run the trains. They are also equipped and trained to act in the field of customer care whenever their intervention is required by passengers in the case of emergencies or special needs thanks to the intercommunication system installed in all carriages.

Recent evolution in FGC's productive management indicators clearly shows a direct relationship between increased customer satisfaction and the number of stations adapted for accessibility, whether newly built or recently renovated. These same indicators show even greater improvement when brand-new trains are introduced into commercial service.

From the point of view of results, the introduction of Design for All as a tool for service improvement has unquestionably proven an excellent policy for the promotion of FGC. A good example of this is the 23 per cent growth in the number of travellers who used the company during 2001–2006, a period during which the population grew by only 5.3 per cent.

FGC is now completing its adaptation programme (see Figures 8.11–14), incorporating further facilities for those with auditory or visual impairments in a move that will also improve the quality of the service in general. For instance, messages announced via the PA system will be transmitted simultaneously in text format to information screens in the stations. This focus on taking all groups into consideration is one of the distinctive features of the Design for All programme.

Figure 8.11 A textured and signed strip on the platform promotes safe and comfortable access

Source: FGC Photographic Archives

Figure 8.12 A standard gap signals to users with visual impairments the distance from the textured strip to the edge of the platform

Source: FGC Photographic Archives

Figure 8.13 The textured strip runs the whole length of the platform

Source: FGC Photographic Archives

Figure 8.14 FGC train carriages are also fitted with special sections that can be raised or lowered, allowing those using wheeled devices easier and safer access to trains

Source: FGC Photographic Archives

The road that leads to universal accessibility is a long one, and poses numerous unexpected challenges. One of these concerns developments in wheelchair design that have recently highlighted difficulties regarding the gaps between trains and platforms at some stations (see Chapter 10). It seemed that this problem had been resolved, but it has arisen again as a result of the increase in the number of electric wheelchairs, which are significantly heavier and less manoeuvrable. This has forced FGC to work rapidly to modify platform edges, as well as adjusting the maintenance parameters of its rails and rolling stock in order to reduce the gap even more. This is the final step in achieving the total conversion of a conventional railway network in the Barcelona Metropolitan Region into a service aimed at mobility designed for all.

In these efforts, FGC recognizes with gratitude the invaluable help offered by the people who make up the disabled community. Over the years, they have worked together to identify shortcomings and find solutions, in a process which has been costly in terms of resources, but has at the same time produced rewarding results.

Istituto Europeo di Design

ALESANDRO MANETTI, Director

The Istituto Europeo di Design (IED) owes its establishment in 1966 to the intuition of its President, Francesco Morelli. Since then, it has become a 100 per cent Made in Italy international network of excellence, operating in the fields of training and research in the disciplines of design, fashion, visual arts and communications.

Above all, IED is an evolving educational system dedicated to reinventing itself on a daily basis. Its mission is widespread and clear: to offer young creatives a thorough training – both theoretical and practical – and to convey to them the design knowledge and mindset that will accompany them throughout their lives.

IED is far more than a school: thanks to its unwavering commitment to innovation, it is a melting pot where new generations of professionals are constantly emerging. IED is a powerhouse of ideas that develops creativity through its range of undergraduate courses, masters courses and advanced training courses.

Since it was founded in 2002, IED Barcelona has promoted design as a tool to improve everyday life, concentrating in particular on the metropolitan environment. IED's implementation of Design for All has a twofold focus. On the one hand, as an institution with a responsibility for educating the next generations of design professionals, IED has implanted Design for All in the syllabuses of its various faculties – fashion, design, visual arts and communication – with a special emphasis on social sustainability (see Figure 8.15).

Towards this end, its projects tackle a wide variety of issues of strategic importance for the shorter-term future, like a new range of spectacles (Indo Eyewear, 2006), a new car design (see Figure 8.16) and means of public transport such as taxis in Barcelona (Master in Interface Design, 2004). It also seeks to find solutions for minorities in society (such as the elderly or sick children) that can be beneficial for the whole community. In the sphere of design for children, in 2007 IED collaborated with CasaDecor to redesign nursery school environments. In the area of fashion design, Caterina Foletti created the radically creative Senecta Collection to make fashionable clothing available to older women (see Figure 8.17), for which IED was awarded a special prize.

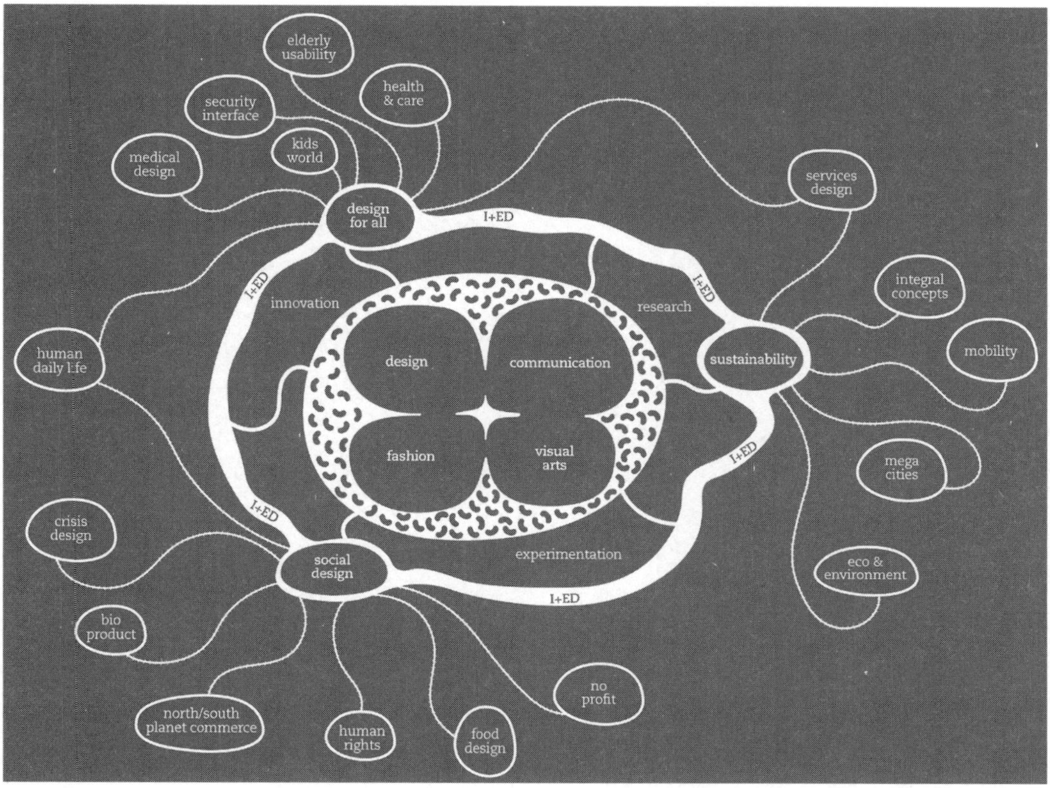

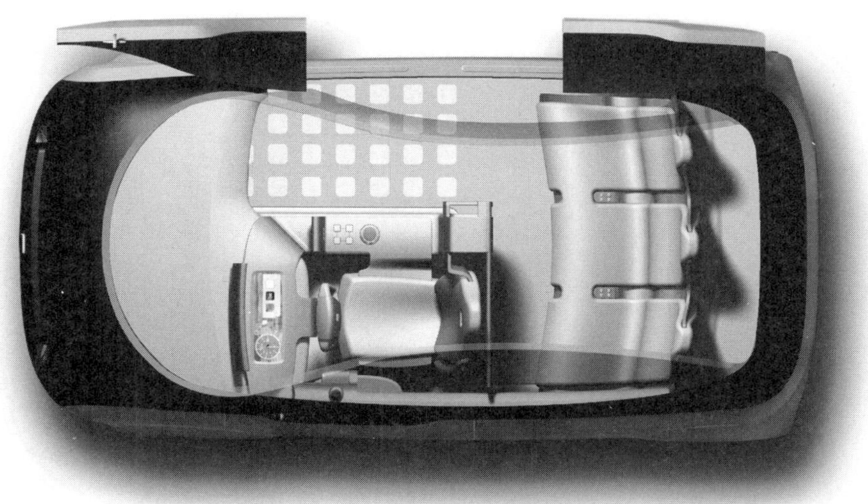

Figure 8.15 Tree showing areas of design taught at IED
Reproduced with permission

Figure 8.16 A car prototype conceived by IED designers
Reproduced with permission

Figure 8.17 A model showing a dress from the Senecta Collection created by IED
Reproduced with permission

The second focus of IED's application of Design for All is embodied in its Solar Bus Stop (see Figure 8.18), developed with the company Copmar in collaboration with I+ED, IED's department devoted to investigation and innovation making use of didactic resources as a key factor in experimentation. I+ED stands for "investigation + education", embodying IED's strategy to use professional training – students and professors/professionals ("education") – to promote research and development ("investigation") to provide assistance to companies that wish to use conceptual design as a key factor in positioning their products and services in the market. I+ED's mission is to analyse, understand, experiment and to develop new tools that anticipate future social developments and the new needs they will bring to light.

Figure 8.18 IED's Solar Bus Stop deployed in Barcelona
Reproduced with permission

As its name implies, the Solar Bus Stop uses solar panels not only to provide lighting at night, but to power LED panels giving access to timetables, information about delays and accidents, and local advertising. Its innovative and functional design provides a wide range of services while optimizing the use of materials, resources and space by incorporating recycled wooden seating and a magazine holder. At night, users can activate the lighting by means of a pushbutton, which as well as improving visibility, promotes a sense of safety.

As well as providing Braille readers for those with visual disabilities, the project is looking into the possibility of incorporating loudspeakers to convey timetable and other information.

While giving access to all these accessories and functions, the Solar Bus Stop takes up very little space, so it can be installed in narrow streets with minimal sidewalks and still allow the free movement of baby buggies and wheelchairs. Its modular construction and simple installation, being anchored by just six bolts and with no need for a connection to the electricity grid, makes it easy to relocate if necessary.

To sum up, Design for All is the foundation for IED's entire professional design education programme.

Oxo

ALEX LEE, CEO

Oxo was founded by Sam Farber, at the time a recently retired housewares entrepreneur. Shortly after his retirement, Sam and his wife Betsey spent six months in the South of France, where they passed their time cooking and entertaining friends. Sam, approaching 70, and Betsey both had arthritis, and so found ordinary kitchen tools uncomfortable and difficult to use. He wondered how he could make them better.

Thus inspired, Sam came out of retirement to create a range of cooking tools dedicated to making everyday life easier for everyone, including those with arthritis. The first group of 15 Oxo cooking tools was introduced in 1990. Today, Oxo offers more than 850 products covering many parts of the home. Each product is based on the philosophy of Universal Design, creating products that are easy to use for the widest possible spectrum of users. Headquartered in New York City, its products are sold in over 56 countries.

Oxo is recognized globally as an example of how a well-implemented Universal Design philosophy can also be a sound business strategy. A portfolio of tools that are easy and comfortable to use for a wide range of people, including those with dexterity limitations, translates into a large target market for the company's products. In fact, during 1991–2008, Oxo's compounded annual growth rate in sales was over 27 per cent.

Despite the wide-ranging popularity of Universal Design products, Oxo has never used this philosophy as a marketing position because different segments of the population have their own unique reasons for gravitating towards the brand. Younger consumers prefer Oxo because the products are clever, efficient and fun (see Figures 8.19–21). Older consumers and those with dexterity limitations prefer the brand because the products are easy to use and are also used by the younger, fitter population.

Figure 8.19 Oxo Salad Spinner – the pump action sets the spinner in motion
Reproduced with permission

Figure 8.20 Oxo Salad Spinner – a simple push button operates the brake
Reproduced with permission

Figure 8.21 Oxo airtight container
Reproduced with permission

Oxo is poised to continue to do well as a result of demographic changes and its unique attitudes and values. In the US, the population aged over 60 will grow exponentially in the next few years, as the oldest of the estimated 78 million baby boomers turned 60 in 2006. At the same time, Japanese baby boomers are turning 70. However, this population's behaviour is much different to that of earlier generations. Although they may have reduced strength and agility compared to their younger selves, they do not want to be constantly reminded of their age. Grandma and grandpa now surf, ride motorcycles and take yoga classes.

A large part of what makes Oxo appealing for this particular population is the fact that the brand also appeals to their children, the "Millennials", over 100 million of whom will be aged 18 by 2020. This younger, "hipper" population views the Oxo range as well-designed and fun.

Several years ago, Oxo conducted several brand equity focus groups, where it asked participants (all Oxo customers) to select images of people they thought were likely to purchase Oxo products. The groups consistently picked images of people who were young, professional and stylish; images of older, less fit and less stylish people were deemed unlikely to be Oxo consumers. In reality, the focus group participants more closely resembled those they did *not* pick as likely Oxo consumers, illustrating that Oxo is a brand that helps people feel like who they *want* to be, not necessarily who they *are*. This is not unique to Oxo. For example, most of the premium-brand technical outdoor clothes are worn by people to go shopping or walk their dogs, despite the fact that the brands' marketing may depict a user climbing K2.

In other research, Oxo learned that rheumatoid arthritis patients, who have severe dexterity issues (particularly in their hands), would not part with their Razor phones and iPod MP3 players. These products help patients feel "cool" and "normal", outweighing any difficulty they may experience in using them.

It is important to note that Oxo draws a clear distinction between Universal Design and Special Access Design. From Oxo's perspective, well-implemented Universal Design results in products that assist a wide array of users without their realizing they are being helped. For example, ramps at crosswalks help people on wheelchairs move about a city, but they are also useful for people with strollers, shopping carts, and even people wearing inline skates. When this feature is not in use, it blends into the background, and because it is used by a wide range of people, there is no stigma associated with it. On the other hand, bathrooms designed for people in wheelchairs usually include metal grab bars and higher toilet seats that make a very distinctive special access statement. While these features make tasks easier for a specific portion of the population, they are often uncomfortable or difficult for the general public to use.

Oxo does not consider this type of access to be Universal Design (though Oxo does recognize the need for special products to address the small percentage of the population with severe dexterity problems, and licenses some of its designs to a company called North Coast Medical). Constant reminders that products are designed for people with dexterity problems would pigeonhole them and limit their appeal. This is especially true for those with the most to gain from this design philosophy, who look for products that help them feel normal. Universal Design is about enabling and inspiring, not patronizing.

9 Examples of User-focused Products and Services

In this chapter, we will describe a very small sample of services and products that were developed to satisfy customers' wishes and needs. Some of them were developed using participatory processes, others by progressively adjusting the management of the company to the needs identified, while in other examples a focus on users' behaviour inspired creative design. All of them have one thing in common: they exemplify some of the phases of the HUMBLES method.

Frozen Food Home Delivery Service – Eismann

Eismann has operated a home delivery service for deep-frozen products for more than twenty-five years. During this period it has continually adapted to the needs and wishes of its customers, since their satisfaction is one of its main objectives. It currently has with more than 2.5 million customers in nine European countries.

Figure 9.1 A selection of Eismann frozen foods
Reproduced with permission

Eismann's flexibility and strong customer orientation have meant that it is constantly winning new customers by providing a timely service that is tailored to their needs with a wide range of high-quality products. Direct contact between Eismann's agents and its customers builds trust and promotes enduring loyalty.

Dry Cleaning and Laundry Home Delivery Service

Continuing the emphasis on satisfying customer needs, this relatively recently emerging service traditionally catered for commercial concerns such as the hotel trade, beauty salons and hairdressers.

If your washing machine has broken down or you do not have time to complete a wash, or if you need a suit dry cleaned but don't have time to visit a shop or queue, such services can collect your clothes from your home and return them to you clean and dry. Some services will collect clean clothing and iron it for you.

Monodose Packaging

This type of packaging allows small quantities of commodities such as foodstuffs, pharmaceuticals, or cosmetics in liquid, paste, granule or solid form to be supplied in convenient dispensers. It is a popular solution in the hotel trade.

Such packaging makes it easy to dispense small or measured quantities, and may be resealable. It is an ideal way to serve liquids on trains and planes. The design of the packaging is crucial – for instance, if it is triangular, the container is a lot easier to empty completely.

It is also useful for dry meat products for domestic consumption. Such packaging must help to conserve the product while being easy to open. An example would be Selva's rolls of cooked ham.

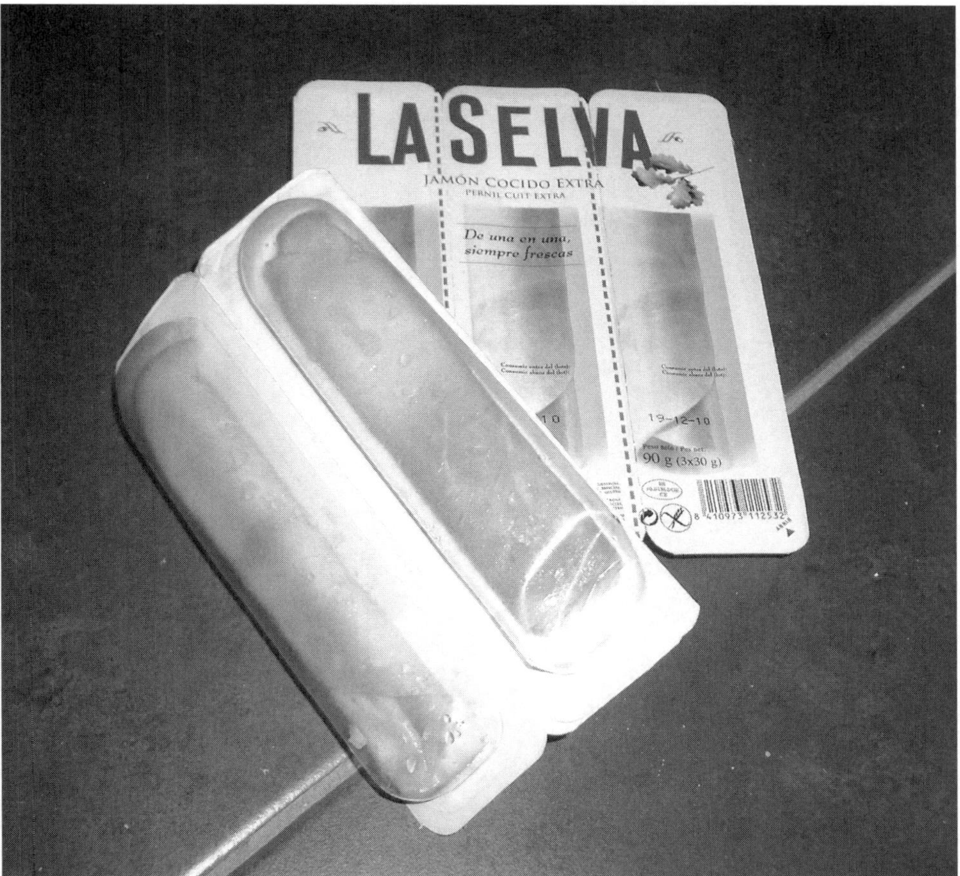

Figure 9.2   La Selva monodose packaging
Reproduced with permission

Pre-cooked Products

Tiredness, lack of time and lack of inclination to cook have made pre-cooked products popular. They often take the form of complete meals that are ready to consume or need minimal preparation. Some of them need to be heated in an oven or microwave, in which case the packaging must obviously be able to cope with high temperatures.

Pasta Packaging

A number of food companies, such as Pastas Gallo, have proven the value of focusing on practicality to offer innovative and efficient solutions to help improve the quality of food and make life easier. One example is easy-to-open resealable pasta packaging, which allows cooks to remove the quantity they require then store the rest, secure in the knowledge that it will remain fresh.

Figure 9.3   Pastas Gallo resealable pasta pack
Reproduced with permission

The Marquina Oil and Vinegar Cruet

In 1961, designer Rafael Marquina's cruet sets won the Gold Delta Design Award, and they are probably among the most widely copied objects in the history of design.

Marquina's reinterpretation of this everyday product features a transparent conical glass flask with a funnel-shaped mouth that makes it easy to refill, and a spout with a ground glass base incorporating a slot to collect stray drops and allow the entrance of air. It is a sober design that resolves with style and efficiency the problem of dripping. It recovers every last drop of oil or vinegar, it prevents spillage, the flask's transparency means users can identify the liquid it contains, and its shape makes it stable and easy and safe to handle.

Figure 9.4   Marquina oil and vinegar cruet
Reproduced with permission

The Milà Washbasin Mixer Tap

The mixer tap designed by Miguel Milà (Delta Award 2005) is characterized by its ergonomics, allowing it to be operated with the hand or elbow. Locating the lever in front of the water spout helps to avoid drips contaminating the tap body, making it easier to keep clean. This is one of the few tap designs that saves energy by dispensing cold water when the lever is in the central position.

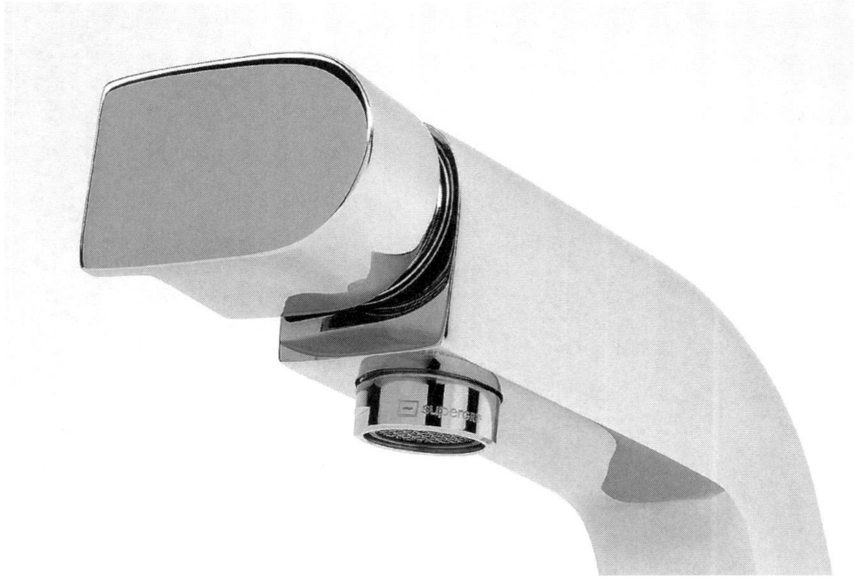

Figure 9.5   Mixer tap designed by Milà (dispensing hot water position)
Reproduced with permission

Folding Funnel – Normann Copenhagen

This design by Normann Copenhagen of Denmark solves the problem of how to store multiple funnels without taking up too much space. It consists of a ridged rubber collapsible funnel that can be folded like an accordion to adapt to containers of different sizes. It can be used with cold and hot foods, and is dishwasher-safe.

Figure 9.6   Normann Copenhagen's folding funnel
Source: Normann Copenhagen, www.normann-copenhagen.com

Ice Cream for Diabetic People

When summer arrives, there is a considerable increase in the consumption of certain products that are traditionally associated with it, such as ice creams and refreshing beverages. These products usually have a high sugar content, so are generally unsuitable for diabetics. However, being diabetic does not necessarily mean having to renounce these delights completely. Diabetics need access to specific nutritional information so they can judge whether the product is suitable for them. Manufacturers of ice cream should ensure that their products' packaging addresses this, since low-calorie ice creams are not necessarily safe for diabetics to consume.

Glucose Tests for Diabetic People

Thanks to technological and design advances in recent years, it has become easier for diabetic people to determine their blood glucose levels in order to control them. In the past, such analyses could be painful, complicated, and sometimes even dangerous. Nowadays, simplified testing kits are commonplace, so it is possible to carry out the tests quickly and easily, avoiding disturbance and possible embarrassment.

Mobile Phone Banking System

Hal-Cash is a system that allows users to transmit money to any mobile phone and withdraw it instantly from cash points and terminals associated with the system without the need for a credit or debit card. The service is not offered by all banks, but the number is increasing.

Hal-Cash is available via participating cashpoints and electronic or telephone banking services. The person sending the money must indicate:

- the bank account which will be charged
- the amount to send
- a deadline for withdrawing the money
- a secret four-digit password
- the mobile phone number the money will be sent to
- a mobile phone number to allow confirmation of the transaction by text message.

Once the transaction is accepted, the system sends two text messages – one to the person authorizing it, and the other to the addressee of the funds, notifying them of the sum available for withdrawal.

This banking system can be a great help in emergencies, providing instant access to cash at any participating outlet.

Retractable Mouse Cable

Nowadays, the mouse is an essential item of computer equipment for most people, and despite the emergence of other technologies with similar functions, such as touchscreens, it remains the most commonly used interface. The drawbacks of its traditional hard-wired connection have led to the development of a cable that can be retracted into the body of the mouse.

Figure 9.7   Retractable mouse cable by Logitech
Reproduced with permission

The bebéDuE Medic Anti-colic Baby Feeding Bottle with Temperature Sensor

All parents know the fact that once a baby bottle has been prepared, before giving it to the child it is vital to place a few drops on the back of the hand or on the wrist to check the temperature of the liquid. With the aim of preventing accidents and after lengthy studies, bebéDuE devoted itself to producing healthier and safer products for babies, launching the bebéDuE Medic baby bottle. The bottle incorporates a temperature sensor that changes colour, providing a warning if the temperature is over 37°C.

In addition, its unique air circulation system eliminates negative pressure and avoids the formation of air bubbles during feeding, so that the baby only takes in liquid, considerably reducing the risk of colic and indigestion. This means that the baby does not need to suck so strongly and the flow is constant, making it easier to control the rate of feeding and avoiding problems such as liquid or air entering the baby's ear canal.

Figure 9.8   Example of a baby feeding bottle by bebéDuE
Source: bebéDuE Spain (S.A.), www.bebedue.com, www.bebeduemedic.com

Makeup Paintbrush

Traditionally, people have used their fingers or a sponge to apply a makeup base. Nowadays, the major cosmetic brands and makeup artists advise the use of a special paintbrush. Because of this, Yves Saint Laurent, a constant innovator in this sector, launched the Perfect Touch makeup base, the first to incorporate a paintbrush applicator. The base's tube design features a rotary opening and closing mechanism that keeps the makeup fresh and the paintbrush in optimal condition for each application.

Figure 9.9   Makeup paintbrush by Yves Saint Laurent
Reproduced with permission

The Ausonia Black Salva Slip

Ausonia, a manufacturer of sanitary towels and panty liners, keeps improving its products to adapt to the needs of modern active women and trends in feminine personal hygiene. Its personal customer care service, which can be accessed via its website or by phone, is complemented by its educational school programme "Adolescence and You", which has already helped more than three million adolescents to accept and adapt to the changes they go through during this developmental stage. These innovations allow Ausonia to obtain customer feedback and stay in touch with the needs and expectations of present-day women. One development that has resulted is a black panty liner that offers all the advantages of traditional ones while being suitable for use with black underwear.

Male Body Razors

Currently, body shaving is becoming a common part of the daily grooming routine of men, which has led, Braun, the market leader in this sector, to introduce its bodycruZer razor, which received the Red Dot Award for product design in 2009. It is the first male razor in the world to combine an electrical trimming system with Gillette Fusion razor technology to achieve a comfortable and close shave, even under the shower.

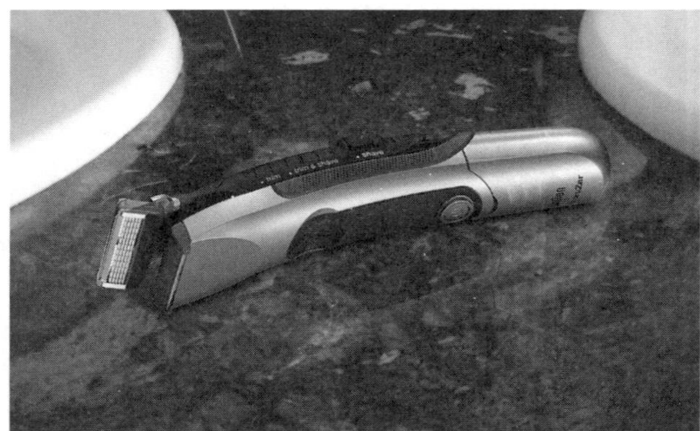

Figure 9.10 Male body razor by Braun
Reproduced with permission

Configurable Mouse

Currently, most computer mouses can be configured for left-handed use through software that allows customization of the buttons. However, generally speaking, most gaming mouse devices have ergonomic designs catering only for right-handed players, which means that left-handed gamers have been forced to use their right hands.

Until not so long ago, most companies making computer peripherals did not take into account the needs of the approximately 200 million left-handed gamers around the world. However, some of them have made efforts to address this sector. Now some, like Logitech and Razer, have launched left-handed video game mouses featuring ergonomic design of and high-precision laser systems that enable more precise control.

Nappies for Child Urinary Incontinence

Although child urinary incontinence is very common, its causes are very diverse, from emotional problems to certain types of disability. With the appropriate protection and a correct attitude in treating a disease that is usually temporary, we can help children to enjoy a happier childhood. The company TENA is convinced that incontinence does not have to prevent people from leading a full and happy life, so its Tena Pants plus product allows adults and children who suffer from moderate to acute enuresis to wear absorbent underwear that offers maximum security while being discreet.

Spiritual Spaces in Airports

The managers of some airports, conscious of their passengers' needs, have observed that they not only drink coffee, connect to the Internet or go shopping before boarding their planes, but many want or need to pray. This has led to the adaptation of some spaces to set up facilities that allow prayer and religious observance. For instance, Barajas airport in Spain offers three Catholic chapels, and two mosques, along with facilities for people from other religions.

Figure 9.11 Chapel in Madrid airport
Source: Aena, reproduced with permission

Replacement Cars

Some insurance and vehicle maintenance companies offer replacement cars (also called courtesy cars) so their customers can use another vehicle while their own is being repaired.

Car Sharing and Car Clubs

Currently, social and personal changes as well as concerns for sustainability have led to radical rethinking of transportation systems. Public transport, walking or cycling stand out as the main options if we want to reduce traffic and the use of private vehicles. Occasionally, though, the use of a private car for journeys is unavoidable, and this has been addressed through car sharing and car clubs in many cities.

Based on the principle that for each type of journey it is necessary to use the most convenient means of transport, car clubs and car sharing are new mobility concepts that promote the rational use of cars, either allowing people with a driving licence to use a car without having to own it, or enabling car owners to share their journey with others travelling along the same route. Car clubs save users the expense of car ownership (purchase, maintenance, insurance, parking, and so on), paying only for the distance travelled and the time the car is in use. Sharing for car owners also leads to savings, as participants can share fuel expenses.

Figure 9.12 Car sharing experience, *liftshare*
Source: Photo © Liftshare.com

Reading University is one of several hundred organizations that participate in the *lift*share scheme, whereby both staff and students share their privately owned cars with other people who are going in the same direction or to the same destination.

TV Captions

Subtitling to provide a written version of dialogue, often in another language, is common in cinemas, theatres and television. There are two types of subtitles: open captioning, which users cannot choose whether or not to display, and hidden or closed captioning, which can be displayed on demand.

Television transmissions nowadays generally use closed captioning, whose primary objective is to cater for those with hearing problems. Ten per cent of world population suffers from some hearing disorder, and only 3 per cent can communicate through sign language, but other sectors of the population also benefit from this facility, which represents a considerable investment by TV channels. In Spain, for instance, national statistics have confirmed that the system is used by:

- 3 million people with hearing disabilities
- 1 million people aged over 65 with hearing problems
- 9 million children in basic education (reading and writing)
- 500,000 children and adolescents with learning problems
- 2 million people with poor literacy skills.

However, the total number of people who benefit from closed captioning is even larger, since many use it to follow news programmes in public spaces like airports, bars and restaurants that are usually noisy, others may use it to help them to learn another language, and so on.

Location of People by Mobile Phone

All mobile phone users, no matter which network they use, can be located through the mobile network or the GPS geolocation system. GPS is already used in the United States and Europe in emergencies, and also to provide certain personal services to users. The ability to locate users through their mobile phone is extremely useful in those cases where the user suffers from disorientation problems such as dementia, or simply to supervise children's journeys.

Nurseries in Shopping Malls

Nurseries in shopping malls and large stores free parents to shop without distraction. These spaces offer children directed play activities, toys, movies and other entertainment, under the supervision of qualified staff.

However, a new phenomenon has emerged in Austria: adult male nurseries, where they can play computer games and read magazines (including *Playboy*) and comics while their female partners shop. The initiative first arose in Salzburg at Christmas time with the slogan "Rescuing the child inside the man", to provide a refuge for men who were fed up with accompanying their partners on shopping trips. There have been attempts to introduce similar schemes in Vienna and Graz in Austria, and Munich, Cologne, Berlin and Hamburg in Germany.

Driver's Seats with a Memory Function

For some cars, the need to adjust the driver's seat to accommodate different drivers has ended with the introduction of electronic adjustment mechanisms incorporating a memory that records the individual position of the seat and seat back. The setting may be triggered by use of a user-specific key. In some models, this function is also available for passenger seats.

Electronic Door Locks

Some electronic door locks for homes or offices rely on readers that memorize an individual's fingerprint. Others are activated through a numerical keypad. Both systems offer several advantages compared to traditional locks:

- They avoid the complex manipulation required by the use of a key, which can be difficult or impossible for some users.
- There is no key to be lost or mislaid.
- All registered users can gain access.
- They make it easier to monitor entrances and exits.

Child Safety for Car Doors

Most private vehicles feature child locks on the rear doors that are operated by a small concealed lever and prevent the door being opened from the inside. In some cases, more sophisticated systems have been developed which lock the rear doors and boot automatically when the vehicle is in motion.

The Tokyo Underground Signalling System

The underground railway network in Tokyo is one of the most extensive in the world. For those who do not speak Japanese, it could resemble a horrifying maze. However, its signalling system, which adopts a different-coloured circle for each line, also identified by a letter, along with a number for each station, makes it easy to navigate. Recently, some lines have started to incorporate displays in each carriage giving the location of steps, escalators and lifts at the next station.

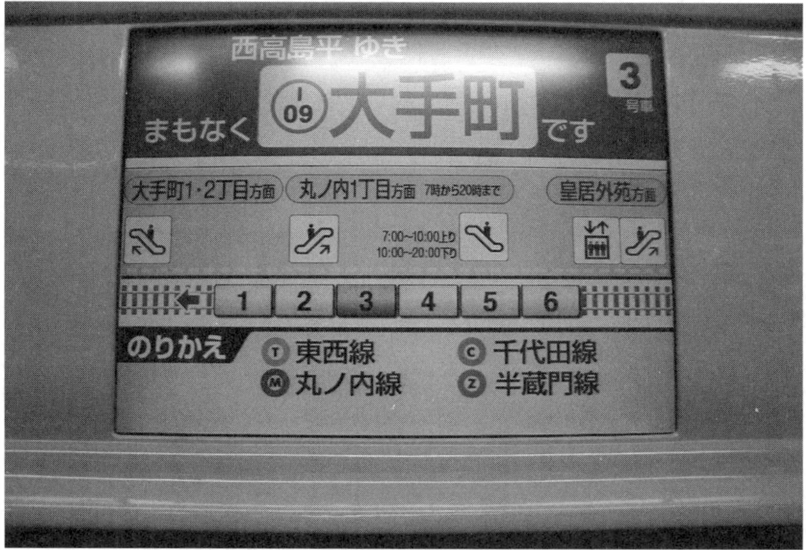

Figure 9.13 A display in one of Tokyo's underground carriages
Reproduced with permission

The Hitachi Lift

Automated announcements in public building lifts so that blind people can tell which floor the lift has stopped at can be very annoying for other users. This is why Hitachi, in collaboration with a panel of users, developed a system that activates the announcements only if a blind user is present.

An elegant solution has been developed through user observation. When they are outside a lift, blind people have difficulty pushing the call button because they cannot see it, so they explore the wall with their hands in search of it. The same applies inside the lift when a blind person searches for the numbered buttons with his or her hand before identifying and pressing the appropriate one. The solution was to incorporate sensors in the button surrounds that activate the announcements if a user explores them with his or her hand.

Kerb Cut 120 – Barcelona

In many cities, it has been common for decades to lower the corners of kerbs to make it easier for wheelchair users, those with limited mobility and those with shopping trolleys or baby buggies to cross the street. However, in 1990, Barcelona was the first city to analyse the design of this urban feature with user participation.

Instead of merely considering the needs of wheelchair users, the designers asked themselves who actually needs a step between the pavement and the road? The answer was: almost no one. Blind people need to know where the roadway begins, but apart from that, the function of the step is to prevent water flooding the pavement when it rains.

The solution – introducing ramps at pedestrian crossings – is helpful to elderly people and those using buggies, skates, wheeled suitcases and so on, but consultations with blind people led to the incorporation of a texture on the ramp and standardizing its width at 120 cm. This means that blind people always know that they can take two steps before starting to cross the road.

Figure 9.14 Example of Kerb Cut 120 in a Barcelona street
Reproduced with permission

Low-floor Trams

In a similar way to lowering the pavement level, low-floor trams in conjunction
with raised platforms at stops allow safe and convenient access to the vehicle for
all users with mobility problems.

Heated Pavements

In Helsinki, when snow turned to ice, it caused many accidents and made
something as simple as walking across the city almost impossible. In order to
reduce the risk of falls, granite chips were spread on pavements, which was
expensive and left a mess to clear up later.

Taking into account that the city had an existing hot water circulation
network, a system was designed that allowed the water being pumped back to
the city's thermal power stations to be reheated and circulated underneath the
pavements. This managed to achieve a surface temperature of 2°C, melting the
snow and at the same time making it impossible for ice to form. This has made
the streets of Helsinki safer and more comfortable in winter.

The New Istututo Europeo di Design (IED) Building

The Istututo Europeo di Design is an educational design centre with branches
in a number of cities around the world. IED's new headquarters in Barcelona
was designed by ProASolutions and FGA Architects, and has been an example of
participative design. The task of adapting a former textile factory of 5,500 square
metres has been carried out through a process in which a team of architects has
interpreted the needs expressed by students, teachers, employees, administrators,
the management board and other collaborators in a number of brainstorming
sessions.

Having defined the architectural brief, several degree projects have focused
on aspects of the building and its use, such as refuse management, lighting for
the central courtyard, furniture for the reception area and the provision of quiet
spaces, with guidance from tutors and the architects.

Figure 9.15 View of the new IED Building in Barcelona
Reproduced with permission

Figure 9.16   The new IED Building, showing the central courtyard lighting
Reproduced with permission

Sunshade Roof Shelters in Singapore

Singapore is exposed all year round to high temperatures and scorching sun alternating with intense, sudden rainstorms. To ameliorate the impact of these weather conditions on its inhabitants, roof shelters and buildings with porches have been extended so that typical journeys, such as home to bus stop, can be made while remaining continuously under cover.

Figure 9.17 Sunshade roof shelters in Singapore
Reproduced with permission

Figure 9.18 View underneath a sunshade roof shelter
Reproduced with permission

10 Case Studies

In this chapter we will present several case studies of companies that have made their focus on clients and users a key element in their constant drive for innovation and quality improvement. Some excerpts from these studies have appeared in earlier chapters of this book to illustrate the HUMBLES method in practice.

Altro and the TOTS Programme

In March 2009, Jordi Masramon, general manager of Altro Supergrif SL, was worried. The world economic crisis, which had started with the subprime mortgages in the US in 2007, had spread throughout the globe, affecting different countries and sectors to a greater or lesser degree. In Spain in particular, the construction sector and allied industries were seriously affected:

"We went ahead with the merger in order to grow, and yet we've shrunk considerably. But we're holding our head above water in this very complex situation. We're exporting about 50 per cent of our production, and abroad some things are looking up; for example, in France we have good retail sales, and they're on the rise. Our sales figures there are better for this year than for previous years, but that's an exception. We're running into difficulties in lots of places, and not only in sales, but in collecting too. Quite honestly, things are pretty bleak in that department. On the other hand, we tell ourselves that it was lucky we carried out the merger because it has forced us to be disciplined. In a way we were ahead of events, although we didn't do it with that in mind; we did plenty of self-analysis, we took lots of streamlining, slimming-down measures that have turned out to be very good for us."

THE STORY OF ALTRO SUPERGRIF SL

Altro and Supergrif officially merged in June 2008 to form Altro Supergrif SL. Altro had been created in 1989 by two partners: Jordi Masramon and the firm Arcon, an importer of technical fittings for the construction industry such as access control systems for hotels and public buildings. Altro started to make products related to construction, including door fittings and bathroom accessories – specialist products demanded by architects. Its products were not for direct sale, but rather made to order. As a result, Altro was constantly in contact with architects, decorators, engineers and designers, who asked it for things they were unable to find in the catalogues. In this way, Altro started to make accessories and structures to support sinks, particularly for hotels. At that time there was an incipient demand, originating from Italy, for designer bathroom fittings. No one in Spain was making them, and imported models were expensive. At first, Altro produced custom-made fittings, and then went on to study how they could be standardized. In 2009, it still maintained some custom production, but standard bathroom fittings accounted for most of the company's output.

The other company involved in the merger, Supergrif, manufactured taps. It was founded in the 1960s, taken over by a multinational, and relaunched at the end of 2002 following a management buy-out by some of its staff. Jordi Masramon explained:

"They're two companies with different origins, but with a series of points in common. That's why we ended up merging them and making them into a single organisation. They're two firms that share a firm commitment to what are often called "designer" products – although I think all products are based on design, but we aim clearly at a medium to high market niche, always looking for those products that aren't easy to make, that make us different and give us the opportunity to be competitive. In our market, all our competitors are 30 times bigger than us, so we use our imagination to seek out unusual or complex gaps in the market. Supergrif and Altro share this feature.

But on the other hand, we came from different backgrounds, and each had its own structure. Supergrif started up as a tap manufacturer; as such, it specialized in one type of product and concentrated on developing everything possible from the point of view of manufacturing, engineering – that is, the more technical side – whereas Altro was much more an "editing" company, in the sense that it carried out the design internally, it managed the product decisions and the ideas, and then it outsourced to the best industrial manufacturers all over the world, depending on the type of product."

At first, Altro designed in-house, with Rubén Mas in charge and with occasional help from other professionals with technical know-how. After the first generation of products, the firm began to work with associations, and through distance learning programmes it came into contact with some professional designers. The pressure felt by the company was also felt by some designers, who were looking for people who could put their drafts into practice. It started to explore some inventions; some prospered, others did not. Some were successes, others were failures, as with all beginnings. One of these projects was approached as a partnership with Supergrif. Jordi Masramon continued:

"We worked in collaboration with Supergrif on the Antonio Miró project. It was proposed as a joint project between the two companies. Paul Vilanova, General Manager of Supergrif, called me and told me he had the opportunity to undertake a project with Antonio Miró, but that he thought it should go further than just the taps, with a wider view, [taking in] the whole bathroom. 'I thought of you, because we could make the taps and you could make the furniture, the accessories and so on,' he said. We loved the idea from the start, because it represented a great advantage

to turn up with the whole package under our arm. Nowadays, this is one of the arguments we offer to our customers."

The partnership was initially a one-off venture, but had two dimensions: first, the product design, which for Altro meant having to innovate, and second, learning about its partner's product and the issues involved in manufacturing a tap. Similarly, neither had the people at Supergrif stopped to think about what was involved in making wooden furniture. So there was an interesting exchange, and they had to learn how to engage in three-way communication and make concessions. If the designer–client relationship is usually a two-way process, in this case the channels were more complicated:

"Antonio Miró took a very active part, contrary to what people might think, as sometimes designers just give a product their brand, their name. He was very enthusiastic about it; this was at a time when he was keen to try new things, as he felt a bit jaded with his sector. We asked him not to just put his name on it, but to come up with ideas, and it went really well, because working with somebody who's not in the trade is a breath of fresh air. It's also true that the first meetings were difficult; nobody understood anybody else, because the experience of each of us had nothing to do with that of the others: in fashion everything changes every three months, everything fluctuates, it darts back and forth. But in the industrial world, to make a tap you have to make heavy investments in moulds. You can't say, "Now I see it differently and I want to change everything." There was an adjustment period, and then some very interesting things started to take shape. He made some very good contributions to the product, which was successful, because they came from somebody with a fresh approach, with no preconceptions."

Product presentation started in 2003, and the series was under way by 2004. The project had two elements: one was the design, and the other, which was very interesting, was the staging of the product. For this, they designed – again together – the marketing of the product: the catalogues for launching it, the presentations, the trade fairs, the whole lead-up. Here, too, they had to learn how to give way and adapt to each other in order to get good results. As a result, they understood that when it came to marketing strategy, there was an early stage when they could walk side by side, finding joint distributors, but there came a time when this would no longer work, because each firm had its own course of action, and especially because in some markets outside Spain it was very complicated to make everything converge. They found a formula that was functional and meant that everything went smoothly yet presented no impediment to each to finding its own way if there were hitches. The experience was very enriching commercially speaking, because at that time the concerted effort of the two companies managed to open the doors of customers who, for one reason or another, had kept them closed for years. It had several advantages, and the initial approach of the project was very successful.

Soon after, the design studio Roviras y Torrente presented the Aeri Project for Altro, incorporating taps it had developed with Supergrif and made for Altro under its brand name. Both projects remained active up until the merger, and this made it easier for the parties to come to an agreement, as they were well acquainted personally and organizationally. Through their collaboration on the two projects, they saw that there was not much sense in keeping the two companies separate, because there was too much duplication. The merger made sense in two different ways: the growth and synergy it would bring, and the logical savings of an economy of scale in terms of physical space – one storage depot instead of two, and one administration department instead of two doing the same work. Jordi Masramon explained:

> "*Our customer profile was the same. There was the odd difference, but in fact, one of the things we did at the beginning was to cross-reference our customer database with sales, and we realized that the level of coincidence was very high: if you took the top 200 customers of each company, 120 were the same, and even in the rest of them, some failed to coincide just because at that particular moment they weren't buying taps, but they had done so a couple of years earlier, and we reckoned it would be easy to get them back. So it was easy for us to bring our positions together.*"

GENERATING NEW ALTRO SUPERGRIF PROJECTS

Despite the recession, Altro Supergrif continued to develop projects. By the end of 2008 it had presented a new series designed by the French studio Ora-ïto. It was a project that Supergrif had started up on its own, but the new company went on to extend it with a view to reproducing in some way the Miró concept – developing a concept with a broad overview of the bathroom. The product was working very well, in spite of the adverse economic conditions.

Altro Supergrif had also developed a new, more basic line designed in-house to replace some of the products in its catalogues. When questioned about the origin of the design ideas, Jordi Masramon replied:

> "*We always keep a sort of open list of aspects to develop. It isn't something that comes out of some meeting where we say, 'We'll do this or that'; it's a series of ideas that are in the air and are being weighed up. For instance, that's how we came up with the 'everybody' idea in the TOTS series.[1]*
>
> *Often when we were doing product development, we talked about the need to find something addressed to people collectively, thinking rather along the lines of a product for public use, capable of contributing more. It's a different story in each case. We have this open list, a sort of 'letter to Santa Claus', and then we try to hone down the ideas. We also have abundant market information from a variety of sources, specialist media, through the associations we belong to. We have sectoral studies; we're pretty up-to-the-minute at the sectoral level. For generating ideas, there's a format of quarterly multidisciplinary meetings incorporating people from the design team, people from the purchasing team, quality, sales. So all the angles are present,*

---

1   *Tots* is Catalan for "everybody" or "all".

because if we talk about something new, they all have something to say: the person in charge of the moulds, of the materials, the head of production ...."

Altro Supergrif defined itself clearly as a market-oriented firm, although like all companies, it had probably made the mistake of neglecting the market on occasions. The TOTS series arose from reflections that arose from a period during which, as Jordi Masramon put it, "we were too engrossed in navel-gazing and didn't take enough notice of outside needs". The change came when Altro Supergrif forced itself to think why it was making certain products and who it was making them for. This was a useful reflection, because the self-satisfaction that comes from knowing that everything is going well sometimes leads us to carry on doing the same things through inertia, without retaining the perspective of the original concept. Jordi Masramon explained:

"We detected a latent demand. We felt that we were missing a product more geared to community use, since the rest of our products were more suitable for private use.

There was a contradiction, because we were doing a lot of jobs in the area of projects, and there we found we could participate when the architecture studios were working on a hotel, but not when they asked us to provide toilets in a public area that had to meet certain strength and durability standards, with a different level of use from a private bathroom. In these cases, we were caught rather off guard, because we couldn't give them an all-round solution. In an attempt to stop projects slipping through our fingers, we tried to find solutions from outside and adapt them, but in this case we didn't manage to offer good enough alternatives. You know how things are when you've got an idea buzzing around your head and all your neurons are on edge."

The architecture and engineering studio AIA Salazar Navarro, located in Barcelona and run by Albert Salazar and Joan Carles Navarro, which had been working for more than fifteen years on public works such as theatres, community spaces, nursing homes, schools and sport centres, and also on hotels, offices and commercial facilities, detected the same problem, but from a professional point of view. It had often been forced to find solutions from different suppliers and companies – fold-down grab bars from one brand, tap and the bathroom fittings from another – and the results weren't good enough for it. So Salazar and Navarro thought, "If we can't find it, why don't we make it?", and started to design the TOTS concept.

There were similarities in key aspects, such as having identified the lack of proposals and the motivation to find efficient solutions, and the two companies brought together two different perspectives that complemented each other perfectly: the manufacturer's and the architect's point of view. Jordi Masramon emphasized:

"We meshed totally. They gave us the rundown, and we loved it because we saw that it filled the gap we perceived that we had, and we jumped in head first."

THE TOTS PROJECT – A DESIGN FOR ALL PROJECT

The TOTS project was a product that fits perfectly into the concept of Design for All or Universal Design. The name "TOTS" was adopted because Altro Supergrif felt that these really were bathrooms for all. Jordi Masramon explained the project in detail:

"One thing we really liked was that we had always thought from our point of view that we could make a bathroom for the handicapped, yet here the approach was different: We're going to make a toilet that, since it's going to be in a community environment, anybody can enter. So it's got to suitable for use by anybody, whether it's a child, someone in a wheelchair or an elderly person.

That is, we opened the spectrum as wide as possible. It's a project that has a lot of positive interpretations. The first is this: a solution for public toilet facilities that is functional for all users. From this starting point, we arrive at some interesting consequences. First of all, the project treats handicapped people on an equal basis, so they can feel comfortable. Nowadays, you go to a public toilet and there's a problem right from the start: there's men, women and handicapped. What's going on here: a third sex? Another category that somebody's invented? Why the separation? And then perhaps, in this day and age, we don't even need to have separate toilets for men and women? At this point, some ideas started to appear that were of quite a sociological nature. Take, for example, toilets in a public place, like a swimming pool; in the case of a single-parent family, if a father has to take his daughter into the shower, where should he do it? In the men's? In the women's? As a solution, we thought: 'In this toilet, why don't we add a module with a shower?' So the toilet is also a place where you can shower and change babies' nappies too, and you go in individually, so there's no need for a division.

A series of very interesting reflections arose as regards use. And then some interesting points were raised about the construction process. If you put a camera in a toilet while it's being built, you'd be amazed how many different workers are involved: one lot for the tiles, another for the plumbing, another one for the mirror, then there's the electrician, and another one to do the flooring. In the end, there are about 15 people involved in fitting out a toilet measuring 2 square metres. And if it's a building that has to be opened straight away, you've got 30 workers there all on the same day, so you can imagine how the job gets done. As well as that, it has very high costs, in all aspects.

The TOTS concept is also different in that respect, because it's a prefabricated product. All the facilities come ready-made from the factory, and all the plumbing and wiring is pre-installed – all the internal assembly is done here. So somebody arrives on site, as when they turn up at your house to set up a kitchen. They find the walls prepared beforehand, they assemble the units, they connect the water and the electricity, and they're done. The same person does the whole thing. And this concept is also very interesting in that it cuts costs, it allows better site management because there's a single person who does the job from start to finish, and it's more efficient in every way. We've made the product self-sufficient, so it doesn't require certain things that are taken for granted when fitting out toilets, like tiling. With this product, it's not necessary, because any parts needing protection are already protected structurally.

All they need is to be coated with a resistant material, and the walls can be painted with a suitable paint. So it has lower costs, and also it's easier to customize. You can give it a different feel; it doesn't have to look like an operating room. Another factor is that there are several sizes, as it comes in modules.

There's a basic solution, which is another of its advantages: squeezing the units into the minimum space while complying with standards and saving maximum space, which again cuts costs. Imagine an office building; if you save a metre and a half of space in every toilet, supposing you've got 25 toilets, in the end that's nearly 40 square metres you've saved. That's another of its strong points. There's space-saving, and there's the aesthetic side. Adapted toilets tend to be the size of a football field, because there has to be room for a wheelchair, and as sanitary fittings aren't designed with this in mind, a lot of room is taken up, to be on the safe side. Here, everything is rationalized linearly. All the manoeuvrability is studied, and it works with the minimum possible space. And then, on this basis, we have added as many ingredients as we could: everything's automated, so you don't have to touch anything, which makes it more hygienic; everything works with photocells. This is also a way of ensuring that there are fewer things to touch, which is positive as regards vandalism problems, and generally there are fewer things to go wrong.

Since we'd got the initial idea right, we went on to develop various aspects that might be of interest, such as customization in corporate facilities. For example, in railway stations the Renfe brand logo can be placed on the panels wherever required, or in a hotel we can follow the corporate image and integrate the product as much as possible; that way, as I was saying before, it's not seen as a handicapped toilet, but as a space with a pleasant design and finish that moreover can be used by all kinds of people. We sought external advice on this issue to have input from the point of view of the users, who were keen to try out the facilities personally. They provided some great input on aspects that we hadn't thought about. They helped us enormously – both in terms of usability of the product and with regard to compliance with standards."

The TOTS project was presented at the Construmat Fair in 2007, and received an award for technological innovation. Before that, it had already won recognition in the Access Awards for products facilitating accessibility.

In March 2009, Altro Supergrif was in the commercial launch phase. The TOTS project had suffered some delays as a result of the merger, but now it was being installed in facilities that had been designed eighteen months earlier. There were TOTS toilets in a congress centre in Sitges, a sports centre in Cerdanyola, an auditorium in Gavà and a nursery in Badalona; TOTS was specified for the new Repsol building in Madrid, and the company had orders for Terminal 4 at Barajas airport. There had still been no full-out communication campaign, yet there was a great deal of interest. The project had made Altro Supergrif change its approach to one of Design for All, even with other projects. Jordi Masramon confirmed this:

"Yes, I'd say it's made us change. It sparked us off to thinking about design that doesn't exclude anybody, and has also given us a different sort of inner satisfaction. Perhaps before we contented ourselves more with the formal quality of things;

we ourselves had to be pleased with the products we made. But in this case you could see that you were actually 'helping', in inverted commas, that you're making things easier for people who have a problem. When we presented it, we thought the technical professionals would value it, but that it might go unnoticed by the public – but in fact that wasn't the case."

The TOTS bathroom is a product for families in which several generations live together. At it says in the introduction to the catalogue: "In Europe there are approximately 100 million people over 65 years of age and 50 million with some form of disability, and with a little luck we'll all come to form part of this group." The product has the advantage that it avoids people with disabilities feeling that they are being discriminated against, as Jordi Masramon explained:

"Yes, it's the idea of unperceived design – things being useful, having a bar to grab when you need it, but it doesn't have to be red, or some great hulking object that's a nuisance for most people and is only of any use to a minority. That's the angle. And ideas have popped up to make modules that might lead us to enter very different markets. For example, although it's only at the concept stage, we've developed a medical module which is intended for nursing homes for the elderly that have an in-house maintenance and control service. This module incorporates scales and an instrument to measure blood pressure; and all this can be connected in order to transmit the information to a central point. Different applications are included in the facilities depending on what they're going to be used for. There's another module, the pet module, allowing people to bath their dog – maybe for an elderly person so that he or she can bathe it in a standing position with all the equipment close at hand. This is the idea – that you can put together the bathroom you need, and even change it at any given moment. It's a product that's getting a very good reception. In this case, unlike our usual way of working, we thought more about the essence than the form – more about the system than the outside finish, which wasn't such a big concern for us."

ONGOING INNOVATION

For TOTS, Altro Supergrif adopted a marketing model that was different its usual ones. The company's products were usually sold through outlets or distributors: bathroom stores with the product on display, sold directly to the end user and requiring an installer who might be working either for the store or independently. With TOTS, it took a different approach. First of all, it was not intended to be displayed to the public in shops, because it was a specialist product. Furthermore, the concept was more prescriptive than usual; it was aimed more at project designers, who had to get to grips with it in technical reports.

Altro Supergrif established a network of distributors selected from among those it already worked with. These distributors were more oriented towards project design and construction, usually had their own installation staff, and were more accustomed to delivering and assembling products on site. In addition, an in-house team was set up to help with the first projects and provide guidance as to how they should operate. In other cases, the team completed the whole job itself, leaving it installed on site, thus offering a turnkey solution. This made it possible to calculate prices more precisely, achieving a product that made sense in terms of costs. Altro Supergrif realized that if it relied on the usual market routines and margins, it might be pricing some features out of the market, so it would cease to be a product "for all". Jordi Masramon added:

"Another issue that is addressed in these facilities is water saving. As we went on adding ingredients, we realized that we could also take that into account. Water use is intense in public spaces, regarding both cost and sustainability criteria, so it was worth taking into consideration. We found some people who had patented a flushing system that worked with much less water and much higher pressure. We carried out the first installations using this system, but never really got it to work properly due to some technical hitches. Yet while we were carrying out these tests, our team got to thinking and came up with a more ingenious method, which consisted of using the waste water from the sink to flush the toilet. It's filtered and conveyed to the cistern. Really, we don't need drinking water to flush the toilet, and as long as it meets certain standards, it does the job."

When Jordi Masramon defined Altro, he always said that design formed part of the company's DNA. He believed that opting for design as a competitive advantage gave the company keener market orientation and competitiveness:

"I don't know what we'd be like without this. I can't picture myself doing anything else, or approaching projects in any other way than seeing design as something fundamental. Design forces you to ask yourself all the questions from the user's perspective. Design makes you think more. And if you think, you can still make mistakes, but it's easier to aim your shots. Companies that don't bear design in mind to such an extent may find that they're carried along by inertia."

Axel All-inclusive Hotels

In spring 2009, Juan Juliá, the founder and owner of Axel Hotels, was sitting in his office near the Axel Hotel Barcelona surrounded by his team, explaining the company's growth plans to two professors from the leading business management school Escuela Superior de Administración y Dirección de Empresas (ESADE):

"I want the company to carry on growing because despite the crisis and the world's economic climate I still feel that I have an opportunity at the present time. It's true that it was easier to capture capital two years ago than it is now but it's also true that there is still a lot of capital on the market that no one knows where to invest because people are reluctant to invest in the building industry or the stock exchange. Projects are thin on the ground. We have several characteristics that match what investors are looking for very well –a brand in a very specific market niche with results and a background that in some way show that things are going well. The result is an attractive product which is even more attractive for investors because it enables them to diversify their portfolios. If they already have a hotel portfolio, it's still a diversification because it's

another niche in the hotel segment. What's more, our intention is to seek some 50–60 million euros on the market, which is not an excessive amount. That's why I started looking for corporate finance companies able to advise us and help us in the search for the right partner for us."

BACKGROUND

Part of the Eixample district of Barcelona is known as "Gayxample". Located right in the middle of it, at the crossroads between Aribau and Consell de Cent streets, is the Axel Hotel Barcelona, a three-star city hotel catering for gay customers. In 2009 it already had 66 rooms, and an extension offering some 40 more rooms was under construction, scheduled to be opened in spring 2010. The hotel was a success and had very high average occupancy rates. In addition to the hotel in Barcelona, the Axel Hotel Buenos Aires opened in 2007, and more recently, the Axel Hotel Berlin.

The positioning of Axel Hotels was unique: although other hotels and resorts catering for gay customers did exist, they were mainly in the holiday sector. Axel hotels, however, were located in cities and served partly as business hotels. Rooms at the Axel Hotel Barcelona featured plasma TVs with broadband Internet and laptop connections, in addition to the Axel Business area with access to a colour printer and computers and a small conference room. A new, larger conference hall was also envisaged in the enlargement.

The company was created in 2003 when its founder and owner, Juan Juliá, an ESADE graduate in Business Administration, after serving as a marketing executive in many multinational companies, reinvented himself as a hotel entrepreneur. In his own words, "Everything started as a dream … a dream of opening a hotel catering for the gay world, my world."

Juan Juliá had always had a hotel and catering background, but the definitive idea occurred to him during a sabbatical year he took when he realized the path his career in marketing would probably take. He then took an MA in tourism, using the hotel business plan as the basis for his dissertation.

The first hotel had come into being with initial funding from a venture capital company, Catalana de Iniciatives. With three hotels now running, he was thinking in terms of opening another ten hotels with the same market focus over the next five years.

Juan Juliá prided himself on his detailed knowledge of the market and the competition. Before beginning the project, he spent two months travelling around the world visiting specific hotels. When he returned, he knew exactly what he wanted. His target market was the segment of gay people visiting Barcelona for business or pleasure and looking for a suitable place to stay:

"A gay hotel is like any hotel catering for specific customer needs. A golf hotel tells customers about the best courses nearby, the easiest or most difficult ones. Well, a gay hotel provides information about where you can go and dance, meet people, and so on. At the same time, the hotel atmosphere makes gays feel comfortable and at home, and although it sounds ironic, it makes them feel like one of the family."

This was the key to the hotel's positioning: it would provide the information required by gay customers and create an atmosphere where they could feel comfortable. It wasn't just a hotel that was "homo-friendly", a hotel where gays felt welcome, but a hotel that expressly described itself in its literature as "heterofriendly" – a place where straight people, and indeed absolutely everyone, would be welcome, although the aim was clearly to provide an atmosphere where gay customers would feel perfectly at ease. Juan Juliá continued:

"The philosophy of the hotels remains the same. They are still hotels that focus on the gay business or leisure market. We use the word 'heterofriendly', a term we have registered, to convey the idea that our main users are still the gay community around the globe, but that we welcome straight customers, such as, for example, businesswomen, who are delighted to come to Axel because they feel very much at ease in gay company and can unwind and enjoy good service in a good location. We are also making inroads into the corporate markets with the closest links to our community: fashion and technology. But the market of virtually all hotels is the same, and the type of hotel is the same. The thing is that we haven't done what other chains have done – making all hotels identical. The one thing all our hotels have in common is the departmental handbook: the way the telephone is answered must be the same, so must the check-in procedure, waiting at table – these are the things you'll find the same in all Axel hotels. But if you go to the Axel Hotel Barcelona or the one in Buenos Aires or Berlin, their appearance is completely different. Each one has a different mother and father. I like this approach too, because it adds an element of surprise."

Although the slogan was still a "heterofriendly" hotel, in a way Axel was gradually shifting more towards the concept of a hotel "for everyone":

"Our hotel is aimed at gay customers, that's our main target, but we've also seen that the hotel attracts other people who are not gay but who are interested, too. So as long as you make it clear that this is a hotel for gays but that there is no objection to you, a straight person, being here, no one will be surprised to find you in the hotel.

But you must know that you're going to be mixing with gays, because if no one tells you clearly and you don't know that Axel is designed with gays in mind, you might book a room and perhaps not feel at home amongst gays. When someone like that arrives, they might feel uncomfortable and make the other customers feel uncomfortable, too. This is pointless, which is why we say that we are 'heterofriendly'. We make this perfectly clear to avoid any complaints."

Therefore, the hotel's approach had to be forthright, and even if customers were good at finding information, the message had to be clear and simple. As Juan Juliá said:

"A bad sale, as I say, can be worse than no sale. In other words, when results fulfil or exceed expectations, there's no problem, but when you arrive expecting something completely different, then you're sure to have problems."

DESIGN AT THE AXEL HOTEL BARCELONA

Since its creation, design has played an important part in fulfilling the company's aims and building this particular business model. Design was already a prime consideration when the search began for a suitable location and characteristics of the building for Axel's first hotel, in Barcelona. The briefing Juan Juliá prepared for the estate agents stipulated:

"I want a building with a Noucentiste[2] feel on a corner in the upper area overlooking the sea, between Balmes and Villarroel Street and between Aragón and Gran Vía (an area covering some ten blocks)."

The result was a building with a façade very typical of Barcelona's Ensanche district, with fully restored external windows and modern, well-equipped rooms with en suite baths, large beds, four pillows, bathrobes provided, and so on. Juan Juliá was personally responsible for the design, and he conveyed what he wanted to the hotel's interior designers, whom he knew very well, in the following terms:

"Imagine that I have to live in this hotel six months a year. Set up a hotel where I would be comfortable. No fitted carpets, I hate them, no bedspreads. Above all, make bold proposals – not black, white and grey –with plenty of colour. That'll go down well with gay customers. They don't want boring places; they love bold ideas with different colours and different materials."

The architect's brief was to create the largest possible number of rooms for a three-star hotel. Several layouts were suggested, and the chosen one was then worked on by the designers. The aims of the interior design, like the design of all the items and accessories, were directly related to the corporate strategy. For example, the rooms did not have wardrobes with doors, but open metallic structures for hanging clothes, it being understood that since clothes were very important for the gay segment, it was not necessary to hide them: on the contrary, it was important to make them visible.

The product design briefing was also given by Juan Juliá himself. However, although he knew exactly what he wanted, he was often unable to explain it. Being aware of his difficulty in conveying his ideas, he surrounded himself with

---

2   Noucentisme was a cultural movement with political influence that emerged in Catalonia in the early twentieth century.

professionals who knew him well. "I like them being able to grasp the ideas I explain in a couple of words," he explained.

Juan Juliá maintained a strategy based on proactive design while being very functional. He told the architects and designers:

"I don't want to create Philippe Stark-type hotels. A hotel has to be comfortable, and even though the gay community appreciates image, what you want when you go to a hotel is to sleep and unwind, so no matter how much design you incorporate, if the bed is awful and you can hear the people in the room next door, you'll be in a foul mood the next day."

As a result, the beds at the Axel Hotel Barcelona were the same as those at the Florida Hotel (a luxury hotel that had just opened when the one in Barcelona was being built) and those soon to be used at the Arts Hotel, another very luxurious hotel in Barcelona. In Juan Juliá's words: "If you sleep well and the room is pleasant, you'll be delighted. So we mustn't lose sight of our basic business aim: a restful night."

Although they were completely different, the internal and external designs of the hotels in Berlin and Buenos Aires were the work of the same architect responsible for the enlargement of the Axel Hotel Barcelona. Juan Juliá explained why:

"It's much easier for me to work with the same architect, even at the international level. He seeks out local partners who, in the case of the hotel in Berlin, adapted the project to comply with legislation there. He also found a local architect to give it a Berlin touch. Working with the same architect suits me because I can forget about a considerable part of the work, because he knows what I need and what Axel guests need. Otherwise, every time there is a new project, with a new architect I'd be obliged to explain everything all over again. Since he knows exactly what I'm looking for, I avoid lots of problems.

What's more, since he's a young architect, he knows me very well and he knows the Axel customer very well. He also knows how to give each hotel a distinguishing feature, including things that Axel guests appreciate, such as transparent elements and space, interaction. This has been a great advantage for me, and if I want to do more things in the world, I want him to be part of the project."

The architect provided ideas which Juan Juliá selected and tailored to suit each hotel and each city. The hotel in Berlin, for example, was black and gold, which Juan felt was very much in keeping with the city:

"The city is very modern, in vogue, very dynamic and young. There are two sides to the gay world in Berlin: the glamorous side of the trendy, in vogue place where new designers and new music hang out, then there's the toughest part of Berlin how it's always been: cabaret, sex. The architect understood all this really well, and merged it into Axel by using black and gold. But it's black and gold outside and in. The façade is black with the occasional gold touch. It's really awesome."

The mutual understanding between architect, designer and owner was 100 per cent. When Juan Juliá entered for the first time before the hotel was finished and saw the ground floor where the restaurant and bar were to be located, he said, "But it's like a dark room." The architect laughed and said that it wasn't finished, "Everything will have wooden panelling, there'll be green curtains, the walls will be golden." Rather dubiously, Juan Juliá replied, "Well, I trust you." Later, when he saw it finished, he realized that the architect had understood him perfectly:

> *"That's the thing, you can't deal with everything yourself, and you have to trust people as they explain how the project is going. Because sometimes I can't imagine the ideas in the architect's mind, that's something I'm unable to do. Good communication and having the same strategic approaches helps a lot because it saves you a lot of work and eliminates part of the stress that working with people who don't understand you might cause."*

The Axel hotel design was completely different from that of a conventional hotel, and was always in search of excellence. Juan Juliá declared forcefully:

> *"We aim for excellent service and design. When I opened the hotel in Barcelona, for example, it was amazing, but now it's lagging behind a bit. That's quite normal, six years have gone by, but now we're updating it again with the enlargement.*
>
> *The design world changes really quickly, what's in fashion now won't be in a few years. When I did the hotel in Barcelona, I tried to avoid making a Philippe Starck-type hotel with so much design that it becomes overbearing after four visits. I wanted something comfortable and well-designed. In any case, I completely renovated all the hotel's bathrooms last year, after five years. And next year we'll update the public areas and the rooms. This is one of the things about catering for gay guests: since they always like being up to date, you have to make a bit more of an effort in this respect."*

The Axel Hotel Berlin has 87 rooms, and in 2009 it was the largest in the Axel chain. Following the enlargement in 2010, the Axel Hotel Barcelona has 102 rooms, making it currently the group's largest. The smallest one is the Axel Hotel Buenos Aires with 50 rooms, although Juan Juliá describes it as "spectacular". He said proudly:

> *"The New York Times came to the opening ceremony on 31 October 2007. They published an article that ranked the Axel Hotel Buenos Aires 26th in the top 50 places to stay in 2008. It really is amazing."*

UNDERSTANDING CUSTOMERS

Juan Juliá had access to very valuable information: he really was an expert in the gay market, to the extent that one of his first projects was to set up a consulting company, Axel Consulting. These projects were sidelined while he concentrated on hotels and developing the Axel Hotels brand, which was beginning to become a global benchmark in its segment. Understanding his hotels' customers was virtually an obsession:

"We conduct separate quality surveys for the hotel and restaurant, asking about the service, facilities, whether the booking matched expectations, the atmosphere and setting. We also try to talk to customers.

Gay customers talk a lot. I always tell our staff, 'You have to be professional and give excellent service, but you have to be very approachable,' because this is what our customers want. There's a degree of proximity, but a slight distance, too. This is completely different from when you go to a Ritz Carlton, but on the other hand, it lets customers talk more and tell you more things and explain how their stay went. In fact, hardly a week goes by without us receiving an email from a customer who has been in one of our hotels saying, 'Thanks for a wonderful week … so-and-so was very helpful.' And this gives you information. We've even received handwritten letters. We put them on the noticeboard so staff can see them, because they're important for them, too."

Up to this point, ideas had basically come from Juan Juliá himself, who in 2009 had a fine team of professionals: a managing director, a human resource manager, a finance manager, a quality manager, a systems manager, an expansion manager, two persons in charge of marketing and commercialization, and the latest team addition, someone in charge of revenue management for all the hotels. In addition to plenty of market information, customer surveys and trips, including visits and stays in hotels, brainstorming sessions were often held in which all management staff participated. Juan Juliá was a great believer in teamwork, and was used to getting the rest of the team involved in his concerns:

"I always ask people for their opinion. I think it's useful because they might suggest something or say things that hadn't occurred to you. Now I leave the brainstorming sessions up to my Managing Director, and then I speak to him, although my office door is always open and I really do encourage an open-door policy, so people come and see me to comment on doubts or concerns. In this respect, I think my management style is a bit paternalist."

FGC – Railways for All

In May 2009, Oriol Juncadella, Operations Manager of Ferrocarrils de la Generalitat de Catalunya (FGC), was closely following the progress of the company's trains on the displays in the modern Integrated Control Centre at Rubí. This system enables demand to be monitored in real time and compared with the demand curve on the same day the week before. Constant monitoring makes it possible to foresee unusual shifts in demand, such as those resulting from demonstrations. In the case of a demonstration or another event such as a football match, it is possible to see how many people are travelling to Barcelona, and consequently schedule the appropriate number of return trains. This was particularly important during the mass demonstrations of 2003 against the war in Iraq, when large numbers of people were seen to be travelling into the city centre in mid-afternoon, enabling far more return trains than usual to be scheduled from 8 p.m. onwards.

Because of FGC's exponential growth since 1996, network management has been extremely important, although growth rates have been falling since December 2008 due to the shrinking economy, dropping by 5 per cent in the transport system as a whole, and 1 per cent for FGC – a figure which would, in comparison with previous growth rates, affect future budgets. Oriol Juncadella explained:

"The problem is that our growth capacity is extremely limited. We now have a departure every two minutes – that's 30 trains an hour. At peak times we're totally stretched with an incredible occupancy rate of 93 per cent. According to industry standards, anything above 80 per cent at peak times verges on discomfort. We're well above that. We're now working on an essential project to increase line capacity to 40 trains an hour and convert the Plaza Cataluña station, currently a terminus, into a through station. Its six tracks will be done away with and it will become a through station. A full train will pull in, passengers will alight, then the train will move off and another will come in from the depot."

THE HISTORY OF FGC

When FGC came into being in September 1979 as a public company, it was entrusted with operating those railways in Catalonia that did not belong to the Spanish national rail service Renfe. The lines in question were run by Ferrocarriles de Vía Estrecha (FEVE), a state-owned company privatized a few months earlier. FEVE had in fact done little during its time in existence, being more of a temporary solution. FGC was the first public company to be established following the restoration of the Generalitat of Catalonia. From the outset, the Generalitat's model for railways consisted of investing in dilapidated production assets to bring them up to a minimum standard and starting to create a first-rate service. Oriol Juncadella explained:

"The work involved several phases. We started with the Vallés line used by some 500,000 people in that area. It had an urban stretch in Barcelona, making it just like another metro line in the city. FGC started with this line, investing heavily to rebuild infrastructure, redesign stations and install signalling wherever necessary. From the outset, trains were bought, too – 111 units in all. This first phase was followed from 1996 onward by a second phase, known as Metro del Vallés, involving the addition of new four-coach trains able to carry 500 passengers. Signage and terminology were revolutionized somewhat, and the Metro del Vallés brand was created, a brand that was very well received and is now well established. In the urban area, throughout Barcelona, all stations were completely redesigned in response to the need to extend their platforms to enable up to four coaches to pull in. All this was done during that period. Then, in the late 1980s and early 1990s, it was decided to buy those new trains and extend the platforms. Increased demand from Vallés was beginning to make itself felt."

It was a colossal project involving the enlargement of two stations: Provença station, built in 1929, and Muntaner. This investment implied an upheaval for

Metro del Vallés, extending its platforms and doubling its tracks to be able to handle one train every 12 minutes on each branch line, five trains an hour at Sabadell, and five trains an hour at Terrassa. The Barcelona University track was also constructed at this time, meaning that students no longer had to walk to the campus or catch a shuttle bus to Bellaterra station. As a result, the line needed new investment to enable it to cater for 40 trains an hour. Oriol Juncadella continued:

"This management model, based on updating infrastructure and making services as competitive as possible, began with the Llobregat line about fifteen years earlier. Obviously, replacements were carried out every year, but with no heavy investment because the main priority was the first line, the Vallés line, handling 70 per cent of the demand."

The Llobregat line along right bank of the Llobregat river (connecting locations like Sant Vicens dels Horts and Sant Andreu de la Barca) was metric gauge, unlike the international 1435 gauge Vallés line, and was distinguished by the fact that it carried not only passengers, but also considerable volumes of goods. It took salt from Sùria to the Solvay PVC factory in Martorell. It also carried potash for use as fertilizer from both Sallent and Sùria to the port of Barcelona to be exported. Since 2008 it had also been shipping cars from the SEAT factory in Martorell to the port of Barcelona to be exported by sea. This added up to a total of six off-peak trains a day with no disruption to passenger services.

The Llobregat line accounted for 30 per cent of FGC's demand. The town itself had a population of 150,000, in comparison with the 500,000 of Vallés. Another factor of great importance was that the Plaza España station in Barcelona (the terminus of the Llobregat line) was located away from the city centre, so its urban sphere of influence was very small and it was only used for travel to and from the lower Llobregat area, Sant Boi, and so on.

The new trains introduced on the Llobregat line in 1998 were the first in Spain to have a lower central section, because one particularity of this line was that its platforms were not at the same height as the floor of the train, but 50 cm lower, making it necessary to take a step up or down when boarding or alighting. To make these trains accessible for disabled people, the centre coaches had a lowered section of floor in the middle to make this part of the train the same height as the platform. This innovation was introduced at a time of great debate about lowering floors in the tram industry (some trams' entire floors had been lowered, in others only 30 per cent of them) and a series of initiatives throughout Europe, but this was the first such initiative for trains.

In 2003, FGC was commissioned to build the Montserrat Rack Railway, which acted as a functional offshoot of this line, meaning that trains could depart from Montserrat. Maintenance of the Montserrat Rack trains was in fact carried out in Martorell, so trains went along the usual line, then upon arriving in Monistrol, continued along the rack and up the mountain. Oriol Juncadella:

"Other things handed over to us included the Gelida funicular railway, transferred to us in 1986. It was a municipal concession that was falling apart. It was transferred to us, and we applied the same model. Then there was the La Molina ski resort and the Vall de Núria ski resort, including the Vall de Núria rack railway. The Núria Rack Railway looks great now. Thanks to the investment made, Valle de Ribas is no longer the rundown area it was a few years ago. The same goes for La Molina, and more so this year with the ladies' ski championship. We've put La Molina on the map for many people. What else …? We were asked to bring an old train that used to run between La Pobla de Lillet and Castellar de Nuc back into service. We did that in 2004. It's a tourist service with a 60 cm gauge – in other words, yet another gauge we didn't have. And finally, in 2005, the first Renfe line to be transferred to an Autonomous Region was transferred to us: the Iberian-gauge Lleida–Pobla de Segur line.

The thing is that in this instance, we didn't apply the FGC model. We have in fact carried out the first phase, re-laying the track – 20 million euros for laying the track where it should be. The remodelling of Plaza Molina station currently under way is intended to adapt the station for disabled people. Since we are applying the inclusive design, providing lifts for people in wheelchairs is not enough: we are also enlarging the lobby, letting daylight in, and so on."

QUALITY CULTURE

Design for All can be found throughout the FGC system: in station management in the form of customer service officers, in the stations with automatic ticket machines[3] adapted for the blind, and direct helplines connected to the Station Supervision Centre, customer service and emergency desks embracing the hearing disability protocol, access gates that cater for wheelchairs, pushchairs, bicycles and so on, public address systems on platforms to announce the next train, public address systems on trains to announce the next station, together with notices in Catalan, Spanish and English, visual and audible door-closing warnings and intercom systems in the carriages connected to drivers trained to deal with persons with disabilities, and spaces on board for wheelchairs, pushchairs and bicycles. Of a total of 68 stations, 90.7 per cent had already been adapted by 2009, three were in the process of being adapted, and the other four were at the design stage, bringing the eventual total to 100 per cent.

Recently, ECOM, a Federation of Spanish private organizations for the disabled, posed their latest challenge: the interface between trains and platforms. This problem had been pinpointed many years earlier, but since it had proven so difficult – indeed, virtually impossible – to solve, it was felt that the solution was for people in wheelchairs to overcome the problems themselves. But things changed as time went by due to the increasing numbers of people in wheelchairs, in addition to the more widespread use of electric wheelchairs, which are heavier and handle completely differently to conventional ones. Oriol Juncadella admitted:

---

3   The ticket machines won the 2002 Transport and Infrastructure Service Access and Inclusion Award at the European Disability Forum.

"There are more electric wheelchairs every day, so we have a problem. Some rail operators say, 'What does the law say?', and the European Interoperability Standard stipulates a maximum gap of 50 cm, but we strive for 5 cm as the maximum for all users. This is difficult to achieve because the behaviour of our rolling stock is dynamic. The train's position in relation to the platform is a random variable depending on many factors, mainly track wear and tear and passenger load. So it's obvious that an allowance must be made. This is not like a lift. The general public don't understand this, and because we are managers – albeit in the public sector, but still basically managers – if there is a solution, we have yet to find it."

He went on to explain that FGC had carried out extremely expensive in-house work to bring about a change in culture to address the issue:

"First of all, a platform is an item of infrastructure measured according to civil engineering standards with a tolerance of 5 cm. In other words, measurements are not exact. If you conduct a topographical survey of all platforms and all stations, which is what we have done, you'll find that platforms are not straight, they are polygonal. If no one had pointed this out to us, we would not have fixed it, but we have to. And this is an in-house concern, because as far as the Platform Manager is concerned, this platform is perfect. But when you measure it properly, it's not. This is one thing, then there's the track. Tracks are measured more accurately than other civil engineering works. Track maintenance tolerances are measured in millimetres, but there's the additional difficulty of the time of day when track maintenance is carried out. Track is mounted on a bed of gravel: sleepers are laid on this bed, and the rails are nailed to the sleepers.

Track maintenance entails a machine inserting arms that vibrate underneath the track, then gravel being added or removed to raise or lower the track – in other words, the height of the track can be altered. And not just the height: the track can be moved horizontally, too. This work is carried out at night, at specific times. And when the maintenance team finishes work, they have to get out of there quickly to let the first train go past. What happens if the track is too close to the platform? The first train can't get through – a national disaster.

So what is the track maintenance team's first thought? – To try and cover themselves: if they have to be 1 metre from the platform, they're better off aiming for 1.2 metres and avoiding a major problem. And finally, there's another party involved: the operative in the train, the one who adjusts the train's suspension. So we had to speak to these three pillars of the company, make them understand the problem and seek a solution to minimize the gap. That's what we're doing at the moment. We're bringing about this change in culture. That's right – a change in culture. I always tell the three of them that they don't have to worry, we are simply talking about a general situation that doesn't affect any of them directly, in certain respects the track is fine, the platform is fine, the train is fine … it's what comes between them that's not."

FGC began work on boarding and alighting in conjunction with ECOM more than two years ago. ECOM's preferred solution was to have no gap at all, but FGC, knowing that this was impossible for practical engineering reasons, undertook instead to make the gap as small as possible. Oriol Juncadella reflected:

"The question is, 'What is the smallest possible gap?' The company's baseline is, 'How far can we go?' But at the same time, we wonder how far we can safely go. So we carried out some research in conjunction with ECOM. We set up a test bench and asked ECOM to provide disabled volunteers. They managed to involve 72 people in wheelchairs from all over Catalonia. We got them to do some tests with a platform whose relative position could be adjusted so we could analyse the margin between acceptance and rejection. These 72 tests helped us plot a chart with a green zone with an acceptance level of 95 per cent. This means that if the difference in height is less than this level, it is acceptable.

We had to carry out this ergonomic study because despite searching everywhere, we couldn't find any relevant literature. Having said this, we discovered two other things. One is that the green zone on the chart increases depending on the type of wheelchair. Wheelchairs with inflatable tyres, for example, rise up slightly more than those with solid wheels. We also discovered that wheelchair passengers who use public transport regularly are more confident. Hence, something needs to be done in the realm of training, practising and eliminating fear. So we came to the conclusion that we must aim to be in this green zone of the chart. And we are looking for solutions to deal with the problem. As regards existing platforms, we are going to try to raise the platform edge and bring it closer to the train to be in the green zone. We won't do this for the full length of the platform, though, just alongside the two doors on each train used by people in wheelchairs – one at the front and another at the back. This is a question we had to negotiate with ECOM.

One last point about the gap between trains and platforms concerns stations located on a bend. Some stations, like Sant Gervasi and La Floresta, are extremely complicated because the curve makes it impossible to add a permanently deployed structure.

We tested a prototype with some Swiss engineers who are developing the mechanics for a platform extension that is embedded in the existing platform and then unfolds when the train stops in front of it, bridging the gap. We have been testing this since October 2008, and we now have enough information to make the final prototype. We need to fine-tune a few reliability aspects, and above all, how this system interacts with trains when unfolded, because if the extension doesn't fold up, the train can't move off. And vice versa, when the train is entering the station, the extension cannot move at the wrong time, because it may be crushed.

These are the sorts of issues we are fine-tuning, but we have already found a solution for curved platforms. As regards the phase we are in right now, ladies and gentlemen from ECOM are in fact paying us a visit tomorrow to check out an entire route we have planned for them via several stations where this solution has already been implemented, and at La Floresta station so they can finish testing it and give it their approval.

And that's the story of what we call the final challenge. Are we looking forward to finishing it? Yes, because we feel – and this is confirmed by everything we have done so far – that as you improve accessibility through inclusive design, you make stations much more attractive for everyone, and this increases the facilities' appeal."

FGC had already used closed circuit TV in stations to run ad hoc studies to find out how many people with pushchairs, wheelchairs, shopping trolleys or bicycles made use of this type of facility for the disabled. It measured this, and in fact only 3 per cent of passengers did so because they had no other option:

"But this means nothing to us. We know that 33 per cent of the population will take advantage of these facilities at some point in their life. We are working for the future, right? We are working towards a system that doesn't exclude anyone. That is our philosophy."

IKEA and Design for All

THE COMMUNICATION OF DESIGN WITHIN THE COMPANY

Within IKEA, visualizing home lifestyles is the responsibility of the Communication and Interior Design Department, run by Antonella Pucarelli:

"This means that I am responsible for exhibiting, for how we put the products on show in an IKEA store and the whole communication part. Everything you see in an IKEA store is done by the people in my department and the store's other departments."

Each store has a team of 20–25 people who take care of all the product solutions and suggest how to display the product. There is a team at each country's headquarters whose job it is to develop what they refer to as "media" – the room-like composition constructed to show how a living room, for example, can be furnished. In Spain, it is an eleven-person team, each responsible for one media. They also design whole sections of houses, called "home", and through that, design whole 35 or 55 square metre houses, with all the rooms. They have one person who is ultimately responsible for this, who is very knowledgeable and experienced in household design:

"This activity demands constant development and training for those people who work in that aspect of the stores. We also have specialists in lay-out, graphic design, and visual merchandising, who are the ones dealing with the downstairs part of the shop..

This team runs all the store's teams, totalling around 400 people across Spain and Portugal. This is our competitive advantage because, as we have said before, we do not only sell a product, we sell solutions, and the customer has to be able to see them and also see new things which correspond to the latest trends. It must never be forgotten that home life is changing a great deal and the customer has to be aware of the changes."

The company conveys the idea of design being for everybody in a specific in-store document, to express, for example, what "democratic design" means, and that a product's functionality and aesthetic value does not have to come at a high price. As well as the stores, this kind of communication is used on the Internet and in public relations. Internally, this communication is part of the information and knowledge pack that staff receive at the beginning of their time with the company.

MARKET INFORMATION

IKEA has mechanisms in place to obtain feedback from users, and processes all customer complaints and suggestions using purpose-designed systems. There is always a direct relationship with the customer. Someone from customer service gathers all the input together and sends it to the heads of sales in different areas, and they then report to the headquarters in Sweden, where product development takes place. It is said that there is a direct line to product improvement, and there are a number of examples of products that have been improved through customer input.

Apart from this, IKEA invests in global market research, mainly looking at megatrends, to see how people's lifestyles are changing – for example, how technology is affecting home life. This is all invaluable input for the staff who are developing the products, and also for the stores, which are looking at ways to represent these social changes. At a national level, IKEA has a marketing department which carries out analysis.

PRODUCT STRATEGY

IKEA's proposal is not based on giving customers the best possible quality, but giving value for money. It is aware of other companies that aim for the highest possible quality using the finest materials, but that has never been IKEA's focus: the aim is to give the best quality possible at a reasonable price.

IKEA has a product portfolio with some 9,800 items classified according to the store, because each carries either the full portfolio or a reduced version, depending on its size. Part of the portfolio is fixed, and is only updated in terms of adding new colours or products. For example, in the kitchen section there is the Faktum system, which forms a basic structure for renovation in terms of finishes or new elements. Although it is a fixed system, it also allows customers to add accessories, giving them some freedom in replacing their furniture. On the other hand, there are some new additions which account for about 20 per cent of annual turnover. These new additions may later become part of the core catalogue, or they may not, as is the case for seasonal Christmas products.

All stores contain a Swedish food section, because it is important that the stores be recognized as Swedish. This was the founder's idea. In the same way, all the non-commercial zones, such as the entrance, the restaurant and the goods on sale, have to convey their Swedish roots. There are also a few small local adaptations, so the restaurants always serve a local dish of some kind.

With the same philosophy in mind, the names of the product brands are all in Swedish, which sometimes means customers have difficulty pronouncing or remembering them, depending on their own language. To begin with, one person was responsible for naming all IKEA's products. In most cases, the names come from geography, nature or the product region, and all mean something in Swedish – they are not invented. This is an important and complicated job, because it is vital to ensure that the names work in other languages:

"Although Romance language speakers find the pronunciation difficult, it's strange how in-store, we use the product name: 'Bring me the book in the Billy' (that's an easy one). And our customers – our fans – do it, too: 'I've got a Billy' or 'I want to sit in a Pöeng.'"

SUPPLIER POLICY

IKEA has a very strong relationship with its suppliers, who are asked for their full commitment, not just in terms of quantity, but also in the way their products are produced. Their contracts are very long because of all the strict requirements they set out, including matters connected with the environment and child labour. There are very strict internal regulations, and there are internal staff and external consultants whose job it is to ensure that they are complied with. With such strict regulations in place, the suppliers need to be absolutely committed. This is a long-term relationship, since the suppliers sometimes have to accept the need for specific investment in resources, machinery or whatever else is necessary. The whole relationship is based on the idea of environmental protection. One example of this is that the wood used has to come from forests where reforestation and sustainability can be officially guaranteed.

As for the production infrastructure, IKEA Holding owns certain production lines, but also brings in third parties. In either case, regulation has to be very strict to comply with the minutely detailed requirements.

In terms of logistics, the main principle is sustainability: having the lowest possible environmental impact. Take the case of a single product – a table, for example – which is made from components produced in various parts of the world. The idea is that the various suppliers send the components directly to the stores or the regional areas. In Spain's case, for instance, IKEA has a plant where all the different items are gathered together:

"This year we have set up a company in Portugal to produce some of our best-selling products. So this means we are not receiving products from other countries, only Portugal. The idea is to decentralize production as far as possible in order to minimize environmental impact and emissions – and transport."

The result is that even though products sold in France or the USA may have been produced in different countries, they adhere to the same design and quality standards.

PRODUCT DESIGN

The organization's corporate culture is the basis for a great many products, and its origins were in Smaland in the south of Sweden, where IKEA's founder,

Ingvar Kamprad, was born and raised. Smaland was the source of IKEA's values: simplicity, humility, saving and responsibility were all evident in the lifestyle, attitudes and customs of the place where IKEA began:

"Let me tell you an interesting story – it's about how one of our star products, one of our best-sellers, came into being. The question being asked about some products was, 'How can we reduce weight and cubic space, and so bring down the price?' The fact is that a lot of our products came into being in this way. Among other things, people were thinking about the materials that our suppliers threw away, and they came upon this material which is used to make doors, the stuff which is left over when a certain type of panel is cut which helps to give it shape. This material was being thrown away by the suppliers, and it was decided in IKEA that it should be used to make these little tables, the Lack tables.

Many of our products are now made using this technology, this kind of structure, which is then covered with some type of material: wood, laminates and so on. Creativity: the challenge that faces our designers is to find solutions by thinking about totally different things, different sectors, different ways of manufacturing, different ranges. For example, we have a chair which was shown at the ExpoZaragoza[4] in the Swedish pavilion where we also held two conferences to put forward our ideas about the environment. We showed a chair which was made of plastic, but 100 per cent recycled plastic, from a supplier's waste material. There are many such examples.

Look through the catalogue; this is how we are trying to communicate the concept of democratic design in our catalogue: Why do designers like IKEA? Because they're mad about design … all projects commence with the desire to do it better. It's a challenge! You cannot make a bed, a bedside table and a wardrobe for less than 100 euros. It's impossible! But then we start thinking, drawing, visiting factories, and we get so involved that it's hard to stop thinking about it. It becomes an obsession. You start to go mad. All you think about is how to achieve a design that looks like your splendid drawing, how to package it in a flat pack and how to do it at a price that allows people worldwide to live with your contribution to design. This is the famous plastic chair I mentioned above. It can be completely dismantled.

Another case is the Norden table, which is made from boards of material which has been unused during the manufacture of other products. Sometimes the idea for a product comes from the material that one wants to use because such huge quantities are being thrown away – 'Why waste it?' – and they start to think about how they can use it. So sometimes it comes from the material, sometimes from a great creative idea, a design sketch, always remembering that it has to be an IKEA product, and has to satisfy a lot of demands.

The Lampan lamp is another example of cost-effectiveness. It can be taken apart and takes up very little space, as the base fits inside the shade. So it occupies half the space in transport, which means reduced CO_2 emissions.

The product doesn't come about through a designer's need to gratify his or her self-expression, as a tribute to an individual personality (whose signature is all-important), it comes from the recognition and appreciation of an opportunity and from a way of finding a solution to a specific household need, and making it affordable for all.

---

4   This refers to the *Exposición Mundial de Zaragoza* in 2008.

IKEA's stance has broken the mould, particularly in Italy, where a very interesting discussion was caused during the 1980s. In fact, nowadays, it's impossible for us in IKEA to get into the Milan Furniture Fair, which is one of the global reference points. There's no way.

At IKEA, the creativity is the expression of the end-user ... that's why I came here."

IKEA DESIGNERS

In the beginning, IKEA worked with unknown designers. Its first pieces of furniture came from local production, after which Ingvar Kamprad set up his own production system and decided to collaborate with designers who signed their work:

"Currently, most designers are freelance, but in Elmtaryd, the city where the founder lived for some time, and where the IKEA headquarters are now, there is a team whose job it is to come up with the products, create and develop them. So part of the production is in-house, using a team which designs the product from its conception, focusing on functionality, aesthetics, environmental impact and, obviously, the retail price. This means having to think about how it breaks down into parts so that it occupies least space, the transport costs, which also affect the environment, and so on. It is using these guidelines (aesthetics, price, design, functionality, and low environmental impact) that the work is done by the in-house team and the freelance designers, most of whom are working exclusively for IKEA.

Most of the freelancers come from the Scandinavian region of Sweden, Finland, Norway and Denmark, because the idea is that the rest of the world sees IKEA design as Scandinavian."

Although Ingvar Kamprad is, in theory, no longer involved directly in management, he was still active throughout 2008 and took an active role in IKEA's design decision-making, as Antonella Pucarelli explained:

"Yes, that's quite right, he still gives us input, he's very active. He actually decides everything right from product design, the way we present the product, the retail organisation, store distribution – it's amazing to see the energy he has, his positive attitude. When he visits the stores, right from early morning he talks and talks, putting across the company values, how we have to connect with the client ... It's incredible."

IKEA's Swedish organization is the managing body in product development. There are people in charge of range development who provide input to specific areas, and sales managers who are in charge of the various business areas. Products are classified first by business area, and then product area.

There is quite a centralized method of working in the various markets. At a certain time of year, the sales manager contacts all those in charge of sales in the various countries in order to seek their input, but obviously the larger markets carry more weight than the smaller ones. The main markets in Europe are Germany with 42 stores, followed by France, Sweden, Italy, Spain and Portugal. There are also stores in the USA, Canada, Russia (undergoing incredible growth) and Asia (China and Japan).

COMPETITION FOR IKEA

IKEA has such a specific business model that large-scale direct competition is unlikely to arise. Antonella Pucarelli explained why:

"We have a lot of competitors who are out to copy us, but they are not in direct competition because they are so much smaller. To be IKEA, you have to have IKEA's organization, which is incredible. We do have some local competition, but major European chains like Carrefour or Leroy Merlín may be able to compete in terms of one product or another, but not across the entire range. IKEA's strength is that it offers everything – absolutely everything – you need to furnish a house. We have competitors in specific product areas, such as textiles, for example, or sofas or chairs, but nobody else has the whole range."

Habitat could possibly be a competitor to a more limited degree, and using a different business model, resembling IKEA's, offering good design at comparatively low prices. Habitat was founded by Terence Conran in 1964 and eventually ran 80 stores across Europe. By 2008 it was part of the IKANO Group, owned by Ingvar Kamprad and the Kamprad family:

"Habitat is connected to IKEA; Ingvar Kamprad has shares in it. The prices are different because they work in different sectors. But there is, for example, a table in the Habitat catalogue designed by Ingvar Kamprad."

THE FUTURE OF IKEA

Ingvar Kamprad wanted to build an ownership structure and organization that could be maintained independently and had a long-term vision. Since 1982, the IKEA Group had belonged to the Stichting INGKA Foundation, which has its headquarters in Holland. In 1986, Ingvar Kamprad retired from management, but in 2008 he was still a consultant with INGKA Holding BV, the parent company of all the group's firms, which also has its headquarters in Holland. IKEA Services BV and IKEA Services AB, with nine units in Holland and Sweden, backs the work of all the group's firms, from the industrial firm Swedwood to the property sales businesses of the stores in the various countries:

"The company's main challenge is to stay true to its philosophy. It is a challenge, because expansion is connected to large numbers, which are connected to major impact, which means huge responsibility. Apart from this question, it has to be said that our objective is not only to be number one in Europe and the States, but also in China, Africa and South America.

So the question is: how we can we be affordable for that kind of market. This is one of the questions about the future which is often asked, along with others which crop up during research into raw materials, about the goal of reducing CO_2 emissions. Basically, for IKEA the whole thing is to remain true to its principles, to its values.

The second generations represent a very important question, because up until now, the business has been the spirit of its founder, his ability, his vision, his incredible vision – he is an absolute visionary. I believe that characters like him turn up once every hundred or two hundred years. He has named his successors – he has three children who have studied business administration, although I think only one of them will actually be there in the future. The founder is looking at systems to protect the concept, to guarantee the future development of the business and on a financial level he is setting up more protective elements. But really, his spirit is just amazing: he's still throwing out fantastic ideas, like the range for pets. After all, they're part of the home, too."

IKEA IN THE WORLD

At the close of fiscal year 2008, IKEA had 285 stores in 36 countries. These stores employed more than 127,800 workers. The numbers of visitors to the stores wordwide in 2008 approached 565 million. In fiscal year 2008, the IKEA stores had a global turnover of 21.2 billion euros, a 7 per cent increase over the previous year, IKEA Food achieved sales of 957 million euros, there were 450 million visitors to the website, 198 million catalogues in 27 languages, and 21 million IKEA Family members in 18 countries. In terms of global sales and purchases, 82 per cent of IKEA product sales were in the European stores, 15 per cent in the USA and 3 per cent in Asia-Australia. Germany had the company's highest turnover (15 per cent of sales), followed by the USA (10 per cent), France (10 per cent), the UK (7 per cent) and Sweden (6 per cent).

IKEA relies on 1,380 suppliers in 54 countries. The great majority of IKEA's products are bought in Europe (67 per cent), Asia (30 per cent) and North America (3 per cent). IKEA has 38 distribution centres in 16 countries, 41 purchasing offices in 30 countries and 49 Swedwood factories in 11 countries

CORPORATE SOCIAL RESPONSIBILITY

IKEA's vision is to improve the day-to-day life of people: its customers, collaborators and suppliers. Behind this vision lies IKEA's organizational commitment to its surroundings – both social and environmental – and its awareness of the important role that companies can play in most social conditions that people experience and the natural environment in which they operate. This commitment reflects a way of doing business which the company hopes will have a positive effect wherever it operates.

To pursue this goal, the company has taken on a very ambitious commitment: IKEA's business practices must have a positive impact on people and the environment. In order to strengthen this commitment globally, in December

2004 the IKEA Group decided to sign up to the United Nations Global Compact, an initiative created by Kofi Annan in 1999 which co-ordinates efforts to achieve a more sustainable and fairer economy. Its members promise to align themselves to a series of principles covering the areas of human rights, the work environment, the natural environment and the fight against corruption. IKEA reflects the Global Compact's principles in its strategy, its corporate culture and its code of conduct. This commitment entails a way of doing business with clear objectives:

- to be the best business to work for in its sector
- to be a proactive business, known for its environmental concern
- to be a business which is involved with the local community.

Being the best business to work for in its sector

IKEA's human resources concept is to offer employees the chance to grow, both personally and professionally, while taking on the commitment to create a better day-to-day existence for both customers and employees. This is why IKEA gives its employees the chance to take part in activities in different areas of the company, and to take part in working groups with colleagues from very different professional levels.

IKEA offers and expects a high level of involvement from its employees, so that they can take on progressively greater responsibilities, which requires a willingness to learn and flexibility on the part of its workers and management – both fundamental values in the organization.

One of IKEA's main objectives is to develop a human team which reflects the society in which it is functioning in terms of diversity and gender. For this reason, the question of equal opportunities at work is a priority for IKEA: IKEA's management currently comprises 52 per cent men and 48 per cent women. IKEA is seeking to address this imbalance through the Gender Equality Act.

In 2008, it launched a recruitment campaign aimed at women capable of taking on management-level jobs in its stores. There are currently five female store managers in IKEA Iberica.

PEOPLE STRATEGY

IKEA wishes to employ people from a wide range of backgrounds, and takes on those who show an understanding of customer expectations, who identify with the company's ideas and values, and who are willing to put in the effort to make them work. These values, the cornerstones of IKEA's corporate culture, include: leading by example, simplicity, a constant desire for renewal, humility and willpower, daring to be different, unity and enthusiasm, and an ability to both take on and delegate responsibility.

This is how IKEA has put its people strategy into action – an innovative strategy which the company will implement over three years in an attempt to integrate human resources and business, with two clear aims:

1. to become a reference point as a major employer in Spain, and definitively the best company to work for in the distribution sector
2. to improve its employees' skill levels.

As well as offering its employees better working conditions and better access to information, training and development, IKEA's primary aim is personal development. It seeks to offer people good working conditions, motivation, and a high level of adaptation to each of their personal and professional needs. Therefore, one of the fundamental concepts of IKEA's corporate social responsibility policy is directed towards its employees.

One of the constants in IKEA's philosophy is a high level of customer orientation among its employees. IKEA promotes the idea of professionalization of its workforce, and a higher level of qualifications in its teams, with the overriding aim of offering a better service to its customers and professional opportunities for its suppliers. Its business is based on a solid and stable foundation of specialists.

What does IKEA's people strategy offer its employees?

New compensation policy

IKEA's new compensation policy for its workers aims to improve their technical qualifications and increase the level of the customer service on offer. The new salary structure also includes job-specific extras, in order to offer professional development depending on the specialization and contribution to the company of the various positions.

Social benefits such as the pension and savings plans, maternity benefits, the canteens and staff birthday celebrations are all included in the new compensation policy.

Training

Employee training and growth are of key importance to IKEA, and the company's corporate culture revolves around its workers. This focus on employee training means that customers are offered a higher level of skill, which in turn leads to a better shopping experience.

This is why the whole IKEA workforce is offered a wide range of programmes and courses, from job-specific training to international company training, in fields such as organization, the environment, corporate values and safety in the workplace. The IKEA training plan has three elements:

1. **The training plan itself** – with objectives, activities and technical content aimed at improving skills
2. **Management** – co-ordination and practical aspects which ensure that the objectives set are actually achieved
3. **Monitoring** – the ability to measure development through training.

IKEA also measures the level of satisfaction among its workers, giving them the opportunity to assess and voice opinions about their managers' leadership in complete confidentiality and anonymity.

The main advantages of IKEA's new performance and development assessment system are that it makes manager–worker communication easier, and it helps to identify opportunities for professional development or ways to maintain and improve performance.

BEING A PROACTIVE BUSINESS KNOWN FOR ITS ENVIRONMENTAL CONCERN

Products and materials

IKEA is working to ensure that its products and materials respect the environment, as well as being safe for its customers from a health perspective. These environmental requirements are applied throughout the product's whole lifecycle. From the initial design of the product, attention is focused on the raw materials that will be used (recycled and renewable) as well as the packaging (flat packs) used to ship each product – which has a direct bearing on transport, distribution and storage.

Recycled materials

The IKEA PS Ellan chair is made from a mixture of wood fibres and recyclable polypropylene. It needs no assembly tools and is transported stacked, which means fewer emissions, as transport space is minimized.

The designers responsible for the development of IKEA's products and its technical team are all highly conscious of the need for safety, quality and sustainability. The final aim is to reduce, as far as possible, the impact of the company's activities on the environment by ensuring that its products have been manufactured in socially responsible way.

The main raw materials used in IKEA products are wood, cotton, metal, plastic, glass and rattan, and the organization works hard to obtain the largest possible proportion of renewable and recyclable materials.

Combating climate change

IKEA actively tries to reduce the carbon dioxide emissions produced as a result of its operations, in an attempt to slow down the rate of climate change. IKEA is aware of the direct and indirect emissions produced through its activities, and wishes to play an active part in minimizing them. The actions and projects are specifically designed in accordance with IKEA's processes and value chain, so as well as reducing emissions, it reduces operational costs, and IKEA can pass on these savings to its customers. Reducing emissions demands ideas and projects, but above all it requires the involvement of all the groups that make IKEA's business possible: suppliers, distributors, customers and the employees themselves. The main areas IKEA is currently working on are efficient product transportation and reducing carbon dioxide emissions.

Distribution is a key point in IKEA's business concept. It is very aware of the importance of transporting products efficiently, hence IKEA's insistence on flat packs. IKEA's aim is to avoid transportation by air, so every inch of transport space – be it lorry, boat or train – is used, meaning fewer journeys are needed, less fuel is burned, fewer emissions are produced, and as a result, costs are kept down.

IKEA works very closely with its transport providers to control carbon dioxide emissions and put plans for their reduction into place. Developing technology (for instance, to measure a lorry's full capacity) and searching for more sustainable transport alternatives are aspects which the company takes very seriously in this area.

Transporting less unnecessary air means lower carbon dioxide emissions: for example, the PS Vallö watering can is stackable and is designed to maximize the efficiency of space usage on each pallet, thus reducing both transport costs and emissions.

RAW MATERIALS

Wood is one of the most important raw materials for IKEA, and can be an excellent choice in environmental terms as long as it comes from responsibly managed forests, because it is renewable, recyclable and biodegradable. IKEA does not use illegally logged wood. IKEA's long-term corporate aim is to obtain all the wood for IKEA products from forests with responsible management certification. Currently, the Forest Stewardship Council (FSC) is the only forest certification standard that IKEA recognizes. The company also has its own forestry specialists, who work with suppliers on site. Their main job is to promote the development of sound forest management by sharing information and knowledge.

The World Wide Fund for Nature (WWF) has formed a strategic alliance with the IKEA Group to collaborate on key areas of sustainability: responsible forest management (an area already covered by an earlier strategic agreement in 2002), sustainable cotton production, and reduction of carbon dioxide emissions in order to ameliorate the effects of climate change.

IKEA supports sustainable cotton production: along with the WWF, IKEA trains cotton growers in agricultural schools in Pakistan and India to use water more efficiently and support sustainable production of this raw material. Most cotton plantations use huge amounts of water, artificial fertilizers and pesticides during the production process. IKEA is working to ensure that its cotton comes from sustainable resources.

SUPPLIER MANAGEMENT

IKEA has a collaborative relationship with its suppliers, always with an eye on the long-term, integration of them into the company's value chain. To do this, IKEA has the IKEA Way (IWAY) code of conduct, which draws together the requirements the company sets in terms of social and environmental matters, both for itself and its suppliers, in the purchase of furniture and interior decoration objects, distribution and marketing products, including the catalogue and food products.

PROMOTING SUSTAINABILITY

In matters of sustainability and climate change, IKEA works with its suppliers to raise awareness and provide training in social and environmental concerns, improving energy efficiency, promoting the use of renewable energy, reducing emissions and auditing compliance.

Since 2006, IKEA has been running its IKEA Goes Renewable project in its stores and premises, which includes a number of initiatives in order to increase company energy efficiency by 25 per cent. The aim is to move to the use of renewable energy (biofuels, geothermal energy, wind and solar power) in all the organization's premises worldwide.

Sustainable people transportation

IKEA is working on sustainable mobility plans so that visitors, customers and employees can get to its stores by public transport. To do this, it maintains an active policy of collaboration with public administrations in order to improve bus and train services to its stores. When it plans to open a new store, a crucial priority for IKEA is to ensure access to a good public transport system. The company also runs awareness-raising campaigns about sustainable transport. To encourage customers to use public transport, IKEA offers a home delivery service.

In 2007, IKEA replaced its fleet of staff vehicles with a hybrid model from Toyota, with higher performance and lower fuel consumption, which means very low pollutant emissions.

Water

IKEA has carried out an audit of water use to draw up action plans for how to reduce water consumption. In some stores, rainwater and air-conditioning condensation are collected for non-drinking uses.

IKEA GreenTech

IKEA GreenTech is a research and development project that aims to develop new ecological solutions, including solar panels, energy efficiency, water conservation and purification, alternative electricity sources, and low-emission materials and products.

Through IKEA GreenTech, the company will be investing 50 million euros into innovative environmental product companies over the next five years.

BEING A BUSINESS WHICH IS INVOLVED WITH THE LOCAL COMMUNITY

The IKEA Group takes part in a wide range of social activities at the international, national and local level. IKEA surrounds itself with a wide range of experts in order to find real solutions which support the fight for all children's right to a safe, healthy childhood and access to a good education.

IKEA has links with UNICEF and Save the Children, both of which adopt a holistic approach to improve the health of women and children, create access to a good education, and give women the power to attain a better future for themselves and their communities.

"€1 is a Fortune!" – an international initiative

The "€1 is a Fortune!" campaign is an initiative arising from the alliance between IKEA, UNICEF and Save the Children. The aim is to support projects led by these organizations to improve living conditions and children's education in developing countries.

In collaboration with its customers, IKEA donates 1 euro to these projects for every soft toy sold over the Christmas period. The campaign takes place in IKEA stores all over the world, and the donation is independent of the price of the toy sold. Thanks to the campaign, IKEA has given UNICEF and Save the Children 11 million euros over three years. In the third year of the campaign, it raised 294,269 euros in Spain alone.

A local initiative – IKEA Colabora

IKEA Colabora ("IKEA Collaborates") is a social action framework created by the company in Spain. The aim is to promote national as well as local initiatives connected to each store's activity through three kinds of initiatives:

1. **The IKEA Colabora Foundation** – this makes an annual donation of 90,000 euros to non-profit organizations involved in social action projects in Spain, aimed at improving the quality of children's lives in that country. IKEA's employees choose the winning projects. To ensure the IKEA Colabora Foundation's success, IKEA is working in collaboration with Fundación

Lealtad and Economistas sin Fronteras. In 2009, IKEA redesigned the scheme to offer support for environmental projects in alternate years.

3. **Donations of IKEA furniture and products** – all IKEA stores make such donations to local organizations.

4. **Volunteer work** – IKEA supports employees' participation as volunteers in projects supported by the company.

This initiative's success depends on the full involvement of each and every IKEA employee. To achieve this, IKEA runs in-house campaigns to raise awareness and set up compulsory social and environmental responsibility training programmes for its employees.

All IKEA employees must incorporate respect for the environment and sustainability into their everyday work, because each and every one shares responsibility for IKEA's commitment.

Nespresso – Luxury for All

PAUDEX Switzerland, (March, 2009) – Nestlé Nespresso S.A., the worldwide pioneer and industry reference for highest quality portioned coffee, has announced 2008 sales of 2.262 billion CHF (€1.35 billion) – more than double its 2006 sales. In 2008, the company marked its eighth consecutive year with an average of 30% or more year-on-year growth, reaching the 2 billion CHF milestone two years ahead of initial projections and solidifying its position as the fastest-growing business in the Nestlé Group.

"Our 2008 results are satisfying because they reflect our deeply rooted culture of innovation and our commitment to highest quality in everything we do," said Richard Girardot, CEO of Nestlé Nespresso. "Our ambition is to become an iconic global brand, building on our proven coffee expertise, unstoppable drive for innovation, unique business model with our privileged and direct relationships with our customers."

Vincent Termote, Managing Director of Nestlé Nespresso Iberia, was reading the press release about the results of Nespresso in his bright office in the Bonanova Promenade in Barcelona and could not help feeling satisfied with the success of the product in his markets – Spain and Portugal. Despite the world economic recession, in five years Spain had achieved third place in the market and Nespresso Iberia was about to open its sixth boutique in Barcelona. He thought over the reasons for the success of Nespresso. The heart of the Nespresso concept was quite simple:

- **Great coffees** – the selection of the best coffees supplied in perfectly measured individual portions in hermetically sealed capsules
- **Machines** – a full range of elegant and well-designed coffee machines
- **Service** – a personalized 24/7 service through the Nespresso Club.

Nespresso's slogan is: "Providing a perfect espresso – very high quality coffee with a consistent body and exquisite cream – we guarantee consumers worldwide can enjoy their passion for a perfect coffee."

THE HISTORY OF NESPRESSO

Nestlé was founded through the merger of two earlier companies in 1905, and by 2009 was the largest food chain in the world.[5] Coffee was one of its most important product lines, with strategic brands like Nescafé, the instant coffee invented in 1968. The Nespresso brand coffee supplied in capsules was a relatively new category that had a bright present and a promising future. Around the world, every minute of the day, around 8,000 cups of Nespresso coffee were being consumed. According to a study by AC Nielsen, in 2008 capsule coffee represented 5 per cent of coffee on the market by volume and 10 per cent by value. The forecasts for 2015 were 12 per cent and 25 per cent respectively.

In the 1970s, Nestlé had a dominant position in the instant coffee market, which represented 30 per cent of world coffee consumption, and Nescafé was the leading brand. However, in the market for roast and ground coffee, which represented most of the remaining 70 per cent of coffee consumption, Nestlé only had 20 per cent. The idea of Nespresso arose with the intention of penetrating this sector of the market, and more specifically, the gourmet market that was the fastest-growing one. Nestlé started researching an espresso system with the aim of providing the same quality of coffee found in Italian coffee shops. Research centre staff went to Italy to investigate how the system worked and how coffee was being made in Italian coffee bars. It took those three years of investigation and several patents to create the Nespresso system, which consisted of individual capsules of 100 per cent recyclable aluminium containing 5 grams of roasted and ground coffee for exclusive use in specially designed coffee machines. The capsules protected the coffee from damage from exposure to sunlight, air and humidity, and allowed simple preparation with the guarantee of a high-quality result.

In 2008, Nestlé defined ten key dates in the constant innovation process of Nespresso:

1. In 1976, Nestlé's Innovation and Development Team was inspired when an employee visited Italy and decided to develop the secret of the perfect espresso through his own licensed system. And they managed to do it in way that had been unexplored to date: preparing coffee at home and in the office, away from traditional espresso bars with their huge machines.
2. In 1986, Nestlé founded the company Nespresso SA. In collaboration with Swiss manufacturer Turmix, the Nespresso system was launched into the office market for coffee in Switzerland and Italy. Capsule production was

---

centralized in the factory in Orble, Switzerland. Later, the system would be offered to the wider consumer market.

3. In 1996, Nespresso SA celebrated ten years of success with 3,500 points of sale and 180,000 members of the Nespresso Club. The system was also launched in England, Malaysia, Singapore, Taiwan and Hong Kong. The same year also saw the launch of the Nespresso Professional System to provide coffee machines and first-rate coffee in portions to small and medium businesses, premium hotels, the restaurant sector and many airline companies.

4. In 1998, Nespresso SA widened its range of products, and in collaboration with the Italian manufacturer Alessi launched a machine of groundbreaking design. It marketed this strategically important development by launching its largest ever advertising campaign in the European media and widening its horizons with a redesigned website.[6]

5. In 2001, the improved ease of use and ergonomic design achieved through the launch of the Nespresso Concept machine led to record sales. Nespresso SA started to build a new production centre for coffee capsules in Orbe, Switzerland.

6. In 2002, the construction of the new facilities of production in Orbe was complicated, and its production capacity increased by 400 per cent to address future growth objectives. A more exclusive and convenient version of the system was introduced, with the aim of widening the range of machines on offer. The introduction of Nespresso Boutiques provided an additional presence in major cities, while online orders increased 94 per cent during the year. By 2008, e-business would represent in 30 per cent of the company's income.

7. In 2003, at the Convention Sintercafé in Costa Rica, Nestlé Nespresso SA announced the launch of its Nespresso AAA Sustainable Quality Program, designed to promote the production and distribution of sustainable coffee of very high quality. Nespresso announced its co-sponsorship of the Alinghi team, which was defending the 32nd Americas Cup, the most important sailing competition with the oldest sporting trophy in the world.

8. In 2005, the revolutionary Nespresso Essenza coffee machine helped to position Nespresso as the European market leader for espresso machines.

9. In 2006, Nespresso hired the Oscar winner George Clooney to star in a 50-second commercial called "The Boutique" that was shown on European television stations and in cinemas. With Le Cube, Nespresso established new standards in innovation and design of coffee machines. The faultlessly polished aluminium Nespresso Siemens model by Porsche Design was a success among design lovers interested in top-of-the-range machines.

10. In 2007, as symbol of its global expansion, Nespresso inaugurated its Boutique brand with a 1,500 square metre outlet on the Champs Elysées in Paris, whose grand opening event was attended by international stars such as Sharon Stone. The expansion of Nespresso continued in new strategic markets such as Asia (Hong Kong, China, South Korea) and Latin America (Argentina and Brazil). The company invested a total of 150 million Swiss francs in its new

---

6   See www.nespresso.com.

Production and Distribution Centre in Avenches, Switzerland to cater for global growth.

THE NESPRESSO BUSINESS MODEL

In public speeches, Vincent Termote has explained the reasons for the success of the Nespresso concept:

> *"One of the innovations of the system is the route to market. We do not sell to supermarkets, through the classic distributional channels. We have chosen another model for very specific reasons: preserving the quality of our coffee. The capsules must be hermetically sealed to maintain the quality of the coffee for 12 months. Despite this, with a conventional distribution we could not have been able to guarantee this quality, which is an obsession for Nestlé. However, in reality, the success of the system is based on what we call the Nespresso Trilogy."*

First pillar – high-quality coffees

Vincent Termote went on to explain the Nespresso trilogy, whose first factor is the coffee itself:

> *"You have to take into account that a good cup of coffee does not only consist of having the perfect raw ingredient, but it is a vital starting point. Only 1–2 per cent of coffee produced worldwide meets our quality standards – that is, we buy the best coffee. After sending it to Switzerland, we carry out a split roasting (which consists of toasting each consignment of coffee separately to reveal it at its best), then we blend it, grind it and pay a lot of attention to quality control, but this is still not enough to deliver good cup of coffee. From the farmer's work to the production in Switzerland, we take care of all the details, even sustainability. We have 16 varieties of coffee, which I think is a key element of our success: there are flavours for everybody. There are 12 espressos – short coffees – and within these coffees there are three that are single-origin (one from Brazil, another from Colombia, and one from India); and then we have four lungos – long coffees.*
>
> *Within this range we also have three decaffs, a lungo and two espressos. And they all have the same organoleptic profile – that is, it is not the origin of the coffee that necessarily makes the difference, since, apart from the three single-origin lines, the others are blends. What is of interest to our specialists in Switzerland is that they all have the same organoleptic profile – one flavour per capsule – and this is the key point for consumers, since they will always achieve the same coffee result. This does not happen in a bar, since there are distorting elements, such as if you use more or less coffee, or the machine is not well calibrated. In short, a non desirable variability is introduced."*

To provide high-quality coffees, Nespresso begins by rigorously selecting only the best green coffee beans that its specialists can source. Gourmet coffees make up only 10 per cent of green coffee production, and within this proportion, only 10–20 per cent will be of sufficient calibre to meet Nespresso's high quality standards.

Once the beans have been selected, several processes take place in the Orbe production centre, including blending, roasting, grinding and packing, before the coffee can be enjoyed in the cup. As with wines, each of the Nespresso Grand Cru coffees offers a unique flavour and aroma profile. In 2008, Nespresso offered 12 Grand Cru coffees of very high quality, nine espressos (producing a small 40 ml cup) and three lungos (smooth but intense coffees to be enjoyed in a larger 110 ml cup). In 2009, it offered 16 varieties, among them three single-origin coffees.

Nespresso's AAA Sustainable Quality Program

Vincent Termote explained the importance of sustainability for Nespresso:

> *"The first element of the trilogy is coffee – the best coffee that can be bought – but another thing that is important is that Nespresso acts to promote greater sustainability than exists nowadays, and for our efforts we have received awards like the Green Globe Award, among others. With the AAA project (AA is the best coffee, AAA is the one that corresponds to our concept), what we do is to help our producers to deliver that high-quality coffee. We offer support to the farmers to produce a better-quality coffee, we pay more, and we even guarantee that 75 per cent of what we pay goes into their pockets. Classic sustainability programmes consist of ensuring the money goes to the farmer and not to the intermediary, and this can encourage producers to produce quantity and not quality, which drives prices down and thus has an adverse effect. We work on the quality part, and this is ensured by supporting farmers financially and also socially, by setting up schools. We are carrying out this project aggressively: we are talking about 20,000 farmers; we are talking about 40 per cent of our production through the AAA programme, which has also been recognized by the World Bank."*

Nestlé Nespresso wants to improve the quality of life of coffee farmers and their communities, while at the same time safe ensuring the supply of high-quality coffee in the future. In 2002 it announced its official relationship with Rainforest Alliance, the leading non-governmental organization devoted to improving the sustainability of farm production. The Rainforest Alliance is a key partner of in the AAA Sustainable Quality Program.

Nespresso and its suppliers work together with more than 15,000 farmers that participate in the AAA programme to ensure that practices on farms are geared to supplying better-quality beans in economically feasible ways while respecting the environment. The coffee producers that participate in the programme are rewarded not only economically, but also with a long-lasting relationship with Nespresso. Nespresso currently buys 35 per cent of its coffee through this programme, and its Gran Café Volluto is made 100 per cent from this coffee. By the end of 2010, Nespresso expected to buy 50 per cent of its coffee through its AAA Sustainable Quality Program, which offers many benefits:

- **An increase in the price of high-quality coffee** – Nespresso pays up to 10 per cent over the market price
- **Establishing systems** – the procedures established ensure that 75 per cent of the price is transferred directly to the farmers
- **Quality improvement** – training and committing farmers to produce better-quality coffee reduces the proportion of beans rejected from 50 per cent to only 5 per cent
- **Development of long-term loyalty among the farmers** – about 70 per cent of farmers in the key regions have participated in the programme over the past four years.

Since 2002, Nespresso has embarked on numerous projects. For instance, in 2004 it provided materials to small-scale coffee producers in Colombia to help them improve productivity and quality. It also carried out a major programme of reforestation of indigenous species in Costa Rica and contributed to the extension of school buildings in the Ixhuatlán region in Mexico. In 2006, it announced a $500,000 partnership with the International Finance Corporation (IFC) to support the Nespresso AAA Sustainable Quality Program. Through this association with the IFC, it has been able to dramatically expand the scope of the programme and carry out substantial improvements in the sustainability of farming practices and quality of crops in the three major regions in Central America that cultivate coffee, including Costa Rica (La Georgia and Orosi), Guatemala (Huehuetenango) and Mexico (Ixhuatlan).

By mid-2007 the company had received prestigious awards for its commitment to sustainable quality, including the Rainforest Alliance's Corporate Green Globe Award for businesses that show an extraordinary commitment to sustainability, and the Coffee Quality Institute's Leadership Medal of Merit Award for its vision and role in development and leadership.

In August 2007, it held its first AAA Summer Campus study programme in Costa Rica. For 14 days, 20 international students chosen from the 1,100 who had expressed an interest worldwide attended to learn about sustainability in coffee production. The learning experience included two days of practical training at INCAE, the best Latin American business school, they participated in a debate about sustainability and learnt about the origin and trade of coffee and its contribution to Latin America's economy. The students visited farms that benefit from the Nespresso AAA Sustainable Quality Program, and learnt all about the coffee manufacturing process in the ECOM mill in Santa María.

They also had the opportunity to learn how the Rainforest Alliance is working to implement the best sustainable practices in several sectors, such as tourism and farming. The final days focused specifically on the AAA Sustainable Quality Program, including a full training day about how farmers can use TASQ, a self-assessment tool developed in collaboration with the Rainforest Alliance to improve the quality of coffee. The Summer Campus ended with presentations from the students, who shared all they had learned and gave suggestions to improve and promote the programme.

Given the success of the first AAA Sustainable Quality Coffee Forum at the IMD international business school in Lausanne, Switzerland in 2005, in November 2007 the second one was held in Costa Rica, the place of origin of the AAA Sustainable Quality Program, to exchange ideas with 80 professionals from all over the world about how to improve the impact of the programme. The Minister of Trade of Costa Rica, Marco Vinicio Ruiz, opened the forum, at which non-governmental organizations like the Rainforest Alliance, Techno Serve, teachers from INCAE and the CATIE Tropical Research and Higher Education Center, Nestlé and Nespresso executives participated, as well as suppliers and experts in the industry. Using the knowledge gathered at the forum, Nespresso conducted the closing session of the 21st Convention of Sintercafé, attended by executive managers from the world's main coffee companies.

Second pillar – the coffee machines

The second factor in the trilogy is Nespresso's coffee machines, as Vincent Termote explained:

> *"At Nespresso, we are obsessed with the quality of the coffee in the cup, and this cannot be ensured without designing a good machine.[7] Nespresso is the only label that creates its own machine designs. The range includes 30–40 models of different colours, functionalities and shapes. It is a wide range. From a briefing, the technicians and design team work on this issue to produce the machines we want for the different markets. We work with many designers, but we can say that historically, what really made a difference was working with Les Ateliers du Nord of Lausanne. This is the main team that works on our machines because they know the Nespresso technology. The machines are manufactured in Switzerland by an original equipment manufacturer (OEM). Afterwards, for each country, we choose the associates that are going to take care of the distribution of machines and do not participate in their manufacture. There are minor exceptions, like Porsche Design and Lattissima, where we have worked with Porsche, Siemens and Delonghi. We have also worked with Miele on a built-in machine. But most of the machine range is designed by Nespresso itself."*

The apparent simplicity of the machines hides very complex technology to achieve the required quality of coffee. Over years of research, Nestlé has registered a great number of patents for Nespresso machines. The machines are manufactured under licence by external companies and sold directly through international manufacturers that, in turn, distribute them through selected small appliance retailers. In 2009, Nespresso was collaborating with DeLonghi,

---

7   The process of making good coffee consists of three stages. The first involves soaking, where the coffee is sprayed with water to expand it; the second is airing, where air flows through the humid coffee, creating small irrigation channels, and the third is extraction, in which water flows through the coffee at high pressure and temperature.

Koening, Krups, Magimix, Miele, Siemens and Turmix. Before this, it had worked with Matsushita, Philips, Alessi and Jura.

Collaboration on these brands is very profitable, Vincent Termote observed:

"For instance, when we get into a market where we do not have brand awareness and no one knows what Nespresso is, in this situation, if a consumer goes to a shop and sees a Nespresso machine, maybe they will not trust us much, but if they see Krups and Nespresso together, their impression is more favourable. The seller network and the Krups team already exist, they have been established and are ready to sell coffee shops and other Krups products. This gives us reliability in a new market. The associate buys machines and later distributes them with a strictly defined contract from Nespresso regarding opening of points of sale and the distribution network."

The machines are marketed in department stores and specialized shops within the distribution network Nespresso has set up to maintain its brand positioning. When entering new markets, Nespresso seeks the approval of opinion leaders when distributing the machines, avoiding shops that are not in keeping with the Nespresso brand image. Thus, it is very important for the company to keep a close eye on its distributors. If it cannot find partners with the appropriate level of brand approval in the market, it trades directly using the Nespresso name. For instance, in Japan, the USA and Brazil, it sells machines under the Nespresso brand, since these countries lacked a suitable market leader.

Nespresso offers a full range of machines with a large variety of functions, designs and prices, some to be used at home (B2C – business-to-customer) and some for hotels, restaurants and offices (B2B – business-to-business). All its machines have been specifically developed to complement and promote the aroma, cream and flavour of the selected coffees.

Nespresso is constantly innovating, and it regularly launches new coffee machines: the most important innovation in terms of machines in 2007 (2008 in the case of some countries like Spain) was the launch of Lattissima, an advanced design that provides espresso beverages based on fresh milk at the press of a button. In 2001, Nespresso launched the revolutionary Essenza machine, and sold 3 million of them. In 2005, it introduced a colour range reminiscent of sunny Capri days. In 2006, it launched more new colours: the "Glam Rock" range. In the same year, it launched the first Le Cube machine. With striking well-defined corners and available in four colours, Le Cube personified cubism – minimalist, pure – and appealed strongly to design lovers, becoming one of the best-selling Nespresso machines to date.

Designed for coffee connoisseurs, in 2006 the Siemens Nespresso by Porsche Design machine was introduced. This machine combined the knowledge and experience of three premium brands – Nespresso, leader in the single-portion gourmet coffee market, its partner Siemens, the leading manufacturer of home appliances, and the Porsche Design Studio – to create a coffee machine that was completely automatic with a one-touch cappuccino function. In 2009, it introduced a new design of machine, the CitiZ, with two models of CitiZ&Co capable of making two coffees simultaneously, and the CitiZ&Milk to make white coffee.

The B2B range also introduced three new Nespresso Gemini Generation machines in 2006: the Gemini CS200 and CS220, with a double-head system to make two coffees at once, and the Gemini CS100 with a single head, aimed at small to medium-sized businesses. In tandem with this, Nespresso introduced a special payment system for medium-sized and large companies in the summer of 2008.

The role of design in the Nespresso machines

Creating coffee machines with a balanced, perfect design incorporating the latest technological advancements is Nespresso's hallmark. In 2001, Nespresso launched the Concept, the first machine that was functionally designed around the capsule system, abandoning the traditional shape of coffee machines. For these machines, the well-known designer Antoine Cahen managed to introduce colour and a new radical shape while maintaining ease of use. This unique machine redefined the market for espresso machines, and thanks to the success of its sales, the coffee market itself, as Vincent Termote explained:

"With machines, we started with square models. If we talk about design the Nespresso Concept Machine, a round model combined the practical idea of incorporating a receptacle for the empty capsules with ease of use, which entailed assuming a risk, since we did not know whether the consumer would be ready to welcome such an innovative and revolutionary design in the world of coffee machines. However, Nespresso means innovation. Nespresso had already innovated in creating the category in 1986. We are always innovating. That was a risk, but it created this machine that was a key element in the spread of Nespresso.

Nespresso has been an operation in which for years we have been refining the system, we have polished the model. In 2001, when we launched the Concept, it was a boom. It won awards and became a cult object. Since then, our machines have always had a great design. This is the first step. Then we launched Le Cube and Lattissima. There is a new range that has been launched this year. It is called CitiZ – eight models, three different families. It is an urban concept, a compact machine. The idea is that more than 50 per cent of people live in cities and spaces that are limited.

So far, we have been talking about machines for the B2C market, but we also design machines for B2B. For an Arzak,[8] to have a beautiful machine at sight is always important, as it is in the breakfast buffet of a four- or five-star hotel. Little by little, we conquered the field, because the consumer who has one at home also wants one in the hotel. In Spain, we are in more than 25 per cent of locations

---

8   A famous restaurant in San Sebastian that has three Michelin Stars.

with a Michelin star and we are working with the best. Last Monday, I met with Ferran Adrià.[9]"

Nespresso's emphasis on design led it to launch an international design competition in 2006 it. For its second competition in Milan in 2008, Nespresso partnered with international designers like Patrick Norguet, Alfredo Aeberli, Ineke Hans and Constantin Grcic, who served on the jury.

Nespresso machines have won many awards for their integration of design and technology. In 2005, the company was awarded the prestigious Red Dot Best of the Best Award by the Design Zentrum Nordrhein-Westfalen in Essen for attaining the highest quality in the international design of products through its Nespresso C90 (Compact Line). Two years later, Nespresso was honoured with another Red Dot Award for its Nespresso Siemens machine by Porsche Design.

Third pillar – the system

Vincent Termote clarified how Nespresso markets its machines:

"In terms of coffee, we control absolutely everything. In terms of machines, sales are carried out by our partners or Nespresso itself, but Nespresso always takes care of the marketing of our machines itself, because obviously, having different partners, we do not want different countries project different images. Thus, we must ensure that when a machine is on the shelf, the consumer understands that it is not just any model, but only works with a particular brand of capsule – Nespresso's – so this is a closed system.

For us, it is very important to be distinctive at points of sale, and in fact this has been one of the major battles in distribution, because we want to control our image. We have fought to establish a really distinctive and premium image in distribution. This is taken care by Nespresso itself – maximizing visibility at points of sale, all the communication and media work, everything marketing-related is run by Nespresso.

The sales of our machines are complemented by selective distribution. Although we have different distribution methods, we always focus on department stores that really reach the consumer profiles that have a certain affinity with Nespresso. We also bear in mind retail chains that specialize in household appliances, in particular reliable ones that have enormous power as prescriptors and can explain the system."

He went on to explain another unique approach to marketing:

"The coffee and machines are two business pillars. The third is the Nespresso Club, which is a customized service made up of different elements: the Customer Relationship Centre, which includes the Internet, and our boutiques. Why did we choose this model? As I mentioned earlier, we are trying to avoid selling Nespresso machines through supermarkets or shops that cannot offer the advice and display standards we want. These are part of our service that is important to us."

---

9   Ferran Adrià, considered by many the best chef in the world, runs the restaurant elBulli, also awarded three Michelin Stars.

The Nespresso Boutiques

Nespresso's boutiques offer a window into the heart of Nespresso and a key point of sale, generating around 29 per cent of its annual sales in the home market. They also serve a critical role by developing client–label interaction, aiming to providing a venue where customers can enjoy the perfect coffee experience.

Working together with Nespresso, the well-known French architect Francis Krempp has contributed to creating many stylish Nespresso Boutiques around the world, including those shops in Paris, Zurich, Amsterdam, Rome, Moscow and Sydney. For the new markets, the Boutique Bars work as window displays to promote the values of the brand, introducing visitors, as well as their family members and friends, to Nespresso's products and services. The tangible emotional space that Krempp has created inside the boutiques encourages coffee lovers to feel part of the Nespresso lifestyle, allowing them to choose the latest accessories to complement to the coffee machines they may already have at home.

Each new boutique, strategically placed in important metropolitan shopping areas, takes the coffee lover on a voyage of discovery. Coffee specialists are on hand to help them select their preferred variety of Nespresso, as well as letting them try out the Concept, Essenza, Le Cube and Lattissima machines so they can choose the one that best fits their needs. Stimulating all five senses, each boutique presents a wide variety of coffees as well as providing ideas about how to make and enjoy the experience of the perfect coffee in the comfort of their own homes.

Typifying the growth of Nespresso, there were 117 boutiques around the world by late 2007. Together with the new boutiques Nespresso hopes to open in Europe, it also expanded into East and South Asia, North America and Latin America, with 175 boutiques in 30 countries by the end of 2008.

Branding

Vincent Termote clarified the importance of branding to Nespresso:

"Why did we decide to sell coffee directly? As a brand, we aim to become an icon of perfect coffee worldwide. This is our ambition, We have already achieved this in many different countries. We have recently entered Latin America and China, and obviously, in these markets we have not yet reached 100 per cent.
We want to become an iconic brand. We are starting to occupy a niche, we believe we are a cult brand, but we want to reach as many consumers as possible."

Nespresso's ambitions rely on its focus on the quality of its brands:

"For us the most important thing is the quality of the coffee. The quality of the product has also been part of the Nestlé philosophy. In this sense, we are perfectionists – we sometimes even approach paranoia – we are perfectionists and expect perfection.

We are constantly pursuing improvements in the quality of our coffee. If we compare consumer preference for our coffee with another well-known brand, in Italy, where clients are even more demanding, three consumers out of four prefer Nespresso. It speaks for itself. Why? Because of the quality of the coffee and the quality of the machines."

NESPRESSO'S COMPETITION

Rival espresso coffee systems exist, but they are hampered because Nespresso has protected its technology very well with a multitude of patents, as Vincent Termote emphasized:

"When we speak of technology and patents, we're talking about more than 1,000 patents and a machine that operates at more than 19 bars of pressure. Pressure is very important to extract the coffee from the capsule and to produce the cream that traps the aromas within the cap. The quality of the cream also allows us to see whether or not the coffee is burnt. All these details make the consumer go for Nespresso.

At international level we have a lot of competitors in many markets. In the pyramid of Nespresso competitive advantages, we saw that the first thing is the quality of the coffee in the cup. I can assure you that all the Nespresso capsule systems are of a very high standard due to their technology. The second factor is design. There are some competitors that are trying to make machines with a better design, but in this field we are also outstanding. We managed to be different. Regarding the third competitive advantage, the service, we could say that our Nespresso Club is unique – there is no other brand that does what we do.

The factors of variety and selection are also covered by other brands, but not to the same extent as Nespresso. However, most of the other brands are addressed to a much less demanding market. Some of their models are sold in supermarkets, thus they have the advantages but also the disadvantages of these distribution channels. Today, we keep being the leaders in our segment – we have created it and we lead it."

Nespresso's approximately 17 per cent share of the coffee machine market has shown dramatic increases, by 6 per cent in 2000, 15.2 per cent in 2007 and 17.1 per cent in 2008:

"In Spain we have almost three times more, we are talking about 45 per cent – that is, one in two espresso machines sold today is ours, and the concept has had a fantastic welcome. In Barcelona, it is 80 per cent."

Vincent Termote continued, unable to hide his satisfaction:

"Word of mouth works very well, it is like a snowball. We have set out without advertising anything, only sponsoring events: golf, horse riding and sailing. We sponsored the Copa América in Valencia in 2007. The presence and exposure for our coffee gives us a real advantage. In short, today competitors are trying to get in because it is the only category that is really growing in the coffee market. We have created a new category. Traditional distribution methods do not pose any problems because we

ensure that we invest in other categories. In fact, Nestlé has created another system that is a little different from Nespresso's – let us say it is more multi-beverage, it is for a consumer who is maybe a little more demanding about his or her coffee and also wants to consume hot chocolate. This system is a bit different from ours because it is sold through supermarkets, which allows Nestlé to occupy a greater share of the market.

We may have competitors, but we are very aware that we have advantages. Apart from this, it is very important for us to keep working with humility and enthusiasm to always stay a step ahead of our competitors. This is an advantage we want to keep. The idea is to keep on working without making much fuss about it.

However, the future holds a lot of questions. Will we be able to maintain this growth? Will we really some day be able to offer our product to everybody in the world? What are the limitations? What are the threats that will come up in the medium term? What actions should we take?"

Santa & Cole – Person, City and Planet

In March 2009, the whole world was deep in crisis. Starting nearly two years earlier in the United States with the property market crash, followed by unprecedented havoc in the banking world, the slump in production and sales had spread throughout all sectors of all economies. In one way or another, firms like Santa & Cole were bound to feel the effects of such a major shake-up. Chairman and founding partner Javier Nieto Santa was worried, but also full of vitality and showing the great future vision that characterized him:

"In 2007 things went very well for us, 2008 was fine … 2009, I've no idea. To be honest, I don't know if the government's plans are going to work. January and February went terribly and we tightened our belt, but well, other than that, we've kept going. I think at the moment we've got the best generation of products in the history of Santa & Cole, and hunger sharpens our wits. I reckon this situation will wreak some big changes, because socially we'd reached the point of repugnance. I hope there'll be changes. They'll affect us in many ways, and all for the best, if we're still alive, because right now that's the essential requisite: to survive."

HISTORY OF SANTA & COLE

Santa & Cole was founded in 1985 by Javier Nieto Santa, Gabriel Ordeig Cole and Nina Masó. The name was taken from the second surnames of its founders, and the symbol – two unequal eyes looking though a pair of glasses, the "fertile eyes" of the title of a collection of essays on design – symbolizes their vocation as editors and the importance of having their own point of view about the objects they design and sell.

Santa & Cole define themselves as design editors. Their function is to edit – that is, to select those objects in which they recognize themselves, and to manage the most suitable means to enable a designer's idea (or an existing design) to take shape and be put on the market. Javier Nieto Santa explained:

"Our company's raison d'être has always been industrial design, an art consisting in finding the best in each object in order to offer a more pleasant user experience in our everyday lives. Our business is to seek out and choose from among an extensive number of objects those with a great history which precedes them, or with a humble success to discover; a selection that contributes more than just matter: serenity, culture and wellbeing."

In 1987, Santa & Cole started to develop its indoor collection with a series of lamps that shed a warm light – something that was totally opposed to what was in fashion at the time, the "halogen bulb with a twisted tube". However, their commitment to human warmth and visual comfort was received with great enthusiasm. The Basica lamp, the first design signed by the Santa & Cole team, was the work of Santiago Roqueta, an indispensable figure in understanding the development of industrial design in Catalonia. In that same year, designers such as Miguel Milá and Beth Galí made decisive contributions to the first Santa & Cole catalogues, with emblematic products such as the TMM standard lamp and the Lamparaalta street lamp.

Santa & Cole is the product of several takeovers (such as that of Disform in 1994) and distribution agreements that have gradually built the company as it exists today. Some significant examples of this are the agreements reached for distribution in Spain with two firms: in 1987, bulthaup (Germany), a benchmark brand in kitchen furniture, and USM (Switzerland), specializing in office furniture.

In 1989, Santa & Cole became the agent for La Cornue France, a company dedicated to the manufacture of hand-crafted top-of-the-range cookers. Likewise, five years later, in 1994, Ingo Maurer entrusted Santa & Cole with the distribution of its lighting products in Spain.

Santa & Cole's founders' vocation as editors of design also came to be applied to the classical function of book publishing. In 1991, Santa & Cole started publishing design monographs, convinced that the books they published and the objects they edited were inseparable and had the same objective: to foster a more sensitive and less banal material culture. In 2005, the book publishing function was spun off and became a company in its own right: Ediciones de Belloch. The publishing house continued its work with the same determination as in the early days, with four collections of books: *Clásicos del Diseño* (*Design Classics* – biographies), *Contemporáneos del Diseño* (*Contemporary Designers* – also biographies), *Los Ojos Fértiles* (*The Fertile Eyes* – essays on design) and *Biblioteca de Gestión* (*Management Library* – essays on management), the last of these in collaboration with ESADE.

In 1988, four years before the Barcelona Olympic Games, Santa & Cole embarked on the development of street furniture hand in hand with those who were to be the protagonists of the transformation of Barcelona: the municipal technicians, landscapers and architects in charge of the projects for the Olympic areas and the conversion of the city. The company assisted them and edited some of the elements that were designed for the event, which subsequently formed Santa & Cole's first catalogue of urban elements. The success of this work was due to the close communion that existed between all those involved and the trust placed by politicians in the architects who led the work inside and outside the city council, together with the companies that gave them support and believed in the environment that was being built during that magical period. More than twenty years on, Santa & Cole's Urban Division represents 70 per cent of its turnover, and it has continued to work to realize a vocation: to contribute towards the harmonious development of cities. This has influenced their concept of Design for All.

By 2009, Santa & Cole had become highly internationalized. The company started up in a small street in Barcelona called Santíssima Trinitat del Mont, and it was in this original workshop that it made the prototypes of lamps such as La Bella Durmiente and La Colilla. Two years later, after much remodelling and a visit by Gerd Bulthaup, it became the showroom for Santa & Cole lamps and bulthaup kitchen furniture. As the company grew, with various distribution agreements and takeovers, Santa & Cole's spaces also grew, with the opening of two shops in Barcelona and offices in Madrid, Bilbao, Valencia and Malaga.

Internationalization started very early. Santa & Cole had been present in the markets of California, Florida, France, Germany and the Netherlands since 1988, but it was in 2004, with the opening of its first subsidiary in Italy, that it reaffirmed its commitment to the international market. In 2006, Santa & Cole signed an exclusive distribution agreement with North America's leading company in outdoor furniture and landscape architecture, Landscape Forms. This provided an opportunity to build transatlantic bridges between Europe and the United States. Thus, in 2007, 35 per cent of the firm's sales were exported to over 35 countries. In July 2008, a new showroom was opened in Frankfurt, and Santa & Cole France opened in 2009.

The Santa & Cole business group had acquired the Belloch site in 2002 with the aim of promoting a knowledge park linked to communication and design. By 2009, the park housed the headquarters of Santa & Cole and other enterprises such as Telefónica's Corporate University. Parc de Belloch has a surface area of 125 hectares, including almost 45 hectares of agricultural land, and was the origin of Santa & Cole's Forestry Division. Belloch lies 30 kilometres north of Barcelona, and has ideal climatic characteristics for growing trees, shrubs and other plants for Mediterranean and Continental climates. With its Forestry Division, Santa & Cole went beyond just extending its Urban Division catalogue, combining living elements (trees) with urban elements (street lamps, benches and so on), thus providing architects and landscapers with a more balanced range of possibilities, with the aim of improving the material quality of life in cities.

The following mission statement can be found on Santa & Cole's website:

"We are concerned by the sustainability of the environment and good relations between nature and the city. We want sound and freshness, shelter and seasonal variation, changes of colour and of shape, small formats and big individuals. Because the combination of urban elements, lighting and trees is the best to help us to humanize our cities. We are thus planting our seed of responsibility with the future, convinced of the enormous value of the natural design of social spaces, where trees, shrubs and plants again occupy their refreshing space between the asphalt and the cement."

Santa & Cole's activities have been recognized by the National Design Award (1999), the Prince Felipe Award for Business Excellence (2006) and the Design Management Europe Award (2007) in the medium-sized company category.

THE BUSINESS PRINCIPLES OF SANTA & COLE

Javier Nieto Santa, Chairman and founder of the company, reported:

"For nearly 25 years now, Santa & Cole has lived for industrial design, an art consisting of focusing on everyday objects in order to seek a better user experience, thereby leading us to reflect upon material culture. Hence we edit elements of domestic and urban furniture and lighting, plant elements (which are living matter) and books (which are likewise alive) – a range that is only apparently unconnected, converging upon a single concern: not to accumulate, but rather to select; not to enjoy quantity, but rather quality."

Santa & Cole's policies are organized around four core themes:

1. structure, strategy and knowledge
2. editing policy
3. the importance of design
4. knowledge management policy.

Structure, strategy and knowledge

For Javier Nieto Santa, clearly the only way to earn more (the end objective of any strategy that seeks to ensure survival) is to have asymmetric competitive advantages that are not easy to obtain. And if these are exclusive, then so much the better. Considering that the only legal monopoly which is socially acceptable is that of intellectual and industrial property (brands, designs and patents), Javier Nieto Santa was of the opinion that these so-called "intangible assets" are so relevant that it is far more worthwhile to be the owner of knowledge (the editor) than to be the (subcontracted) physical producer of products or services based on this knowledge.

However, if protectable knowledge (in the sense of intellectual and industrial property) is the key to developing one strategy or another, if strategic exclusivity is increasingly focused on whether or not we hold certain "knowledge rights", then it is also true that a company's human structure is decisive. Javier Nieto Santa argued:

> *"Knowledge is generated by people ... and a structure that generates knowledge makes it possible to implement a strategy altogether different from one that doesn't generate it. We like to declare that we're proud of the people who form Santa & Cole."*

This explains why Santa & Cole defined itself as a knowledge industry. It strove to generate, contract, protect and spread knowledge, expressed through physical products with good design, the *gute form* of Bauhaus and Ulm: constructive solidity, aesthetic sobriety and functional quality – a trilogy which even becomes an ethical rule, especially in these times of such material waste on a planetary scale.

Editing policy

Santa & Cole has lent its brand name to the editing of lighting products and indoor furniture, urban elements, books and plant elements for urban reforestation. It has also defended the interests of certain leading manufacturers in Spain (including, the German firm bulthaup in the field of kitchen furniture, the German company Ingo Maurer in interior lighting, the French firm La Cornue in cookers, and the American company SubZero in cold appliances). These product groups were very different from each other, but had a shared sales network and common prescribers: the professionals involved in a project, interior specialists, designers, architects, urban planners and landscapers interested in contemporary design with an original quality.

Santa & Cole contracts out 100 per cent of its production to a large portfolio of suppliers, mostly in Spain, but also in other countries:

> *"We don't manufacture with our own hands. We're editors. Our task, in terms of catalogue products, not special or one-off products, can be summed up as follows: selecting what should be included in the catalogue (new products) by reviewing both the proposals of our designers, who are our authors, and our original commissions; developing those proposals technically; contracting out and financing the production of the various components; and then storing, selling and collecting payment for the finished products – and throughout the process, defending the ownership of our edition rights against any intrusive third party, and also our authors' creative value."*

The importance of design

The best protectable industrial design, plus whatever related knowledge is required for its reasonable commercial development – this is the essence of Santa & Cole's strategic worldview. As editing is its *raison d'être*, registered design is not just an aesthetic choice, but the basic pillar of its differentiation strategy. Santa & Cole works only with protectable original designs, either registered by its authors or generated in its in-house departments. It defines its criteria for selecting designs in this way:

"Our philosophy of taste is eclectic and modern rather than futuristic and postmodern. We are interested in rationality and balance, silence as opposed to stridency. And we are particularly motivated by the fact that we are the standard-bearers of a fine range of Spanish design throughout the world. For the most part, the creators of the objects we edit are internationally renowned designers and architects from Spain. This is because we value their ability to contribute ideas, new reflections and attitudes towards the objects, new perspectives on the world that, together, we help to project."

Knowledge management policy

It is true that the beginnings of Santa & Cole followed the pattern of the product-centric editing company that edits in order to enlarge a catalogue, in the hope that its products will later be of interest to its target market. However, in later years the company gradually underwent an internal transformation of its organizational culture towards a project-centric model, in which its mission is to contribute knowledge to its clients' specific needs and help them solve their project problems: anything from how to light up a seafront promenade to how to lay out a kitchen, furnish some offices or a home, adapt and humanize large public spaces, or integrate trees into the urban fabric. However, it does not sell projects as such, but the elements that might be used to make projects a success; not architecture, but rather materials: its knowledge merely seeks to back up the common sense of the professional advice it gives its clients.

The Parc de Belloch project should be seen in this context of the importance of knowledge as an essential element of Santa & Cole's strategy. It consisted of the creation of an innovation campus linked to a new top-rank academic institution promoting the best expression of the talent of contemporary Spanish and Hispano-American designers.

SANTA & COLE AND DESIGN FOR ALL

For Javier Nieto Santa, revenue was not the issue. It had more to do with ideological principles, and he was convinced that with the end of certain ideologies, new ideologies would emerge. In his opinion, the crisis in the financial system would lead to a new ideological dawn:

"My daughter said to me, 'Why should I eat a banana that comes all the way from Colombia if the energy used to transport this banana as far as my mouth is greater than the energy I get from eating it?' In other words, although you can eat a banana from Colombia, it doesn't make sense for the planet. This is the oil economy, and it may be going down the drain."

Santa & Cole has licensees in New Zealand, Australia and the USA who manufactured its urban elements in those countries. The only acceptable alternative for them would have been to transport the products unassembled. This would have made no sense and Santa & Cole was unwilling to get involved in such complex operations, so it granted the licences and the licensees pay royalties. Santa & Cole helps the licensees, providing them with know-how and coaching them. One of the advantages of Santa & Cole is its very broad product platform. For example, the US licensee manufactured landscaping elements like tables with circular benches, litter bins, cycle parking stands and sunshades. It supplied universities, hospitals and public and private environments – a huge market. But it had never made a street lamp. This was the case with many licensees – they would make a bench, for example, but not a street lamp, because they were put off by having to deal with electrical regulations. Santa & Cole encouraged them and said, "If we managed to do it, so can you." Imparting knowledge was more worthwhile than sending parts.

Javier Nieto Santa emphasized one of his recurring concerns:

"This is why I hope one of the emerging principles will be respect for intellectual property, because if the oil economy collapses, what emerges is intellectual property, which is much more important and nobler."

Ideas of this sort hold a lot of sway over product design, because they influence the selection criteria:

"We're not interested in plastics unless they're recyclable. Of course, this imposes formal conditions, because it affects the structure, the physical medium, the strength. And we're not interested in uses that aren't for everybody. We believe that we're witnessing a revolution of values that is unprecedented for our generation. Forget 1968; forget the hippie philosophies of the 1950s and 1960s. The distance between me and my daughter is much greater than between my father and me. And between my father and me, there were light-years. If you think about the new values, everything is affected – everything: What bulb does the lamp take? How much does it cost? What materials is it made of? What use is it intended for? In what use-situation is this product going to exist? In other words, in a way we're becoming even more bourgeois, because we believe more in the concept of "rurbanization" – mixing, a constant transition between the urban and the rural, without boundaries, urbanization and ruralization hand in hand. Boundaries have always been poorly defined, and they were hideous, because that was where the most wretched people lived: the periphery, the banlieue."

Javier Nieto Santa was quoting the people at the IAAC (the Institute for Advanced Architecture of Catalonia), and its director, the architect Vicente Guallart, who talked of "Gibartar", a new metapolis: the conurbation of Girona, Barcelona and Tarragona, a city running parallel to the coast, almost 200 kilometres long (Los Angeles measures about 150 kilometres) and 35 kilometres across. Gibartar would concentrate the vast majority of Catalonia's gross domestic product. If Gibartar existed, Cardedeu[10] would not necessarily be any different from what it is now, nor would the Maresme:

"Really, we who live on the edge of the big metropolises already live fully urban lives, but regional planning still isn't conceived for this mass use. The conversion to metapolises, which is close at hand, is going to change everything. In the last fifteen or twenty years, in Spain, more land has been developed than in the previous two hundred years. Why have we developed so much land? We have to redefine the concept of nature, and that redefinition will be designed. Isn't that Design for All – designing the concept of nature?"

These reflections, shared by the board of Santa & Cole, led them to set up a new company, Urbiótica,[11] a spin-off that, in collaboration with an engineering group in Sabadell and the School of Telecommunications at the Technical University of Catalonia (UPC), sought to apply to the city the concept that automation brought to the home. The idea would be to have clusters of sensors for multiple areas of the urban environment to measure variables such as noise, traffic or soil moisture for trees, for example, to transmit those measurements to collector nodes by radio,; and finally to interconnect these nodes to a decision centre where the information would be organized through geographical information systems. Javier Nieto Santa anticipated:

"Some might think this is very Orwellian, but with technology it all depends how you use it. The streets are very untechnified; they could be technified a great deal more. For example, there could be sensors measuring the presence of metals, like there are in car parks to show whether or not there are free spaces. Why can't we be told whether there are free parking spaces in Muntaner Street? Why can't we know the moisture level of a tree and its hydric stress? Urbiótica, plus the Forestry Division, plus other criteria, adds up to Design for All. That says everything. Something's happening!"

The Forestry Division accounted for a little less than 10 per cent of Santa & Cole's turnover in 2009, but the company was convinced that it was the division with most potential for transformation. It had given a different perspective to urban elements: what should a street lamp be like if it has to stand next to a tree? And what about the paving? Javier Nieto Santa complained:

"Paving's in a terrible mess, especially considering that paving is the starting point of the city. To urbanize is to pave, after which you can add whatever you like. It's a real mess, and just think: it's a colossal subject. So we at Urbiótica ask ourselves: Why shouldn't the paving be intelligent? What could intelligent paving consist of? Why not have it emit a radio-frequency signal and, say, link it to a stick so that blind people could find their way around the city better? The stick could simply be a receiver that

---

10   Cardedeu is a town near Barcelona where the company had its storage depot, about 3 kilometres from Parc de Belloch.

11   The Catalan newspaper El 9 Nou published the following item on 22 September 2008: "Creation of Urbiótica, S.L., dedicated to the design, development, planning, production, marketing, installation, operation and maintenance of monitoring, management and communications systems in the urban environment, including computer operations, etc. Chairman: Javier Nieto Santa."

vibrates and guides you as you walk. Why not have illuminated paving or kerbs? And why not include a cable conduit? With a cable conduit we'd have connectivity and …. Really, digging trenches is such bad design; having to dig everything up …. And so on, with any subject you like. It's all about paving. And who's studying paving? Some, like the Americans, tarmac everything, and others, like in Lisbon, carry on paving with their little mosaics of black and white cobbles. It's crazy."

He continued to throw out ideas for Urbiótica:

"You've heard of the war of the antennas – the cost it entails for mobile telephone operators to install repeaters and microcells? Of course, that's all revenue for the residents' associations, but if the city councils did it they would be doing big business. The operators wouldn't have to deal with thousands of different negotiators, and a city with mobile, broadband and wi-fi networks is a big advantage. You can manage your parks and gardens department differently, you can manage the traffic, you can manage security, parking, pollution. With Urbiótica, there'll be plenty to get our teeth into. And all that technology is already out there, just waiting to be used. It's the typical case of alteration by design: 'You make industrial curtains out of that stuff? Wow! It's beautiful the way the light shines through it! Well I'm going to make lampshades out of it.' That's what we did with the Moare series, by Antoni Arola – the material was designed for industrial curtains, but if you turn it round, it makes great lampshades. Mostly, that's what design is all about. Design doesn't invent, it applies. It decontextualizes, it transforms …."

Creativity at the service of all was written into the DNA of Santa & Cole. On occasions, it drew up a briefing document on one of its ideas, other times it did not; sometimes it came up with an idea, and sometimes it came from elsewhere. Regardless of who the original author of the idea was, the key moment was when somebody presented something formally: "Hey, that thing we were talking about – I think it can be expressed like this." And this formalization of the idea was never carried out by people inside Santa & Cole – the company made practically no products in-house. But from that moment on, it did everything else: how the product was expressed materially, the economics of it, how it was to be positioned, how it was to be communicated, and so on. Designers working with Santa & Cole were paid royalties. The company had a portfolio of designers who it worked with on a regular basis, but they listened to anyone who called. They looked at everything, they were open to everybody: "Young or senior, established or unknown, it makes no difference to us. We take a look at everything."

The selection criterion was that the product that had been formalized should be of interest from the point of view of the Santa & Cole catalogue; it should surprise, it should be something that would never have occurred to the staff – functionally surprising products, such as a footbath for when you leave the beach, something not very obvious. Occasionally Santa & Cole reaches agreements equivalent to those that artists used to have with certain patrons, who told them: "I'll pay you this much a month, and you just carry on painting." It sometimes does this with designers of renown; paying them a monthly fee, and if something worthwhile was forthcoming, it was deducted from the first royalties.

Nevertheless, Javier Nieto Santa was still unsatisfied:

"We're still missing several products. For example, it would be great to have a lighting product with rechargeable batteries, to keep indoors in the winter and then, in the summer, to take out and put on the table on the terrace, without any need for a cable. It's incredible that that still hasn't been solved. Because the technology – batteries – has been sitting there under our nose for years. We're also missing a good light for working at a computer without glare that's comfortable and doesn't mean yet another cable. To quote another example, we've just brought out a chair for everyday use. It's not very modest to say so, but it's a magnificent chair, it's very twenty-first-century, indoor–outdoor, it's cheap, it's recycled, recyclable, everything. Yet formally it's very Charles Eames, very 1950s. We made it for Belloch – for us, in other words. So in fact nothing's solved and everything's solved. It depends how you look at it."

There is a book by a well-known professor of sociology at the University of Rome, Domenico De Masi, entitled *L'emozione e la regola (Emotion and the Rule)*,[12] on the tension between creativity and discipline in truly creative groups. It concludes with an appendix about Santa & Cole, enumerating the factors that tend to describe a creative company:

1. A creative company is an organization dedicated to knowledge, the production and dissemination of knowledge.
2. It is a company that aims at ongoing innovation of projects and processes, understanding these two aspects as being deeply integrated.
3. It is an organization that concerns itself with aesthetics.
4. The creative company also stands out for the care it takes to act professionally and the importance it attaches to people as individuals.
5. It has great flexibility, represented by business decisions to diversify the product, markets and organizational structures.
6. It is characterized by intensive use of communication technologies.
7. It has an "organic" organizational model; it is results-oriented and ability-centred, is heedful of internal and external communication processes, and values intangible elements such as professionalism and motivation.

The person, the city and the planet – as we left the interview with Javier Nieto Santa, the car radio was announcing the crisis at General Motors, as if to signal the new times ahead.

---

12   Domenico De Masi, *L'emozione e la regola: La grande avventura dei gruppi creativi europei*, Bari and Rome: Laterza, 1990.

Sol Meliá – Hotels for All

"Accessibility is essential for 10 per cent of the population, necessary for 40 per cent and comfortable for 100 per cent of the population."
(Francesc Aragall, Design for All Foundation)

The tourism industry is one in which Design for All has made a big impact and where there has been a major effort to apply its principles. The disabled community worldwide is large, with a spending power of millions of euros, so being able to provide services that do not exclude any individual in society is very important. For these reasons, for our final case study we chose to focus on a hotel chain, Sol Meliá. In spring 2009, we interviewed Federico Martinez-Carrasco, Director of Sol Meliá's Community Involvement Department, in Palma de Mallorca.

THE COMPANY

The Sol Meliá hotel and resort chain was founded in Palma de Mallorca, Spain by Gabriel Escarrer Juliá in 1956. As of 2009, it was the largest vacation hotel chain in the world. It has 304 hotels in 26 countries around the world, and it employs more than 35,000 people. It has a number of brands: Gran Meliá Hotels & Resorts, Paradisus Resorts, ME by Meliá, Meliá Hotels and Resorts, Innside Premium Hotels, Tryp Hotels, Sol Hotels and Sol Hotels Vacation Club.

Sol Meliá's business model consists of three components: hotels, the Sol Meliá Vacation Club and Leisure Real Estate. The hotel component manages the company's 304 hotels, offering a wide variety of experiences for the customers. Due to the large number of brands, a new internal structure emerged which grouped them as follows: Premium Brands (Gran Meliá, Paradisus, ME by Meliá), Meliá Brand, Tryp Brand and Sol Brand, the Innside Brand being managed with the Tryp and Meliá Brands. The goal was to offer its customers a wide array of products and services. In addition, Sol Meliá has four business models for running its hotels: proprietorship, management, rent and franchise. The Sol Meliá Vacation Club offers client companies two options. They can either purchase specific rooms to let to customers, sharing the management of income generated, or they can purchase vacation slots for a specific number of years in one of the hotel brands. The third component, Leisure Real Estate, is in charge of studying the sustainability of the company's assets as well as the management of the condo hotels, as well as analysing ways to optimize the performance of the real estate assets.

In addition to these three pillars, there are other departments that complement them, as Federico Martinez-Carrasco, Director of the Community Involvement Department explained:

"Besides the three pillars of our business, we have several departments that go across all areas and provide support to the business model. First, the Human Resources

Department: there is a clear division within the hotels by brand, and there is a strategic division of Human Resources, a Department of Finance that services and supports the whole company, a Department of Marketing Strategy and an Information Systems and Administration division that provides support to the entire company. Then there are three more areas that are staffed by and answerable directly to the President: the Legal Department, the Office of Strategic Planning and the Department of Corporate Social Responsibility."

The Department of Corporate Social Responsibility (CSR) is made up of the Environmental Division and the Community Involvement Division. The CSR Department developed in a particular way in Sol Meliá. The original Community Involvement Department was created in 2005, directed by Federico Martinez-Carrasco. It reported directly to the President and dealt with any issues that did not belong to any other department, aiming to align all the issues with the company's strategy. Following this, the need to handle many issues regarding the environment led to the decision to create the Environmental Department in 2007. In July 2007 it was finally decided to create a Corporate Social Responsibility Department, incorporating the Environment and Community Involvement Division and Environmental Division. The objective was to have a department that spanned all the company's brands and launch projects that would be adopted by each of them. The issues of disability and Design for All were managed by the CSR Department. The fundamental mission was to create value through a focus on CSR and make it their competitive advantage. In the words of Federico Martínez-Carrasco:

"We want corporate social responsibility to be one of the principal attributes of the corporate brand .... We have a fundamental mission which is value-creation, the creation of value through corporate social responsibility, making it one of our competitive advantages .... We are not talking about specific situations, but of a general way of doing things, so that when someone talks about Sol Meliá, they say, 'These are people who are worried, who care, they have a philosophy ....'"

Each of Sol Meliá's brands operates independently, being differentiated from the rest. Each brand has its own structures and divisions, such as human resources and marketing. However, they try to achieve the highest possible degree of synergy. Each Sol Meliá hotel targets a specific market niche:

"Paradisus is the top vacation brand, the big fancy resorts; the Gran Meliá brand is the top urban brand, the most luxurious; ME Meliá is a brand within the urban sector with a specific target, more modern; the Meliá brand is the one mostly associated with the company, with the largest number of hotels, and then there are Tryp and Innside, more in the middle sector .... The 2008–2010 Strategic Plan proposes a clear market segmentation throughout the brands."

DESIGN STRATEGY

For Sol Meliá, design is very important, and considered key to many areas of the company. As one of the company's principles is to maintain the cultural heritage of the communities where it operates, one of the design strategies that is always present in the renovation of its hotels is to incorporate elements of the host city's culture. Examples include displaying paintings from local artists, representative symbols of the city or pictures of it in the guest's rooms. All the design elements are the responsibility of the hotel's architect, Alvaro Sanz, and his studio, G56.

Design also plays an important role for the CSR Department. The company is currently developing design and renovation manuals for all the Meliá hotels with the aim of establishing basic design elements and guidelines throughout the chain. The CSR Department participated in the definition of the design elements covered in these manuals in order to incorporate the principles of Universal Design in the widest possible way. Federico Martínez-Carrasco explained:

"You cannot imagine a hotel being built now without including design elements addressing environmental issues. You cannot conceive of a hotel that does not incorporate elements of Universal Design, both in renovation and construction."

THE ROLE OF THE END CONSUMER

The end consumer is crucial for Sol Meliá. It conducts regular quality surveys, as customers' perception of the company is very important:

"The customer is our raison d'être, the soul of the company, the end user. We are absolutely clear about this. For example, in these times of budget cuts, the most important thing is that the customer is not aware of them. I mean, we can make budget cuts in other areas, but not when it comes to customer service and quality of service."

Sol Meliá is aware of how advances in technology have affected its industry. Customers now interact directly with the company, making all their reservations via the company website, whereas in the past such interactions were not direct, but through travel agencies. Sol Meliá's CSR Department is working on issues regarding the new, more demanding customers:

"It is difficult because it is a mature segment, so it is very hard to surprise the client. You have to be constantly innovating and looking for new sensations."

The CSR Department has introduced the principles of Design for All in different areas of the company. These efforts began through the recognition that including disabled people in the company's market and targeting a wider set of consumers was essential in the tourism industry:

"Regarding the issue of disability, customers demand their rights. This is one of the issues that is very clear, where the company must adapt to the disabled sector. Before, a customer would go to a hotel and would find whatever, and would accept anything – not today. Today, the customer is demanding, 'Look, I have the same right as that person to have a vacations or a nice stay – would you make it nice?' And in that sense, we have to adapt.

Today, we cannot afford to exclude any segment of the market – we would be committing suicide. In fact, one of the arguments I use in my internal sales strategy is that there is a huge market of disabled people that we have to go after."

The company has a social commitment and understands that it is important to make a contribution to reducing social differences and poverty. For these reasons, it focuses on disadvantaged groups, the elderly and children. Moreover, it is aware of the economic implications if it fails to target this consumer market.

SOL MELIÁ'S EFFORTS ON DESIGN FOR ALL

As stated above, the principles of Design for All are handled by the CSR Department. The management goal of the department is to launch projects, involve departments closely related to a specific issue, and then let them continue with the project from there. It enables others to apply the principles themselves after providing the necessary guidance:

"What we do from our department is to launch the issues of accessibility, which are issues that affect food and beverages, for example coeliac disease, that affect maintenance and training at reception – these are issues that span all departments."

After signing an agreement with the Federation of Celiac Associates (FACF) in 2008, Sol Meliá, initiated a specific menu for those with coeliac disease to be implemented in all its hotel restaurants, starting with the Tryp brand. In addition, the company invested 2,194,366 euros in 17 hotels to build accessibility ramps, adequate elevators, rooms with disabled access, and adaptations to the hotel pools.

There were many challenges and difficulties in the implementation of Design for All. One of the major concerns for the tourism industry was the economic implications of having to revamp their facilities to adapt them in accord with the principles. Sol Meliá tackled this issue through two different strategies. The first one involved the CSR department participating in defining the design elements included in the brand manuals to ensure that Universal Design principles were applied. This means that future construction or renovation projects will take these principles into account from the beginning, avoiding extra costs for the company. This was not an easy task, as all the principles cannot be applied to all the company's brands:

"What we like to pretend is that the concept of Universal Design is applicable to all brands, but what happens is that it is clear that in some hotels, because of their

circumstances, some things can apply and others cannot. It is not that easy, because Universal Design is not easy … for example, some hotels need to have bathtubs because they cater for families with kids, so bathroom redesigns become more difficult if we try to eliminate the bathtubs and replace them with showers. However, reforms in Meliá's hotels take this issue into consideration every day."

The second strategy it used was to concentrate on hotels that were due for renovation, so that the principles were included in the renovation plans and were not the sole reason for them:

"We take advantage of the opportunity of renovation, and starting from there we follow a guide. The guide is the needs the hotel has, depending on its type. … What we do is, when there is a renovation project, we ensure that we implement accessibility features, we take advantage of these moments. We couldn't go to a hotel that has no plans for renovation and decide that they need to do it – we can't do that."

COMMUNICATION

One of the main issues Sol Meliá has identified is communication problems, both internal and external. Communicating Design for All internally is not an easy task as there is a widespread lack of knowledge of what the concept is and what its benefits are:

"The company does not sees it as Universal Design, they still see it in terms of disability and accessibility …. This is something I proposed at a meeting with the architect Alvaro Sans – that we should stop talking about disability and accessible rooms …. If you want to sell a an accessible room to a "normal" client or to someone with no disabilities you won't be able to. But if instead of selling an accessible room you sell a room with Universal Design elements where you have incorporated the latest design features, and in addition it is a more spacious room and a room that you can sell to a young couple, to a family or to an elderly couple, you are talking about Universal Design, and you can incorporate a plus for many motives."

Federico Martínez-Carrasco emphasized:

"We have to stop talking about accessibility and disability, and start talking about Universal Design. We shouldn't think of just one disabled person, we should think of someone who is pushing a baby stroller, a person with a broken leg, a person who is dragging luggage, or an elderly person. The key is to abandon the term 'accessibility' in hotels.

Besides, hotel directors don't like these terms because, although they don't sell accessible rooms, that concept is still there. And clients do not like them; clients still thinks that if they are sold an accessible room, we are going to give them a hospital room. And that continues – we have to do a lot of internal and external education work. Here, the company keeps talking about accessibility and disability, and not Universal Design – that is the continuous battle.

> *One of the outstanding issues regarding the hotel directors is to convince them, because when there is a reform, the director has a lot of influence. The director of the hotel is like the soul of the hotel, and if he is conscious [about Design for All], he will make sure that the principles are included in the revamp. There, in the issue of sensibility and information, is where the big opportunity for improvement lies."*

Communicating externally to the customers was also not easy, for the same reasons. As mentioned above, customers who are disabled do not want to be labelled as "disabled", and those who are not disabled do not want "rooms for disabled", as their perceptions of these are negative. This is a delicate issue for Sol Meliá, as it not only affects the Hotel component of its business model, but also the Sol Meliá Vacation Club. If customers wrongly perceive rooms as being only for the disabled, they will not accept them, as Federico Martínez-Carrasco explained:

> *"The ideal would be that you don't have to tell the client, but that these are principles you implement in the hotel and are transparent to the client. This would be the ideal situation, where the only thing the client perceives is a bigger room and how much good design there is in the room. When you talk about Universal Design, people immediately associate it with disability and accessibility, and even worse, with wheelchairs. I'm going for the extreme case – when people think of disability, they immediately think of someone in a wheelchair, they do not think of an older person or someone pushing a baby stroller, as they can have the same issues as someone in a wheelchair. We are still very far – and in the hotel business it is the same – we are very far from that concept. In fact, every time it is talked about, the example of Confortel is mentioned, hotels from ONCE,[13] then at the internal level they say, 'Let's not enter their field, customers don't associate us with a chain that is geared to disabled people.' The directors run away from this, and these are the great difficulties I have encountered."*

RELATIONSHIP BETWEEN PUBLIC AND PRIVATE ENTITIES

Competition based on Design for All

For the reasons stated by Federico Martínez-Carrasco above, Design for All principles are not usually advertised by Sol Meliá, so it is not easy to recognize which of its hotels have adopted it and which have not. However, Sol Meliá was aware of two hotel chains that were also tackling these design issues, though neither represented direct competition:

> *"Paradores make a lot of noise, they are present in many forums and their presentations are appealing .... However, the renovations performed by them are more complicated because of their hotel typology: every hotel is a monument, so any adaptations must be more appealing, as they are more difficult to carry out. Then Confortel is another*

---

13 Organización Nacional de Ciegos Españoles (National Organization of Spanish Blind People), http://www.once.es/new.

one. Being hotels owned by ONCE, it is clear they adopt the accessibility principles as they go hand by hand. People with disabilities know that in these hotels, they will not have any problems."

HUMAN CAPITAL AND DESIGN FOR ALL

Sol Meliá was completely aware that the effectiveness of its human capital was crucial to diffusing Design for All throughout the company. It was clear that without employee training, there was no way the principles could be applied correctly. Before and after implementing any changes, Sol Meliá made sure its employees were trained about the issues at hand. It was also aware that employees needed to be trained about accessibility and disability, as it was vital to customer relations and the success of the changes being implemented:

"From the point of view of Human Resources, they know they have to give training about disability, they have to inform and train about dietary issues such as coeliac disease, food for diabetics. This is also an issue for the Food and Beverage Department, and the Purchasing Department – they have to buy products from special employee centres.

That is our battle. From here [the CSR Department], we launch the efforts and then each department channels the information, because as I said, our true goal is that this becomes a company philosophy. And how do we achieve this? By making all employees feel it in this way."

One of Federico Martínez-Carrasco's main concerns at the time of the interview was training hotel reception employees in how to communicate with those with disabilities:

"This year, we are going to launch the issue of training in disabilities for the personnel on the front desk."

Finally, Federico Martínez-Carrasco was very aware of the importance of training and communication in all departments. It was important for employees to understand what efforts the company was making to cater for the disabled and have clear idea of the company philosophy:

"The issue of training is very important for me, is something that can be resolved quickly – especially training hotel employees in how they should work, act towards and treat a client with any type of disability.

Each employee has his or her own concerns, but our objective is to analyse these to align the concerns of one worker with the concerns of the company and give them form. Because they have concerns but don't know how to channel them, how to put them into practice, many are confused – 'Corporate social responsibility sounds good, but what does it consist of? Is it social action or environmental concerns? Is the sum of both? Is it more?' – and that is our task now."

APPLICABILITY TO ALL SOL MELIÁ BRANDS

The goal of the CSR Department was to make the concept of Design for All part of the company's philosophy and to incorporate it across all the company's brands. Yet, due to the Sol Meliá business model, sometimes it was not in the hands of the department to introduce the issues:

"We have hotels that are owned, but there are others that are rented. However, both have similar management processes – the owner or renter is in charge of deciding what happens in the hotel, in this case what a department like mine [CSR] can do is limited because it depends on the hotel ownership. There, it depends on the management contract and on the owner. If you find an owner who is conscious about disability issues, when you are talking about a series of investments in the hotel, it is easier for him to accept them if he is interested in Design for All."

AREAS WITH ROOM FOR IMPROVEMENT

Sol Meliá recognizes that there are several areas where there is still much room for improvement. It is looking to collaborate with associations that represent disabled people so that the accessibility guidelines for its design manuals can be defined. It is working on employee training in all issues related to disability and providing employees with information about the efforts it is making. Furthermore, it is aware that it needs more information from customers about these issues:

"One of the main problems we have is that we do not know how many of the clients that come to the hotel are disabled, we don't have that information, and that is a problem. Employees at the front desk ask about this when the client arrives, but this information is not consolidated, it does not go to a specific box in the system."

Federico Martínez-Carrasco concluded:

"This is something we have to work on, especially since we have to demonstrate within the company that we have a certain number of disabled clients, and then compare one year and the next. All these market research studies need to be conducted. This is something we need to work on with our Information Systems Department, but of course this would have to be done with an outside company, and with the economic situation we are in right now, this is not possible. But it will be some day."

Index